BIAFRA
The Memory of the Music

Jim Malia

Published by

MELROSE BOOKS

An Imprint of Melrose Press Limited
St Thomas Place, Ely
Cambridgeshire
CB7 4GG, UK
www.melrosebooks.com

FIRST EDITION

ISBN 978 1 906050 00 9

Printed and bound in Great Britain by:
CPI Antony Row, Bumpers Farm,
Chippenham, Wiltshire, SN14 6LH, UK

Dedicated to

That Band

that Happy Band

that Band of Brothers

---

and the music...?

...like a little flute complaining

a long way off beyond the willow trees

a long way off and nothing left remaining

but memory of the music on the breeze.

Preface

The Biafran conflict of the late sixties resulted in one of the most highly publicised emergencies of all times, arousing, through the skill and courage of the newsmen on the spot, the concern of thousands, resulting in a relief programme larger, according to the International Red Cross, than any since the aftermath of the Second World War.

The aspect of the Biafran relief programme and my part in it, as told in the later chapters of this memoir, is one very small part of a very large canvas; a stage upon which many players had their entrances and some, tragically, their exits.

I had the privilege of working for a while on the airstrip at Uli, receiving supplies flown in from Sao Tome, flown in night after shattering night, in unarmed aircraft facing shore batteries, marauding MiGs, machine guns and bombs, piloted by men courageous beyond the call of duty. The graves in the cemetery near the airstrip are their monument.

And where did those supplies come from? Father Tony Byrne in his excellent book, *Airlift to Biafra*, gives us some idea of the extent of that massive operation. He himself, seconded to Caritas International based in the Vatican, working with Cardinal this, Monsignor that, Cicognani, Gallina, Benelli, Bayer, did much to organise that relief.

And there were others involved he tells us, many others: World Council of Churches, Conference of Missionary Societies, Presbyterian Churches of Canada, Diakonische Werk of Germany. At the same time, despite government vacillation, organisations such as Oxfam, Christian Aid, Save the Children, CAFOD, Concern of Ireland, all played a vital role.

The International Red Cross was a crucial part of the relief operation. Even after the shooting down of one of their planes, national Red Cross organisations took up the role, the French prominent among them, as were also their Médecins sans Frontières and others.

Needless to say, American aid was massive. Night after night huge C97's flew in with tons of Formula 2, enriched cornmeal, vital nutrition in the growing emergency. Catholic Relief Services, supported by the legendary generosity of the American people, appeared to have limitless resources.

North European countries played a vital role; the tons of stockfish among other supplies flown in nightly by Scandinavian and Icelandic airmen provided ample evidence of the part they played. Pastor Mollerup of the Lutheran Church was a power behind the forging of some thirty five organisations into what became JointChurchAid.

And what about the men on the ground? Uli airstrip had been functioning many months before I arrived on the scene. Men of the Spiritan Congregation were there: the legendary Des McGlade, Father 'Gus' Finucane, Harry Mullen among them, working at the sharp end in darkness and in storm with the ever-present threat of bombs and machine gunning.

And our own African Marists, dedicated Brothers working with quiet efficiency night after night supervising Caritas ground personnel, off-loading planes, stacking lorries, escorting convoys back to base.

And that was half the operation. Caritas manned the airstrip on alternate nights with WCC when the operation was repeated with equal dedication and efficiency by the men and women of the World Council of Churches.

It was indeed JointChurchAid, certainly one of the largest, definitely the most dangerous, arguably the most efficient relief programme ever mounted.

And the reason? The men of the cloth and the women behind that operation worked with the selfless dedication of their calling. Also the bulk of that relief was organised on parochial lines. Few world-systems are as efficient as that of the Christian parish.

1

Capitulation

The sun had set. Palm trees stood black against the deepening sky. A single cricket rasped sharply in the darkness and stopped.

I strained my ears, listening to the silence. An aeroplane droned overhead, circling low. A line of tracer bullets arched into the night sky. The silence was shattered by the hammering of a heavy machine gun. Other guns opened up. More tracer streams groped the darkness. Then the throbbing of the aircraft faded. The guns stopped. Silence descended again. I was surrounded and alone, a prisoner awaiting captivity.

It was Monday, the 12th of January 1970. At four o'clock that afternoon the secessionist army had formally capitulated. Major-General Philip Effiong, acting head of state, had offered unconditional surrender of his armed forces to the Nigerian government. Thirty months of civil war had come to an end. Biafra was no more.

I switched on the radio and turned the volume low. The lilting notes of Lillibolero broke into the silence of the darkened common room where I was sitting, signalling the seven o'clock news from the BBC. I bent close to hear. The delivery was solemn; the facts were clear: Third Marine Commando under Brigadier Obasanjo had broken through the southern Biafran defence line, had swarmed across the Imo River, captured the vital stronghold of Owerri, linked up with the Northern army advancing south from the Onitsha sector, had overcome opposition and forced surrender. The fact that Ojukwu, the architect and inspiration of Biafra, had left the country made capitulation the easier.

The news announcer was continuing: mopping-up operations were in progress against small areas of resistance. Concern was expressed for certain expatriates still in the country, some of them British, involved in the relief campaign. The Foreign Office urged those same individuals to remain low and avoid areas of actual fighting until complete order had been restored.

I smiled sadly to myself, switched off the radio and stared ruefully through the darkened window to the line of darker bush beyond. In that darkness around me, even as the Foreign Office warning was being delivered, Federal troops were digging in. An occasional burst of automatic gunfire spoke of the continuing mopping-up operations.

I got up, and with some difficulty in the darkness, I managed to find the remains of a bottle of brandy. It had been harboured carefully against an emergency. I reckoned that now was such an emergency. I poured a measure and settled down in the armchair. My thoughts lingered back over the day.

It had been a long day. I was awakened early by a burst of gunfire.

"What is it?"

I fumbled into some clothes and hurried to join Norbert standing on the veranda overlooking the valley from where the firing was coming.

"Sounds like a Saladin." He strained into the darkness. "The Feds could be here. They were at Angara last night."

It was not a Federal advance unit; it was a gang of looters in a predawn attempt on the refugee food store. They were driven off with a heavy show of firepower.

There was a sudden silence; streaks of dawn light fingered the sky. "What now?" There was no thought of going back to bed.

"I'm getting the orphans away." Norbert was decisive. "The Feds will have crossed the river; it's just a matter of time before they're here. This place could be a battlefield." He gazed across the compound where, already in the dim light, troop movements were apparent against a background of yelling orders, revving lorries. "I've a centre down the valley ready for the children. I'll get them there as soon as it's light enough."

"I'll give you a hand. I've petrol in the Volks."

"What about the airstrip?"

"Closed. The Feds have a howitzer at Awo Amama, well within range. I spoke to Johnsonn."

Captain Johnsonn was one of the many brave men who, night after night, had run the gauntlet of Federal anti-aircraft fire to deliver relief supplies, landing in darkness at Uli airstrip, offloading in desperate haste under constant threat of falling bombs and crackling machine-gun fire from the Federal bomber droning overhead, roaring off to cram in a second shuttle. But now even he realised the odds were stacked too high. Or so I thought.

"OK. You can take the Amike side. I'll send a nurse with you. Grace knows the centre. I'll start moving the children out of here. Meantime, let's have a coffee. It's going to be a busy day."

We made our way down to the dining room. The school in which we had been teaching before the outbreak of hostilities had been commandeered by the Biafran army. The takeover was efficient and courteous. Lines of demarcation were clearly established: the Biafran military took over the main school buildings and dormitories. We were left with the schoolhouse and enough space to continue work in the feeding centre and orphanage.

The coffee was hot from the flask. We sat and quietly prepared for the day ahead. We knew it was going to be a momentous one.

I picked up the nurse and set off at speed along the dusty laterite road. There were two dozen children in Norbert's makeshift orphanage, a converted primary school in the nearby village. Their nurses wrapped them in blankets against the cold harmattan wind and we brought them in relays to their new home deep in the bush, little eyes patient and trusting, in this new crisis in their brief, crisis-filled lives. Norbert was waiting in the temporary refuge.

"Any sign of the Feds?" He was concerned for his children.

"They're at the market crossroads. There won't be a battle, not here anyway; the soldiers are dispersing. What next?"

"Once the children are settled in I'll slip back to the school; I've a few things to collect."

Glancing round the compound, I knew there was little to collect. Norbert, imbued with his native Scottish thoroughness, had left nothing to chance: beds neatly arranged in the whitewashed schoolrooms, thatched shelters erected for his children against the dry-season sun, the storehouse packed high with emergency supplies.

"I'll try to get through to Ihioma. The bush road might be open."

"Go well; take care." There was a note of anxiety in his voice.

Ihioma was the central supply base for Caritas, the international relief organisation. The base had been established as the war became more widespread, the hunger more desperate, the relief operation more efficient. Two of our men were there, expatriate school staff who had stayed after the general exodus. Members of the Marist teaching order, we found ourselves adopting a variety of roles since the closing of the schools. Norbert was kept busy with his refugees, his clinics, feeding centre and orphanages. I had been detailed to the airstrip to help in the reception of relief supplies. The Head, on one of his errands of mercy, had strayed behind the lines and was captured by the Federal army. Lewis was co-ordinating supplies at Ihioma.

The bush road was open. I found myself nosing my way in the little green Volkswagen against a straggling line of refugees hurrying breathless before the advancing Federal force. A barrier blocked my way to the main tarred road. I slowed as I approached, then I recognised the shoulder flash. The area was still in Biafran hands. The soldier halted the car. He was alone, in full battle-gear, tall, professional. He walked slowly over, stooped and peered through the open window.

"Sir, where are you going?"

"Ihioma. Supply base."

He looked at me. His gaze and his tone were level with no hint of military authority: "Sir, why do you not go to your own home? You know that now all is over."

There was concern in his voice. Our eyes met briefly. His handsome sepia face was streaked in perspiration. Slowly he lowered his head so that all I could see was the webbing of his steel helmet and, beyond him, the line of refugees wandering past the roadblock, aimlessly, nowhere, faces strained with anguish beyond anguish. I watched the crippled, broken victims of the horror of the war as they struggled on their hopeless way beneath their meagre loads and I turned to the soldier. He had raised his head. Again our eyes met. There were tears in his eyes.

I spoke to him quietly: "This is our home," I said.

Silently he raised the barrier and I drove through.

There were tears in my own eyes and a scorching lump in my throat. The futility of it all: massacre and flight, thirty months of death and destruction, bloodshed, starvation and now defeat, surrender, fear.

I met Lewis at the gate to the mission compound supervising the distribution of relief to the passing throng. He waved me on to the house. A meeting was taking place, passionate and urgent. Archbishop Arinze was at the head of the table. A speaker was holding forth strongly: "It must be surrender. There is no choice. There can be no more bloodshed. There must be an official statement."

"Who will make this statement?"

"Effiong is acting head of state."

"Where is he?"

"Army headquarters are at Bishop Shanahan College, Your Grace. He could still be there."

Arinze turned to me. "Is the road open, Brother?"

"I've just come through the bush path. That could still be open."

"Lead the way; I'll follow."

A lone sentry was guarding the staff office. "The Head of State is not here. He has gone to the radio station. He is to give an announcement at two o'clock."

The Archbishop's car crunched to a halt behind us. I gave him the news. There was silence. Palm leaves rattled stiffly in the dry-season breeze. The Archbishop's voice was flat and tired: "And so it has come."

Norbert had joined us from the schoolhouse where he had been giving a final check. "We are in their hands now, Your Grace."

"And in God's hands. What will you do, Brothers?"

"We have a place off the road for the orphans. We will wait with them and see."

The Archbishop nodded quietly. He raised his hand in blessing.

The sentry had quietly joined us. We stood and solemnly shook hands. The Archbishop left and we were alone. The soldier turned and resumed his guard post, straightening his shoulders to attention. I looked back as we drove off. He had not moved: the guard at the gates of Herculaneum.

Two o'clock came and went. Radio Biafra was transmitting solemn music but no announcement.

"What do you reckon, Norbert?"

"Giving the troops time to disperse; talk's been rescheduled for four o'clock."

It was an anxious two hours. Intermittent gunfire could be heard all around us. An occasional bullet ripped through the foliage overhead; the sound of heavy shelling thundered in the hills to the north. Suddenly a jet fighter screamed up the valley, black, roaring immediately over our heads. We instinctively crouched for cover in the flimsy palm shade. The MiG climbed and circled and was gone. I looked over at Norbert; his eyes were fixed on the children packed in the clearing. I followed his gaze. The little sea of faces stared at us in silent trust.

Four o'clock. The music ended. The speaker was introduced: acting Head of State, Major-General Philip Effiong was to address the nation. We waited. The music started again, loud and uncompromising: *Finlandia*, the choral piece chosen as the Biafran national anthem. We listened in puzzled amazement then Effiong spoke, calmly, deliberately, solemnly. He spoke of the suffering and bloodshed of the preceding months; the starvation and death of countless thousands. He spoke of the resistance his fellow countrymen had put up, the massacres and expulsions that had caused that resistance and the creation of the state of Biafra. But now it was over. Further resistance was futile. As head of state he called upon all under arms to lay down those arms forthwith and return to civilian life. Now, with the path to reconciliation open, all must seize the opportunity to establish peace and harmony within the Republic of Nigeria. He called upon the leaders of the country, he called upon the God whom they all served, for help in this dark hour.

There was a brief pause at the ending of the speech and then the notes of the Nigerian national anthem broke out loud and clear and unambiguous, its stirring notes trumpeting through the forest, announcing aloud and to the world the ending of hostility, the end of thirty months of civil war. We sat in wondering silence.

Someone tapped me on the shoulder. It was Godwin, our house steward, lab assistant and faithful factotum. "Brother, you must come to the school immediately; there are looters about."

I followed him into the valley, along the trail, up the escarpment and into the school compound. It was deserted. An eerie late-afternoon stillness hung over all. Where troops had drilled and orders had been barked, where, thirty months before, the merry cries of schoolboys at their games had been heard, silence reigned.

The mission house was locked; the store was intact. A thousand hungry soldiers had passed; not a grain of rice had been touched.

"Godwin, go over to the Chief's compound and tell Igwe's wife to bring twelve women to come to clear this store. Tell them to come quickly." They did so, departing with sackfuls of rice, cornmeal, stockfish, salt and flour, and the stern injunction that all must be shared.

Godwin went to lock the store.

"Leave it, Goddy. Open the shutters. Let all see that the storeroom is empty. Now the looters will have nothing."

Godwin smiled at the ruse. "That is good. The looters will have nothing." I nodded. His smile broadened: "And we will have nothing."

In the excitement of the day, the idea of food had not crossed my mind but Godwin, the ever-resourceful, was prepared. He had a supply set aside.

It was dark when we finished our supper of stew and rice.

"That was very good, Godwin. I think you should leave now."

"Why?"

"It will be safer. Go to your house in Igwe's compound. I will stay here. There will be no palaver this night."

After mild protest Godwin left and I was alone.

The world was quiet now. The occasional bursts of automatic fire had ceased. The shriek of a nightbird deepened the silence. I watched, through the blackened window, a few stars twinkling in the silent sky and felt the unreality of the situation baffling coherent thought. Was I dreaming? Was I really sitting alone surrounded by darkness and hostility in the house where, less than ten years before, I had arrived to a hearty welcome, with laughter and friendship and a joy-filled busy life, where academic prowess and sports results loomed large on a horizon peaceful against a background of civil calm and political stability? It was Nigeria, January 1961, three short months after the granting of Independence and the achievement of full statehood. I stepped off the plane in Enugu airport into the heat of the day and the euphoria of Independence. The country was alive with the joy of it: Christmas and Independence and New Year all rolled into one. Little did I realise the grim reality into which I was stepping, a reality that was to lay bare the cracks in the foundations of that euphoria.

2

In the Beginning

Mark met me at the airport. I recognised his cheerful, laughing smile among the throng of cheerful, laughing, surging humanity.

"You're welcome, Jimmy; very welcome. Anything to declare?" He threw the case into the car.

"Bottle of malt whisky. Be careful."

"Spoken like a true Scot."

"Geordie."

"Whatever."

We were bowling along the ribbon of tarred road into the town. I gazed about in wonder at everything that was so new to me, shanty market stalls at the side of the road mingling with brightly painted modern houses, beneath palm trees red-leafed with dry-season dust. A Pontiac swished by; a Bedford truck thundered down. Children waved frantically: "Happy New Year! Happy Independence!"

We slowed down behind a procession of women still joyfully celebrating the event three months after its declaration. 'Happy Independence' was writ large upon their banners and their colourful drapes as they danced their happy way down Main Street to the accompaniment of drums and cymbals.

I had read something of the fight for independence that had been enacted over the years and although the struggle had been mainly verbal and diplomatic it had nevertheless been hard and intense, complicated by tribal differences and the dangers presented by colonial regional boundaries. The dancers we followed, and many more groups and individuals I later met in Eastern Nigeria, were determined that tribal and regional differences would be overlooked. National unity would be maintained. 'Nigeria One! One Nigeria! Nigeria United!' Such were the cries of the day.

We arrived at the school in a cloud of dust and a merry welcome. Lunch had been postponed in expectation of my late arrival. It was a happy meal; the Brothers of the community were a jovial bunch: Scots and English and Irish. Questions abounded about the folk and happenings back home. The bottle of malt was broached. New Year was toasted, absent friends were toasted, Scotland, England and Ireland were toasted; Nigeria was toasted, Nigeria independent, Nigeria and its future. A prayer was said, brief but sincere, and I was on my way far from the comfort and the bustle of the township, through the bush to Orlu and the school where I was to teach, Bishop Shanahan College.

The school, a fine imposing building set off from the road in its own sweeping grounds, had been built shortly after the war with help from a colonial development grant. The men behind the foundation were members of the Spiritan Order, a missionary congregation, French in origin, known familiarly as the Holy Ghost Fathers.

Strong in Ireland with parishes and colleges, the order sent out men to the African mission armed with a vigour, courage and enterprise which, in south-eastern Nigeria, built a branch of the Catholic Christian church flourishing to this day. That combination of vigour, courage and enterprise was, before the ending of this story, to be tested to the limit. It was not found wanting.

Education was the means adopted by the Spiritans for the spreading of the gospel message. 'Educate! Educate!', Shanahan's watchword. Bishop Joseph Shanahan, pioneer of the mission in southern Nigeria, led the way by example, building schools throughout the region from palm-thatched village primaries to storeyed township colleges. The school in which I was to teach had been named in honour of his memory.

Shortly after its completion, Bishop Shanahan College: academic block, technical department, boarding section and all, was handed over to the Marist Brothers, Les Frères Maristes des Écoles. Like the Spiritans, the Brothers were a teaching order founded in France shortly after the Revolution for the restoration of Christianity in that war-torn country. Champagnat, their founder, now venerated as Saint Marcellin Champagnat, was, like Shanahan, an ardent advocate of education. In the middle of the nineteenth century the Brothers came to London in service of the impoverished Catholic community and within a short time they had six schools spread throughout the city centred upon Islington. From London they moved north, to Dundee, and in the 1870s to the Border Country where, in Dumfries, the junior training centre and provincial headquarters were set up.

It was in that junior training centre, *le juvenat* or juniorate, that we learned of the opening of the African mission. Young though I was, sixteen at the time, I immediately made up my mind that, if and when possible, I would be part of that mission. Novitiate, scholasticate, university and three years' teaching later I was asked to take my part. The call to Africa was a far cry from the little prep college on the shores of the Firth of Clyde where I had been happily engaged, but the call was real and welcome and I was more than happy to accept.

And thus I found myself, as dusk was falling, bumping along the palm-fringed road, through the village and up the laterite track to the school that was to be home to me for the next nine years, little realising as we crunched up the driveway, past the school building and on to the to the staff house, exactly how eventful those nine years were to be.

The welcome again was warm. Friends had come in from lonely outposts in the surrounding bush to welcome the newcomer. Supper was followed by an impromptu sing-song accompanied by guitar and fiddle, a ritual I was to learn, very much part of life there. When it was ascertained that I was prepared to scrape the fiddle and croak a song, the welcome was the warmer.

I went down to the market the next day; it was Orie, big market day. Kieran had work to do at the district office and I was left to wander around the stalls. "See a bit of life at the grass roots," I had been advised. I attempted to do so.

"White-man, come buy, come buy."

I took an orange from the tray balanced delicately on the head of the little girl, smiling beneath her load and I gave her a penny. The floodgates opened. There was a rush to sell me everything from onions to cigarettes, coconuts, mangoes, avocado pears, bicycle parts. I was offered shirts, specially imported at cheap-cheap price, shoes, sandals, umbrellas. An old lady offered me a courgette from her little store of vegetables. I was about to take it from her when a voice behind me intervened. I turned. A smartly dressed young man complete with briefcase and furled umbrella smiled and introduced himself, a past pupil of the school. He had recognised the lamb among the shearers: "Before you buy, Brother, you must learn to bargain. I will show you, but first we must celebrate your arrival in our country."

My cicerone led the way to a cabin-bar, offered me a seat at an oilclothed table and ordered two glasses of palm wine. "This is good, mild morning-wine, still fermenting," he explained, "by evening it will be stronger." I sipped at the pungent foaming liquor and decided it was quite strong enough. The bartender asked for three pence. Raphael gave him two pennies and a level stare: "How you say three pence, my friend! You take me for some kind bloody fool! One glass, one penny; two glass, two penny."

We continued our tour of the market stalls, Raphael putting on an occasional histrionic display of bargaining for my enlightenment and eventually we found our way to the industrial section and the 'Orlu United Carpenters' shed, palm thatched and busy.

The sawing and hammering stopped. "Welcome, my friend." I was offered a chair. "Fine chair. Myself I dey make-am." The snuffbox was offered. The tiny pinch I applied to my nostrils was out of all proportion to the cataclysm of coughing and spluttering it appeared to produce. The carpenters were delighted. "Good snuff?"

"Very good snuff."

"Strong pass UK snuff?"

I nodded.

The sawyer went back to his bench well satisfied, stretching his eyes and twitching his nose as the snuff cleared his sinuses.

"Good wood?" I asked.

"Very good wood. Iroko. Strong. Ants no chop-am. This one no good. Wet. Feel-am. No get chance dry proper. Everything now be too quick. Hurry-am! Hurry-am! Feeneesh-am, feeneesh-am! Brother Marcellus, he tell we: 'A ting of beauty is a joy forever'. We make table; fine ting; smooth-am, polleesh-am. Next year for dry season he go split. Pam!"

The age-old complaint of the craftsman: progress in a hurry. I sympathised and we moved on.

I was invited to the chief's palace for lunch. Chief Patrick was waiting for us, Chief Patrick Acholonu, Igwe of Orlu. I was welcomed cordially and invited to be seated. Oji was produced, kola nut with alligator pepper. Kieran, as senior guest, was invited to break the nuts which were passed to the company with all the ceremony of a communion.

"This," explained the Chief, "is oji. He who gives oji, it is said, gives life." The nut was strong and bitter. The palm wine accompanying it was mild in comparison.

"And this," said the Chief, bending down and taking a bottle from his leather bag, "is the oji of your own country." It was a bottle of White Horse whisky. The lunch, of yam and goat's meat, passed in a gentle haze.

School was to open within a few days and I went with Marcellus to Onitsha to buy food for the new term. Onitsha, he told me, boasted the biggest covered market in West Africa, selling everything from a needle to an anchor. I saw no anchor but everything else seemed to be on sale.

The senior prefect and his refectorian were waiting for us with the school cook and their purchases of yam, gari, rice, beans, dried fish and salt. I was introduced and made to feel warmly welcome. Goods were paid for in crisp, red Nigerian notes; transport was arranged and provisions dispatched.

Marcellus had building materials to order and we threaded our way through the market's labyrinth of alleys crowded with stalls, highlife music and laughing, shouting, cajoling market people: "White-man, come buy, come buy!" We came to the building section. Here business was brisk: galvanised sheeting, cement and sand, wood, concrete blocks, window frames, glass, nuts and bolts, screws, nails and tacks. 'Nigeria Independent Traders' were doing a roaring trade. Marcellus ordered what was needed for the biology block he was building, haggled over prices and transport, laughed and bantered, shook hands all round, paid a deposit and left.

"We need some sports equipment," he told me, "a few other items then we can have a spot of lunch and get back."

The trader in sports goods was

Marcellus,
Latin scholar, master builder, clerk of
works, Jack of all trades

more vocal and light-hearted than the builders' merchants: "White-man, what ting you go buy now?"

"What ting you go sell now?" I felt Marcellus had his cards close to his chest.

"You want-am, I get-am; plenty-plenty ting: football, cricket bat, tennis. All ting for sport."

"What of tape measure now?"

"I get-am." The stallholder dived into his stock and produced a builders' tape. "Look at, fine one. One hundred yards. Be very fine tape. Be cloth material; no be plastic. Be leather case, proper leather; look-am now; no be cheap-cheap plastic-plastic."

Already yards of the tape were spewing across the stall and alleyway as the trader with prodigal liberality unwound the measure.

"You like-am?"

Marcellus nodded: "What you say for price now?"

The merchant looked around with caution and lowered his voice: "For you, Sir-Fadder, I give special price; no be price for market. For you I give cheap-cheap price. Na dis way you go be my customer."

"How you say for cheap price now, my friend? Say-am."

"For dis fine tape measure, sir, for you alone, make I say tree poun."

"*E woooh!*" Marcellus rocked back in wonder and consternation. "Na dis man go t'ief me-oh." He appealed to the little crowd clustering around. "How you say tree poun, my friend? Na dis ting no be one poun."

The crowd chorused appreciation at the burgeoning contest. I could feel my embarrassment deepen.

"How you say one poun, my friend? Na you make joke?" The trader was indignant. "Look at now dis fine measure. Quick, make you pay two pound seven and six. I go dash you. Take-am."

"*Pam abuo ego asaa na shishi! Chineke m ooo! Ovuru ivu, enyim.*"

Marcellus' sudden switch into impassioned Igbo convulsed the little crowd still further. His repetition of the price in the stallholder's own language and his expostulation at its considered enormity changed the stakes. The trader was momentarily off his guard but returned to the heightened contest with vigour. Laughing, he shook hands with his opponent: "*Enyim!*" (My friend.)

"*Nwam!*" (My brother.)

"*Iwu onye olee?*" He asked Marcellus where he was from.

"*Awum onye Orlu.*"

Marcellus, despite, I later discovered, his vestigial knowledge of the language, had recognised the Owerri accent. The trader gleefully clasped hands again, grinning from ear to ear. "*Nwam!*" He looked towards me: "And your friend, he sabe speak Igbo also?"

"Na disse man no speak Igbo; speak Geordie."

"Geordie? Na what ting dis Geordie?"

"Be kind English na whe man dey talk for interior."

The crowd looked at me intently with silent interest, I thought, for a Yorkshireman, Marcellus was trailing his coat but I was in no way fitted to plunge into the fast-flowing verbal stream. He produced a tin of cigarettes, long dark cigarillos, and offered one to the trader who accepted it with wonder and delight shared no less by the growing crowd. A match was produced and a cloud of aromatic smoke arose as the trader exhaled with beaming satisfaction.

"Na dis cigar from UK?"

"Fernando Po."

"Ha, na you dey smuggle-am. Be fine ting."

Marcellus handed the tin around the older spectators to the accompaniment of nodding heads and smiling 'tank you's'.

The trader, ever mindful of his occupation, sidled up: "What you say for measure now? You give me good price?"

In the end we discovered that the ring price was twenty-three shillings and the trader was delighted with the bargaining and his thirty shillings. We walked on.

"That was a bit rough on the stallholder."

Marcellus was genuinely surprised at my question. "What do you mean?"

"Well, he asked for three pounds and you gave him only thirty shillings."

"If I'd given him three pounds he'd have been broken-hearted."

"Broken-hearted?"

"That he hadn't asked for more."

We had come to that part of the market where cloth was sold. Cotton is grown in the North and the cloth produced was evident in abundance and with it much, much more: bales and bales of multicoloured cloth stacked high and flowing over, yard upon yard of cloth festooning every stall, draped from the roof space, cascading down in a glorious panoply of colour and gorgeous pattern, boldly printed pattern of unmistakably African design, simple run-of-the-mill Manchester prints, shimmering silks and luxurious velvets, brocades and muslins, linens and laces.

The marketeers, judging by their dress, were Northerners. The flowing agbada and high-piled headgear seemed more appropriate against a background of desert sands and camel trains than a crowded township market. Marcellus greeted a grandfather seated amidst his bales of cloth: "*Sanu, Malam.*"

The old man's jaws stopped chewing and he opened his mouth in a wide grin. The gum he was chewing had discoloured his broken teeth: "*Nagejia.*"

Marcellus picked up a length of lace curtaining and ran his hand beneath it: "For one yard?"

"One pound."

I discovered that the bargaining at a Northern stall was not the hilarious experience we had enjoyed with the Igbo marketeers. The trader whose ancestors had stood poised in conquest at the edge of the Southern Forest was not to be put off his guard by the offer of a Philippino cigarette. A faraway look came into his eyes when Marcellus suggested a price reduction, a faraway look that had in it all the dignity of the son of traders who had travelled the silk roads of the East, whose camel trains had, across the desert, brought silks from Arabia, whose trading posts at Kano had furnished pavilions of emirs and palaces of sultans.

"One pound."

We left him chewing on his aromatic gum and made our crowded way towards the edge of the market, the blaring of the music, the noise and shouting and smells and sunshine.

A shouting, laughing crowd attracted our attention. An outsize lady of monumental proportions, aided and encouraged by her daughter and the stallholder, was trying on a brassiere to the unrestrained amusement of the crowd. She was not happy.

"Na dis one no be big," she protested vigorously. "'E go squeeze me too tight-o!"

"Na dis one pass all for Nigeria, Mama." The stallholder was positive. "No get bigger one for all West Africa. 'E go fit fine. Make you fine lady." The crowd roared with infectious laughter.

It was indeed a merry market. The euphoria that had been so obvious to me on my landing at Enugu and the laughter and light-heartedness of the Orlu market echoed with the crowds that surged around us. The joy of the season was in the air, the crisp, bright, sun-filled dry-season air. I felt a joy to be part of the joy. We had wandered down Bright Street alive with the sound of music, African highlife competing in decibels with Handel's *Messiah*. I was suddenly reminded it was still Christmas, its spirit still alive.

The river Niger lay before us shimmering in the noonday sun, a great sheet of water two thousand miles from its source still on its rolling journey to the sea, the Niger of Mungo Park who had died in his attempt to find its outlet, the Niger of the Lander brothers, captured by tribesmen at this very point of the river and taken, trussed up in war canoes, to the spot that had been their quest, the delta where the Niger flows through its many streams to the ocean. Their report in 1830 caused a great stir and opened up the interior to exploration and conquest. I had read my books and now I gazed in wonder and awe at the mighty river alive with activity. Canoes still plied, not war canoes but traders, heavy laden, their sinewy oarsmen digging deep with paddles in rhythmic motion, their chanting clear across the sparkling water; fishermen upstream were casting nets; a ferryboat chugged its way across the river to the township on the western shore.

We were within the cathedral grounds in the shade of a flame-of-the-forest, its great sweeping branches protecting us from the fierce heat of the sun.

"Bishop Crowther of the Anglican Mission was the first to establish a Christian outpost here, then in the 1880s a missionary Spiritan priest from Alsace and two Irish Brothers opened up the Catholic Mission. They were brave men, died young, malaria." Marcellus pointed to gravestones with their lichened lettering. "Some of them survived, Bishop Shanahan among them. He was the one who really got the mission on its feet. He's buried here. We'll have a look at the Cathedral, then a beer and some chop. Then home."

3

Literature

Term had started. The boys were returning, by car and on foot and in mammy-wagon, three hundred and sixty of them. The Principal, flanked by his body of prefects, was there to welcome them. The school, I learned, was run on strongly democratic lines, the executive very much in the hands of the senior prefects under the watchful eye of the headmaster. The system worked like a well-oiled machine: dormitories were assigned, class lists read out, prefects assumed office, refectorian and assistants took charge of dining-hall arrangements, and all settled down to routine.

The evening meal concluded, school assembled in chapel. The Principal gave his crisp, formal, light-hearted address of welcome; the senior prefect read out brief notices, night prayer was recited; the service and the day ended with the full-voiced singing of the 'Salve Regina', the sound of it, treble and bass, ringing across the compound, the playing fields, the valley and the hills beyond, the same words, the same chant that had echoed across the mountains of eastern France a century and a half before. The school was part of a long tradition.

I was assigned a fifth-year English literature class and found myself hurled into the maelstrom of West African academia: sixty eager students hungering for knowledge, preparing for their Cambridge (Overseas) School Certificate. Shakespeare was on the bill of fare and they were wrestling vigorously with the archaic language of the text. We had scarcely taken up the reading before hands were shooting in the air. In vain I appealed to them to listen to the text, to enjoy the sound of the language before analysing its meaning. Clarification, however, was demanded.

"What does it mean: 'Clerestories as lustrous as ebony'? What are 'clerestories'?"

"A wall with windows, usually above the nave of a church to give light."

"Is not ebony black? How can clerestories be lustrous as ebony?"

"Feste was speaking paradoxically."

"What is paradoxically?"

"What is: 'I did impeticos thy gratility'?"

"Read the context."

"Sir Andrew says: 'Thou wast in very gracious fooling last night when thou didst speak of Pigrogromitus of the Vapians passing the Equinoctial of Quebus. I sent thee sixpence for thy leman? Hadst it?' Then Feste says: 'I did impeticos thy gratility.' What is 'impeticos'?"

"Pocket. I did pocket thy gratuity. I got your money."

"Who was Pigrogromitus?"

"Who were the Vapians?"

"What is the Equinoctial of Quebus?"

This from young lads whose native language was Igbo, who had graduated to West African pidgin, who had started wrestling with standard English in primary school. Shakespeare's light-hearted linguistic frolics presented toilsome learning: Shakespeare pored over and analysed, each line and word scrutinized for its etymological meaning, each meaning further analysed for deeper meaning which Shakespeare himself would not always have recognised.

It was the Nottingham Players who, some time later, cut the Gordian knot: Judi Dench and John Neville and company. They came out to West Africa and presented Shakespeare on the boards. The students loved it. We took a group to Enugu to see *Twelfth Night* and *Macbeth*. Shakespeare in the flesh: Toby Belch strutting and bellowing, Sir Andrew quivering, Maria upbraiding, Malvolio fuming, Olivia pining, Viola simpering. They relished every word and gesture. The groundlings at the Globe could not have been a more appreciative audience, for they were groundlings: not for the Enugu junior audience the ermine stoles and evening-suited elegance of the West End but open-necked shirts and groundnuts and oranges and audience participation. They knew the play, screeds of it by heart, and why shouldn't they join in? The players didn't seem to mind; one of them afterwards told us they loved it, not speaking their words into an empty pit of blackness beyond the glare of the lights but throwing them out and having them hurled back by an audience on their very toes with excitement. The babble of excited tongues as they trooped from the theatre area told well of the audience appreciation.

Upper-school English students.

Macbeth, for the students, was more serious stuff: here was the very stuff of tragedy, here was high drama: Lady Macbeth avowing that she who had given suck would be prepared while yet the babe was smiling in her face, to pluck the nipple from its boneless gums and dash the brains out had she so sworn. Here were witches and deep magic with juju stews as potent as any in their native lore: root of hemlock digged in the dark, finger of birth-strangled babe. Here was Lady Macduff quietly pining for her husband while her child prattled and murderers were battering at the gate; here was her little son, stabbed to death before her very eyes: "He has killed me, Mother; run away I pray." The audience groaned and blinked back tears.

But all was not tragedy and gloom; the Porter at Hell's Gate saw to that. The students in the audience had read the play; they had studied the scene; it had been analysed and explained, vetted for possible context questions, documented and stored away. Now it sprang to life in a way it never had in mission school or convent classroom. The Porter rose to the audience and the audience rose to the Porter. They loved it. They roared with delight as groundlings would and egged him on for more and more he gave, more explicitly. I began to see why the Puritans burned down the Globe. Things were never the same in the English literature class after that scene.

They were bright young sparks in the English literature class. Dickens they loved and took to their own. We were reading *Great Expectations* together. The British Council, that valiant protagonist of culture, had made available David Lean's film of the story. It was a delight to sit with such an audience in the evening as distant lightning washed across the darkened sky and the Bell and Howell projector chattered away whilst we watched on the whitewashed wall that served as a screen, the river mist creeping in from the desolate mudflats, heard the gasp as the convict's face exploded on the screen, the chuckles of mirth at Uncle Pumblechook's idiosyncrasies. 'May I? May I, Mr Pip?' became a stock greeting among the fifth year. They revelled in the beauty of Estella, shuddered at the horror of Miss Havisham, positively roared in approbation at the manliness of Gargery taking on his journeyman, and hissed in suppressed indignation at the termagant Mrs Gargery who did not know her place. "Ha! This woman, she is too much."

But the film did not dull the edge of their literary criticism; indeed it heightened it.

"Did not Joe Gargery have flaxen hair?"

"Yes, in the story."

"In my dictionary it tells me that flaxen is a colour that is light yellow. The person in the play had black hair; also he was not a giant."

Obviously Lean's casting director did not have a West African 'Cantab' literature class in mind when he chose his Joe Gargery.

Their eyes to the minutiae of the book itself were even more keen.

"In this book it says that Bentley Drummle came from Somersetshire. It says he came from rich people down in Somersetshire."

"Yes."

"Later in the book when Pip meets Drummle he says he came from Shropshire. He says to Drummle: 'Something like your native Shropshire'."

I was reminded strongly of the lawyer Jaggers. The speaker eyed me with the air of an advocate: 'Get out of that one, dear Sir.'

I did not attempt to. I congratulated the boy on his astuteness; we checked in other editions and found the same inconsistency.

Jaggers appealed to them strongly, the larger than life, brow-beating, articulate, invincible Jaggers. I wondered how many West African students had taken up law in the steps of Dickens's legal giant. An artful response in class, a felicitous phrase in discussion gained the speaker a thumping of the desk and the acclamation of 'Jaggers! Jaggers!'

It was not simply Jaggers's oratory that appealed to them; many shared his incisive skill in laying bare the bones of an argument. We were reading Hemingway's *The Old Man and the Sea*. A hand kept waving in the air. It was not to be ignored.

"Well, Adazie, what is it?"

"There is a mistake in this book."

"Tell us about it."

"It is the picture on the front cover; either the man is facing the wrong direction or the sun is in the wrong side of the sky."

"Explain."

He did so with remarkable skill, pointing out the minute, consistent detail of the author and the apparent inconsistency of the illustration. I suggested he write to the publishers and point this out, which he did and Jonathan Cape wrote back accepting his argument and promising to have the mistake rectified in the next edition.

African authors were not ignored. There was a growing and understandable reaction against the diet of Victorian literature. I read Chinua Achebe with the prep class. His recently published *Things Fall Apart* was sweeping across the literary fields of the East like a bush fire in the dry-season wind. The students thrilled to him. Here was bone of their bone, flesh of their flesh, of their time and of their place, enshrining in glowing literature the stories of their fathers, home-grown and flowering with the imagery of their land. They knew Okonkwo. They knew his world.

I read the book with an interest bordering on fascination. It provided an insight deeper than any textbook could have done into the ways and the lore of the land, of a generation that had not completely passed away. The book spoke of rituals that covered life from birth to death, the rejoicing at the birth of a child, the goat that was slaughtered to honour the mother, circumcision after two market weeks, the naming ceremony after seven weeks. It also spoke of the darker side of birth: the birth of twins, dragged from their mother and thrown into 'bad bush'.

The book spoke of happier times: Obierika's feast in honour of his daughter's betrothal was a happy time. All the village was invited. The women arrived early bearing gifts of coco-yam and smoked fish, plantain and salt. Young men split wood, fires were lighted, children carried water and the cooking began. Yam and cassava, rice and maize were pounded and boiled. Goats were slaughtered, bitterleaf was chopped, soup was prepared. As the heat of the day cooled into evening the older men arrived. Kola was presented and shared, the palm wine was broached and feasting began. It was indeed a great feast. As night fell, torches were lit. The young men sang songs and the girls danced, the bride among them. Gifts were presented and there was much laughter and merriment and more dancing and music.

Young men and maidens dance and sing and old men die. Ezeudu died and what an explosion of grief rocked the compound! Cannon rent the air, the 'ekwe' talking drum rattled out the news, women wailed and men gave vent to full-chested lamentation. Ancestral spirits appeared, 'egwugwu', dressed in raffia, wearing masks, wielding sharpened machetes, chasing terrified villagers. Darkness fell, the speech of farewell was made and Ezeudu's body was lowered into the earth.

And that, I learned, was only the first burial. Second burial which honoured the name and memory of the deceased took place some time later when the family had gathered resources and a feast befitting the old man's memory could be given. And what a feast! Families courted financial ruin with the expenses incurred in the rites of second burial: gunpowder and cannon, bands and musicians, professional mourners, drinking and feasting, drumming and dancing, as long as the money held out and then beyond into crippling debt.

"Why does the Church forbid second burial?"

I didn't know that the Church did forbid second burial; maybe it was because of the financial burden incurred. I would enquire.

"Bishop Shanahan had a second burial."

"Had he?"

My students proceeded to describe to me the details of Bishop Shanahan's 'homecoming': the gunpowder and the fusillades, the endless processions, the drumming and the dancing. It had been a glorious homecoming for their Father who had died far away from his beloved Igbos, from his beloved Niger. Shanahan had arrived from Ireland, a strapping young man from the Galtee Mountains, stepping ashore at Onitsha at the beginning of the century and he had given his life to the land and the people whom he loved so well and who loved him. He had walked the length and breadth of Eastern Nigeria, trekking as far as the hills of Bamenda; he had talked with chiefs and catechised children, he had built churches and clinics and schools. Above all he had built schools. The toil demanded its toll; his health broke down and he was invalided to the highlands of East Africa where he died. Some ten years after his death his body was brought back with all pomp and ceremony and laid in the Cathedral beside his beloved Niger.

An evening stroll along the little paths winding
through the palm trees, chatting to the children
on the way, learning a little of their language

Some time later I attended a second burial service in a compound near the school. On an evening stroll along the little paths winding among the palm trees, chatting to the children on the way, learning a little of their language, I had been attracted by the sound of gunfire and drumming from a compound. I had been made immediately and warmly welcome, given a seat and a glass of palm wine. The dancing and the music and gunfire continued unabated. The old man had died some time before; now his memory was honoured in a way befitting his life.

I barely made it back in time for Vespers. There was a certain raising of eyebrows when I told them where I had been. Second-burial ceremonies were to be discouraged, *mon frère;* too close a connection with ancestor worship.

4

Religion

Schoolwork was not confined to the literary scene; I had Class Three Religious Education. The question soon arose: who was educating whom?

Things started well: thirty bright-eyed, uniformed students standing smartly to attention as I walked into the classroom. They gave me the now familiar but meaningful words of welcome. I returned the greeting and told them to be seated. They thanked me and sat. The syllabus indicated that the third year were dealing with the Sacraments and in particular the sacrament of Baptism. A short discussion was followed by direct questioning: "What is a sacrament?"

Okereke was on his feet: "A sacrament is an outward sign of inward grace, freely bestowed upon us for our sanctification and salvation." His answer was pat; his smile was merry; his religious knowledge sound.

"And the sacrament of Baptism?"

Thirty hands shot up. I nodded. "Fidelis Okonkwo. Baptism is a sacrament which cleanses us from original sin, makes us Christians, children of God and heirs to the Kingdom of Heaven."

It was obvious they had learned their catechism. I probed a little deeper, a footnote: "What do we mean by original sin?"

Again the forest of hands. "Original sin, otherwise known as concupiscence, is an inborn tendency towards evil said to be derived from the sin of Adam, the original sin."

Questions were followed by answers, clear, correct and confident. I probed even deeper and opened up the discussion. Their knowledge was more than theoretical: Alphonsus with his knowledge of 'book' had acted as assistant catechist. He told us the story in vivid atmospheric detail of his being called to the bedside of an old dying man who desired the sacrament of Baptism as preparation for his entry into the next life but there was a complication.

"What was that?"

Eze had five wives.

"What did you do?"

"You know that polygamy is not allowed by the Church. I explained to Mr Eze." Alphonsus went on to describe in vivid detail the deathbed scene. I pictured the young catechist bending low over the dying man, the whispered urgent message, the silent assimilation of the message in the light of eternity glowing so near. Eze slowly nodded in affirmation. His wives were called. They came stooping low into the darkened hut and squatted in the presence of their dying husband. Eze spoke quietly; Alphonsus bent to hear. Carefully he relayed the whispered words to the wives, their eyes wet with tears, intent upon the speaker. Alphonsus told them that Eze had decided: Anyi was his wife, his first wife, his only wife; the decision was final and absolute. The others, the mothers of his children, were no longer his wives; he renounced them. He was about to receive the cleansing waters of Christian Baptism; he must obey the laws of the Christian Church. I heard in my mind the stifled sobs of the rejected wives. Slowly the old man raised himself from his bed and looked at each of the mothers of his children in turn. Alphonsus took water, poured it on the head of the dying man and pronounced the words of Baptism. Eze slowly lowered himself back on his bed and died.

"What about his wives?"

"Reverend Father came some time after; he said there must be no change; they must continue to share; they did so. After, all were baptised; now all are Christian."

The boys in the class, born storytellers all, had watched intently the expression on my face as Alphonsus spun his tale. Here, they quickly surmised, was an innocent upon whose emotions and credulity even an amateur storyteller could play as upon a stringed instrument. The tales poured forth.

One boy had a sister who worked in a nearby maternity clinic. She could vouch for the truth of the tale. One of her patients, a young mother, had died in childbirth; the babe had survived but would not live. Should she baptise the child? I was about to give my answer pat, based upon my years of study of Christian doctrine when the boy continued, there was a problem: how could she baptise such a baby? The nurse called in Reverend Sister.

"What was the problem?"

"The baby had two heads."

Another boy was on his feet with a tale challenging the very fundamentals of moral theology. This was a true tale because he had seen it in a newspaper; he still had the photograph which he could show me. Other boys had seen it.

"What?"

A girl in a village in the interior had given birth to a child but was it a child?

"What do you mean?"

The father said it was not his; he had nothing to do with it.

"The girl had committed adultery?" I was obviously dealing with students more worldly-wise than the innocent little prep-school boys I had been teaching in Scotland.

Yes: she had committed adultery but with whom? With what?

"What do you mean?"

"The photograph shows a picture of a baby covered from head to toe with thick matted hair."

There was a pause to allow me to absorb the implications. Was such a baby, such a creature, eligible for the sacrament of Baptism? What was the genetic possibility of interspecies procreation? "Who made you?" "God made me?"

"In whose image and likeness did God make you?" "God made me in His own image and likeness." The simplicity of catechetical formulae crumbled before the onslaught of question and anecdote.

"I will take note of your questions."

"Was Jesus a White-man?"

The question was thrown at me some time later after I had completed a piece of work which gave me a sense of deep satisfaction yet which aroused an antipathy which the boys in the religion lesson did little to conceal.

I had come across a life-size metal image of Christ in agony. It was obviously meant to be hung upon a cross, but since its arrival from the home province it had lain in an outhouse gathering dust and losing its coat of what had once been gold paint. Having retrieved it and planned with the school carpenters the cross upon which the figure would be hung, Nicholas and Nathaniel went to work with a will, selecting a solid length of iroko, sawing, planing, mortising, bolting the pieces together and preparing its position in the school chapel.

Meantime I went down to the market to find paint. Gold colour was unavailable but I did eventually find a hard-gloss, brilliant white enamel which I thought would serve and I set to work, cleaning, scraping, scrubbing the figure and applying the paint.

After evening prayer with the chapel to ourselves we hung the figure, bolted it into position and stood back to admire our handiwork. I was well pleased. In the dim light of the sanctuary lamp, the figured glowed with all the beauty of Carrara marble. My carpenter friends' enthusiasm was more restrained.

The following morning I was made to understand why; the reaction of my Third Year students was more explicit: why had I made the figure of Christ

Staff, Bishop Shanahan College

Saint Columba's Prep College

so unequivocally white? I was taken severely aback. The colour had nothing to do with it. My pupils were not impressed. We discussed the matter at length but I made little headway: I had offended their sensitivity. I was made to feel I had committed an indiscretion.

I went back down to the market. I searched the stalls and at last came across what I was determined to find: a tin of high-gloss, enamel paint, brilliant black. After night prayer I went into the chapel armed with brush and paint and set to work with determination. After an hour's energetic labour, I stood back to admire my handiwork. What had been a figure of Christ glowing in the crimson light with all the beauty of white marble, now glowed in that same light with the beauty of highly polished ebony. I was well pleased and satisfied.

The next morning I was confronted with a less than positive reaction from my pupils: Jesus was not a Black-man. I shrugged.

During the day in the parching heat, the paint continued to dry and harden. During the equally dry night, the hardening process continued and the black enamel paint began to crack, revealing with startling vividness the white beneath. When the boys trooped in for prayers the next morning, they beheld, upon the cross, a Christ who was neither white nor black but a beautiful mosaic of both. The boys felt that Christ himself had resolved our impasse. They were well satisfied. Their science teacher's reference to unequal molecular contraction meant little.

5

History

My education continued under the tutelage of the Lower Sixth. I had set an essay entitled 'Independence Celebrations' expecting colourful accounts of those heady days in October when the flag of the new Nigeria had first been raised, when Nigeria had taken its place in the forum of the world, blissful days to be alive, heavenly to be young, et cetera. Some essays I read did deal with the celebrations, briefly, succinctly, but the stress and the burden of the tales I read dealt with the bitter struggle for Independence rather than the euphoria of its achievement.

Certainly the flag had been raised amidst great rejoicing, with fireworks and gracious speeches. A new anthem had hailed Nigeria from a thousand voices echoed and re-echoed throughout the country from city to village, from coastal fringe to desert frontier; dancing and drumming, marching and feasting had marked the dawn of that day of days and long after darkness had fallen on that first day of October in the year of the Lord nineteen hundred and sixty, the fires of Independence burned bright in the night sky.

But the feasting and the dancing and the drumming were but one aspect of Independence, the froth hissing lightly at the brim of the palm-wine pitcher. The draught itself was deeper and more bitter. I was made to taste of that draught to the dregs: here was a neophyte ready for the learning.

The story of the granting of Nigerian Independence had featured widely in the British press: articles from special correspondents had supplied the background information, geographical, historical, political. Front page stories had covered the actual ceremony; photographs had portrayed the event and its leading participants: Princess Alexandra was in Lagos representing Her Majesty the Queen; Sir James Robertson represented Her Majesty's Government. The Prime Minister of the Federation, Alhaji Sir Abubakar Tafawa Balewa was portrayed smiling quietly in this moment of glory; Doctor Nnamdi Azikiwe, architect of his country's independence, was there. All was smiles and handshakes. I had read the accounts with absorbed interest.

And why should there not be smiles and why should there not be handshakes? Sixty short years from the first day of the century to the first day of October 1960 had witnessed the creation of the giant of Africa that was Nigeria, sixty short years during which a column of Empire troops had pacified a country many times larger than the seat of that Empire, had disarmed and welded together warring tribes from steaming jungles to sandy plains; sixty years during which traders and administrators and missionaries had pushed ever further inland from fever-swamp, up treacherous waterways, across mountain barriers to frontiers of the unknown; sixty years during which roads had been built and rivers bridged; railways had been carved through thick forest, laid across miles of open scrubland, cut through mountain barriers, linking town to town, hinterland to port. Schools and hospitals had been built; colleges of higher education were flourishing; trading companies were established, shops and markets expanded; banks and office blocks towered in the centres of commerce. Cities bustled, traffic roared, planes landed, ships came and went; Nigeria had come of age.

And all this in a reign of peace. Where once Lugard's West African Frontier Force with Maxim gun and efficiency had moved from coastal town to desert fort, quelling opposition and establishing treaties, now a uniformed civilian police force, unarmed, maintained order and harmony. Where once a district officer in shorts and sun helmet, seated at a rickety table in a village clearing within the palm tree's shade, had listened through an interpreter to plea and counter-plea, now robed and bewigged advocates in ornate courts of justice expounded law, whilst politicians, duly elected, legislative and executive, were hammering out the finer points of Nigeria's Constitution with eloquence and skill. The Winds of Change had blown fresh; the Torch of Freedom had been handed on; the Mandate of Governance had been ceremoniously bestowed.

The essays I read painted a less euphoric picture: the Torch of Freedom had not been handed, it had been snatched; the Mandate had not been bestowed, it had been wrenched. The illusions which the political pages of the local press had begun to undermine were shattered by the literary onslaughts of the Lower Sixth essayists: their firebrands were lit to dispel the darkness, their pens were poised to cut away the misapprehensions sown by an Imperialist press. I was to be given the facts as they were, and facts I was given, by the ream.

Nigeria had been born amidst toil and sweat and if a great deal of blood had not been spilled, certainly printer's ink had, vat-loads. Nnamdi Azikiwe, I learned, was the journalist who made the ink to flow, not an ordinary hack but one who saw in journalism the power of the third estate. He prepared himself well to wield that power. An Igbo from the North where his father was a pay clerk in the army, Zik, as he came to be known, returned to Onitsha in the south for his education and on to America. There he worked his way through college, as a waiter, as a miner, even as a boxer to eventually gain his doctorate in political science. In 1934 he returned to West Africa, aflame with ambition to set his people free.

The field of Nigerian politics was tinder-dry; Zik set it on fire. The paper he founded was the *West African Pilot* and in edition after edition he poured out protest, propaganda and invective against his country's colonial overlords: 'My country groans, a footstool of Imperialism, a victim of Bureaucracy, a challenge to our Manhood.' His policy rang out from the essays that I read: 'African irredentism, political risorgimento, economic self-determination'.

Puzzled and bemused by the polemic of the essays, stung somewhat by what I considered the gratuitous invective in certain of them, I turned to the pages of history, less rhetorical, more factual.

I delved into the story of European involvement in the area, reading, among others, Michael Crowder's fact filled *Story of Nigeria*. It was the Portuguese, I learned, who made the first approaches, interested in the gold and spices of West Africa. But after the opening up of the Americas it had been the slave trade that attracted the Europeans in wholesale numbers to the shores. Once the New World became part of the European development programme it was soon discovered that there was more money in slaves than in pepper. Twenty-five million souls over the years, it was stated, were rounded up by African raiding parties, marched in chains to the shore-line, herded into barracoons and sold to the European slave traders waiting offshore.

Then in 1807, Britain, by Act of Parliament, outlawed the slave trade and set about its suppression. A quarter of the British Navy, the Africa Squadron of some sixty vessels, patrolled the coast. Its purpose was twofold: to enforce the Act of Parliament abolishing slavery and to protect legitimate British trading interests.

These same trading interests had recovered after the suppression of the slave trade. The value of the palm kernel with its rich golden oil was realised. The machinery of the Industrial Revolution needed lubricant; fossil oil was virtually non-existent; palm oil suited the purpose ideally. Added to that was the value of the oil to the soap industry. The empty wharves of Bristol, Glasgow and Liverpool were now busy with this new traffic. Fortunes were made, massive fortunes and quick. Mary Kingsley in her *Four Guineas* tells the story of a palm-oil trader named Hartze who, on leave in London, was wont to take over an entire hotel in Lancaster Gate complete with staff, kitchen and cellar and there would entertain his friends on the best of everything until his money ran out. He would then pack his bags, ship back to West Africa and rebuild his fortune, a regular oil baron.

Trade in West African waters was profitable but risky. Traders needed protection. The British Government was not loath to afford that protection. In 1849, Consul John Beecroft was commissioned to protect legitimate traders in the coastal areas of the Bights of Benin and Biafra. He did so with a thoroughness that left a heavy mark on any opposition. With the sails of the Africa Squadron fluttering on the horizon, he set about establishing the might of his authority. The King of Bonny Island in the Niger delta was suspected of the murder of certain British merchants. Beecroft sent in a gunboat and forced a treaty from King Pepple reducing him to puppet status. Lagos was still flourishing as a slave centre. Beecroft had the town bombarded and brought within the Protectorate. The King of Calabar was suspected of dealing in human sacrifice; the marines were called in, the town was razed to the ground, the King deposed. McGregor-Laird's ship, *The Rainbow*, was attacked on its journey upstream. A gunboat was dispatched; the shore batteries were silenced; a number of neighbouring villages were destroyed. Traders were protected, slave raiding was curbed, the Protectorate of the Oil-Rivers was established.

In 1863 Lagos was officially annexed and the Colony established. Lagos was well on the road to self-development; traders and missionaries had done sterling work. Even before the gun salute of *HMS Prometheus* echoed over the bay, a westernised African elite, not a few educated in England, were beginning to take their place in public life. That same gun salute was echoed by the voices of the mission-school choir singing 'God Save the Queen'. Trade was flourishing, no longer in slaves but in palm oil, cocoa, rubber. Palmerston's pretext for annexation was suppression of the slave trade; his reason was protection of the trading routes.

This protection was needed on two counts, to defend the trade from attack by tribes in the Lagos hinterland and to curb encroachment from the west by French trading companies based in Dahomey backed by armed detachments attempting a link-up with disaffected tribes to the north.

Some time after my arrival I had occasion to visit the West, Ibadan and its university. It was hard to equate the urbane student life we encountered, the sophistication of the residential area, the cheerful, brisk business of the market place with the direful tales of internecine warfare of which I had read, wars that had rocked the region less than a hundred years before. Where we sat debating the quality and content of the English literature syllabus, the strains of a *Brandenberg Concerto* drifting through an open window, the blood of Yoruba tribesmen had flowed in tribal warfare.

Beyond the sophistication of the littoral, the writ of government was shown scant respect. Intertribal warfare was one thing, but the effect this had on trade and development was catastrophic. Lagos acted with decision, bringing West Indian troops and Hausa constabulary into action against the rebellious tribes, routing them in a screaming-rocket attack and artillery bombardment, foiling the attempted link-up with the French to the west. Residents established Ibadan as the seat of power and set about the task of development. District officers were established, backed by armed constabulary for the protection of trade routes. Treaties were established with traditional rulers; internal slavery was proscribed, human sacrifice forbidden, Christianity protected. Roads were opened up, the Lagos–Ibadan railway was built. Trading stations were set up. The West was pacified.

Further north, however, unrest continued; the Fulani of Ilorin resented the edicts of Lagos. They continued the harassment of trade routes, threatening to push further south.

Governor Carter, of the West, complained to London. The area fell technically within the influence of the Royal Niger Company, a trading group united and organised with great commercial success by Sir George Taubman Goldie. With the granting of its royal charter, the Company had become in effect an arm of the British Government with rights to exclude rivals from its territory, the navigable Niger, to license at a price those companies it did permit to trade and to demand duty on that same trade. To enforce these rights and protect its own, the Company had an efficient and heavily armed field force.

Chamberlain, the Colonial Secretary in Salisbury's Conservative government, instructed Goldie to act. He did so with a show of might. Armed with Gatling guns, Maxims, incendiary shells, electric searchlights and a Whitworth twelve-pounder, he marched on Bida north of the Niger where he engaged and smashed the Nupe tribesmen who had been slave raiding in Company territory, then on to Ilorin. There he brought his artillery into play with devastating effect, reducing the town to rubble and crushing organised resistance with machine guns and repeating rifles. Goldie wrote to London in triumph and in effect: I came, I saw, I conquered.

Success, however, was not complete. Goldie had been stabbed in the back: a French force under Lieutenant Bretonnet had pushed in from the west and occupied Bussa, gaining access to the lower Niger.

This was serious. This was not a matter of hostile tribes requiring a sharp lesson; this was war. Anglo–French rivalry, always smouldering, had been ignited. Chamberlain set up an Imperial field force and put it under the command of Brigadier-General Lugard who, early in April 1898, arrived in Lokoja and prepared to do battle with the enemy. A state of undeclared war between the French and the British existed in West Africa. It was a crazy little war, detachments marching and counter-marching, flag-raising and bugle-blowing, two little insects buzzing at each other on the back of a sleeping giant.

Wilcocks, Lugard's second in command, was instructed to seek out the enemy wherever established. He did so with controlled energy, marching from village to village and establishing or re-establishing British authority over a bemused populace, confronting the French wherever he found them. It was a battle of wits and call-my-bluff with Hausa and Senegalese fingers ever ready on the triggers of their British and French rifles. At Kiama, Wilcocks came face to face with the enemy, dug-in and defiant. The British established themselves within sight of the French position and sent an ultimatum demanding immediate evacuation of the town. The threat of a British advance, flags aloft and rifles levelled, hung heavy in the air. The French were defiant. Wilcocks prepared to attack. It was a tense moment in Anglo–French relations.

Before the attack could take place, a messenger arrived from French headquarters. A truce had been declared; international boundaries had been agreed; the military were to return to base; boundary commissioners were to take over.

Chamberlain's aggressive policy had won the day; Salisbury was able to chart the frontiers of what was to become Nigeria very much in the British interest.

Chamberlain as Colonial Secretary viewed Britain's place in the 'scramble for Africa' with professional determination. Goldie was pensioned off. The Royal Niger Company was dissolved. A field force was officially established and on the first day of January 1900, the newly appointed High Commissioner, Sir Frederick Lugard, read out, before assembled dignitaries, the Order in Council which established as part of the British Empire the Northern and Southern Protectorates, hereinafter to be named Nigeria.

This was a brave claim for even the Queen-Empress to make: two hundred and fifty million acres of tropical West Africa with a handful of soldiers and administrators to make good that claim. But already Mr Lang, the boundaries commissioner, was out with his surveyors and their trundle-wheels mapping and designating streams and rivers, marking trees with a carved 'E', establishing for all to see the borders and the boundaries of the British Protectorate of Nigeria.

6

Pacification

The High Commissioner's task was not confined to office work and speech making. The Fulani were not prepared to allow their empire, the empire of the great Usman Dan Fodio to be taken over by the White-man without a struggle. Let battle commence. The armies of Kontagora and Nupe, northern states holding out grimly against imperial intrusion, gathered in war array, snorting steeds and jingling harness, hooves pounding desert sand, sunlight blazing on burnished spears. War horns blared and battle cries shrilled. Horse and rider shivered with excited anticipation. The British garrison at Wushishi, weakly defended, was singled out. The counter-attack began. Victoria's outpost of Empire was doomed.

Reinforcements were called up. Wilcocks, fresh from the Ashanti campaign, arrived with the main troop of the Frontier Force armed with cannon, breech-loading rifles, discipline and pluck. 'I never served with such fellows', Wilcocks wrote, 'always cheerful, brave and uncomplaining.' Discipline, artillery and the Maxim gun proved too much for Kontagora's cavalry. The Frontier Force smashed the attack and carried the campaign into their territory, burning, slaying, brooking no resistance.

Lugard followed up the victory with a northern advance, establishing effective control from Benue to Zaria, justifying his armed incursion on the basis of his mandate: the suppression of slavery. Even by West African standards, after all, Kontagora had been slave-trading with inhuman cruelty. The Chief was deposed; pockets of resistance were systematically wiped out; the main army continued its advance. Puppet emirs were established in the place of any offering resistance. The walled city of Bauchi was invested, the huge province of Bornu penetrated, 'British' emirs established. Village after village fell; tribe after tribe submitted. Province after province was established.

Sokoto held out. Its Sultan, the religious leader of the Moslem Fulani, allied himself to the Emir of Kano and prepared to resist. Lugard turned south and attacked Kano, entered the city after a token resistance, set up an administration and marched on the city of Sokoto.

In his preparation for conquest the Commissioner had left little to chance. Not only had he insisted on full and modern equipment for his troops but he had spared no pains in their training, drilling his plodding former-constables to an efficiency and combat strength that belied their numbers.

Few sights in face-to-face combat could be more daunting than a Fulani cavalry charge, steeds in tasselled harness, ornate saddles, studded headgear, riders in flowing robes and high-piled turbans, swords waving, spears glinting in the sun, ancient, high-pitched war cries, drums and gongs and squealing pipes. How prosaic in contrast the approach of Lugard's Frontier Force, marching in mechanical columns, forming rigid squares, holding fire in the face of the terrifying onrush of yelling horsemen, then, on command, opening up with rifle and Maxim gun, the dread weapons making an awful anachronism of the cavalry charge, a tactic paid for in the pathetic corpses littering the blood-soaked sands after the repulse. Small wonder the cavalry checked in the face of the leaden hail of death. Small wonder the Fulani withdrew. The Frontier Force dismantled their machine guns, harnessed their howitzers and plodded on.

The town of Gwandu fell; Katsina, on the border of open desert, capitulated. The road lay on to Sokoto, the key point of resistance. Lugard advanced. Outlying resistance was crushed; the artillery opened up with a brief bombardment; the infantry moved forward. Sokoto's army with their Sultan retired and Lugard moved into an undefended capital.

Lugard's speech on the occasion of formal takeover was eloquent. The Fulani empire was no more. The High Commissioner assumed the mantle of their great leader Usman Dan Fodio, he who had established that Empire, whose horsemen a century before had swept in from the west, smashing Hausa resistance, whose emirs had taken over the ancient Habe kingdom. Now force must yield to greater force as the spear had yielded to the rifle and cavalry to machine gun. Sokoto, the Commissioner proclaimed, was now part of the British Empire.

Lugard was firm but conciliatory: slavery was abolished, private warfare outlawed; a justice system would be established; the people and their leaders would be consulted; the practice of the Moslem religion would be respected.

The people of Sokoto submitted but their leader was at large, a Mecca for his followers who flocked to him in his retreat. Lugard trailed the Sultan. The armies met at Burmi and battle raged. Ahmadu, Sultan of Sokoto, hereditary leader of the Moslem faithful, was killed and, with his death, official resistance died.

Pockets of resistance continued, however. A detachment of mounted riflemen of the Frontier Force was attacked and wiped out in a village near Sokoto. The lone survivor, Sergeant Gosling, telegraphed command headquarters. Lugard was concerned; his authority had been challenged. The people of Gwandu grew restless: the arm of the mighty Empire had been shown to be vulnerable. What the village of Satiru did could not great Sokoto do? The capital remained calm. Lugard retraced his steps, attacked the centre of the uprising, executed the leader of the insurrection and turned on Gwandu. Resistance was crushed, the Emir deposed. The North was pacified.

Lugard turned from warfare to administration. Roads were surveyed and built for troop movement and trade; a railway was planned to link with the southern ports; a legal system was established; Residents were appointed and Emirs confirmed in office or otherwise.

The cost was considerable. Despite the victory in the North, the army had to be kept at fighting level and local resistance suppressed, all on an income of £150,000 a year. Small wonder the Commissioner was willing as much as possible to work through the existing Fulani administration. 'I am anxious to utilise their wonderful intelligence,' he wrote, 'they are born rulers.' His system of indirect rule came into being and proved, in the short term, to be successful. Pax Brittanica was established. Lugard left the country to take up the governorship of Hong Kong.

Lugard was essentially a fighting man and from this sprang his regard for the Northerner, a fighting spirit recognising a kindred spirit, admiring the courage of medieval warriors challenging the might of a modern army. As an army man he also admired and approved of their autocratic system of government and was not hesitant in using it to the advantage of his own administration. Such was not the case, however, in the south of the country and in particular the south-east. Lugard failed tragically to understand the mentality of the inhabitants of this region of dense forest and malarial swamp. He failed altogether to understand or even recognise the prevailing form of government that held sway, dismissing it as anarchy without realising that anarchy properly established can be the purest form of government.

Sir Ralph Moor was in charge of this area, allotted the unenviable task of establishing law and order beyond the fringes of coastal- and river-command. Already in 1898 he had launched determined attacks upon the Igbo hinterland but had advanced no further than the outposts of the territory repelled by the fierce onslaught of dane gun, spear and poisoned arrow. Further incursions beyond the Cross River met with similar repulse and Moor realised that to make any real advance, all-out attack was called for.

With the creation of the Southern Protectorate in 1900 such action was imperative. Intelligence reports indicated that the mainspring of the opposition, the power behind the spearmen, the force uniting and empowering the disparate tribesmen, were the People of the Oracle, the men of Arochukwu, the mysterious people of the East whose word was law, whose command went far beyond the confines of their villages, whose influence was a subtle, strangling force in society, commerce and religion. Among the Igbo, the Ibibio, the Efik people and beyond, the power of the Oracle of Arochukwu was recognised and feared.

On an island in a lake within the forest was a cave where was venerated the Long Juju of Arochukwu, venerated not only by the Aro people but also by the tribesmen bordering the region. Many came to worship at the shrine, travelling from afar to supplicate the help of the Oracle of the cave and many, it was said, who worshipped failed to return, entrapped by the guardians of the cave, imprisoned, tortured, sold into slavery or killed and eaten, for the Aro people, it was further whispered, were not only soothsayers but slavers and cannibals as well.

Commissioner Moor had been empowered to act through 'proclamation'. This he took to mean government through the barrel of the gun. He decided to use this power to strike at the heart of opposition. Urgently he outlined his plans to the Foreign Office requesting reinforcements and supplies, stating as his purpose the suppression of slavery, the safeguarding of trade routes and generally the establishment of law and order. Chamberlain acceded to his request with generosity. Moor's commanding officer, Lieutenant-Colonel Montanaro found himself with a well-armed force of some five thousand men and auxiliaries. The wet season gave him time to co-ordinate and train his force and with the coming of the dry season he gave orders to advance. Immense columns of men and supplies began moving on the Arochukwu objective. Local people stared in wonder as line after line of fully kitted soldiers streamed purposefully through their villages and along forest tracks. Little opposition was met.

By Christmas 1901 the army was in position. The village was overrun, a bridgehead secured, a link with the island was formed and the sappers moved in. They worked quickly and quietly and efficiently then left. There was a moment of silence and calm then a huge explosion shook island and lake and forest. The Oracle was no more. The heart of the opposition was destroyed.

The Arochukwu people eventually gave up their cannibalistic practices, their human sacrifice. They settled down to legitimate trade and gainful commerce. Arochukwu itself became a centre of learning established and encouraged by the Scots Presbyterian Mission, bringing to fruition the work of the 'wee Scots lassie' from Aberdeen, Mary Slessor, the 'Queen of Calabar'.

Montanaro's work was not completed with the destruction of the Long Juju. The Igbo does not belong to an autocratic society; there was no keystone whose removal would cause the collapse of the edifice. Resistance continued in the interior. The Third Niger Battalion was pinned down on many fronts in action after action, attempting to establish the authority of the Crown. Traditional rulers were brought under strict control or replaced by warrant-chiefs. Native courts were established, executive clerks were appointed and a body of functionaries, court messengers, in effect native police, was set up. The establishment of law and order went on apace, a difficult task but necessary; they were dangerous times.

Father Jordan in his life of Bishop Shanahan gives us some insight into how dangerous the times were. It was 1906, the wet season, Father Duhaze, a Frenchman of the Holy Ghost Order, had set out on trek from Onitsha, arriving after some mishaps at Uli where he was surrounded by a gang of youths and dragged before the Chief. Ogalunga towered in rage at the sight of this European, threatening to strike him down with the sweep of his machete. Father Duhaze stood his ground, calmly reached into the capacious pocket of his soutane and produced a bottle of champagne. Ogalunga's attitude softened. The pop of the cork signified an end to hostilities. Priest and Chief settled down to an entente cordiale and agreement was reached for the establishment of a Christian school in the village.

Less fortunate was the youthful Father Delaney, imprudently cycling through the bush after dark. He had crossed a deep stream and was making his damp way up the bank when he was set upon by a band of warriors, beaten and dragged triumphantly through the darkness to the village where he was again beaten, stripped and locked in a mud hut. The purpose of his capture and imprisonment became horrifyingly evident when, through a crack in the wooden shutter and in the light of a fire being kindled, he saw an enormous cooking pot being manhandled into position. Panic burst into explosive energy; the missionary hurled himself at the door, sending it flying as he careered into the bush, racing through the darkness, not stopping until he arrived breathless at a Christian compound where he was taken in, given cloth to cover his trembling limbs and guided safely back to his mission station.

The bicycle was a fatal attraction to the inhabitants of the interior. A teacher on the school staff told me the story of a District Officer in the 'early days' who had ventured not wisely and too far into the bush, presumably reckoning that if his bike got him into trouble it would also get him out. It didn't. His bicycle was taken forcibly from him and tied securely to a tree. He himself was macheted, boiled and eaten. The story, I was assured, was a true one. The teacher had had it from his grandmother who had been present as a young girl. "They didn't like White-man," he added with a grin, "too salty."

They were sterling men, the District Officers who took over the running of the country from Montanaro's infantry. Father Jordan speaks highly of them: 'In general the District Officers displayed the qualities for which the Britisher abroad is noted: they were open-minded and impartial, respected themselves, honoured their word and showed grit. They gradually gained the confidence of the African and it was largely through their influence that the pacification of the country was a relatively bloodless affair'.

The District Officer's task was not an easy one but the peace that prevailed at the time I arrived in the country, a peace maintained with apparent ease by unarmed police backed by an efficient system of justice, spoke eloquently of the capability and efficiency of the founders of that peace.

7

The Women

Lord Lugard returned to Nigeria in 1912 taking over the governorship of both Protectorates, the Northern and the Southern.

Changes had taken place in the south of the country since the days of the Yoruba Wars and the pacification of the east. Moor's successor, Commissioner Egerton, had divided the Southern Protectorate into three provinces, West, Central and East and incorporated Lagos into the mainstream allowing it a degree of autonomy and setting it up as administrative centre for the whole of the south. Of the sixteen members comprising Egerton's Advisory Council, however, only three were Nigerian. Expatriate officials were now common on the ground. The mosquito that had guarded the coast so securely had been conquered by an extract from the bark of the cinchona tree: quinine was more effective in opening up West Africa to the European than the Maxim gun. Lagos had its clubs, its port wine and Stilton. Pioneering work was over or confined to the interior. Lagos, under Whitehall, was now the seat of government. The Eastern Province, as a result of this centralization of government favouring Western Nigeria, found itself more and more marginalised.

Lugard had different ideas on taking up the reins of his dual mandate: he set about uniting the north and the south of the country. Within two years of his return he had effected the union. On the first day of January 1914 Nigeria became One; at the stroke of a pen the Protectorate of Northern Nigeria was linked to that of the South. Lord Lugard assumed the title of Governor General of a united Nigeria.

It was no great desire to be united to the South that urged Lugard. His was the North, the North of the open plains and thundering cavalry, the North that he had conquered over mile after blood-soaked mile from Lokoja to Sokoto, the North that now, pacified under his appointed emirs, had taken its place gracefully within the bounds of the British Empire.

Lugard made no secret of his preference for the North. The South and particularly the south-east, he failed to understand, referring to its peculiar form of internal self-regulation as a complete collapse of native rule. His feelings were echoed by many of his expatriate staff who found in the North not only a career but a comfortable living with its more temperate climate, its wider horizons, its open grasslands and well-established class structure that allowed the European to fraternise with members of the ruling classes in palace or on polo ground. It was a man's life and a healthy one. How much more refined, one instinctively thought, than the rat-race of the South with its milling hordes of agitators, its businessmen and trading tycoons and pseudo-intellectuals. God help the poor chaps assigned there by the Colonial Office and God keep them there.

But the North needed the South. Lugard's Frontier Force had virtually wiped out the North's lucrative commerce in humankind. The French Foreign Legion had cut off trade routes to the North. Landlocked by the Southern Protectorate it found itself without direct access to the sea. The North grew poorer as the South grew richer. Ironically it was the despised commercialism of the South that subsidized the North with its annual deficit in administrative expenditure increasing at an alarming rate. A grant-in-aid from the British taxpayer in the period running up to amalgamation was not enough to cover this deficit; thousands of pounds were siphoned from the Southern treasury to aid the North in its genteel poverty. One of Lugard's first acts in assuming dual control was to centralise the treasury in order to guarantee Northern solvency. Again at cost to the South he took control of railway development, linking the North to the southern ports, thus breaking the landlock, guaranteeing access to the sea.

It was not only in financial manipulation, however, that Lugard stacked the dice in the North's favour; it was even more obvious in the geographical nature of the divide that he revealed his prejudice and lack of political foresight. The erstwhile Northern Protectorate, Lugard's North, was left intact, a colossal giant overshadowing the minor provinces of the Southern Protectorate which were broken up even further in the Governor's determination to divide and rule.

There was an immediate outcry against the obvious imbalance in this partitioning. The influential *African Mail* under the editorship of E. D. Morell advocated strongly the break-up of the North into two regions. Lugard's deputy governor, Temple, in the North made a strong case for breaking up the region even further into three in line with the South. Lugard would have none of it. Nobody would interfere with his sacred North. It was to remain intact. After all, when and if it came to a question of regional voting the North would need an electorate at least equal in numbers to the combined southern regions. Little did Lugard realise the seeds of discord his decision sowed.

The Governor did little to help matters internally. He lost no time in relegating Commissioner Egerton's Legislative Assembly to the status of Lagos Town Council and replaced it with a Nigerian Assembly that was by the nature of its constitution no more than a talkshop: 'The Governor shall not be required to put into effect any resolution passed by the Council unless he sees fit'. Thus spake the Order in Council constituting the Assembly. In any case, of its forty members only twelve were Nigerian and of these half were government appointees.

When Lugard left Nigeria in 1919 he was under the impression that he had left behind a native administration that would bring peace, order and harmony to the South and particularly the south-eastern region. How utterly wrong he was became dramatically obvious when, within ten years of his departure, the system exploded in the face of its administrators. And it was the women of the region who caused the explosion.

Lugard was used to the political and social system of the North where the woman was regarded as a non-person. He presumed that such was the case in the South. He could not have been more wrong. Though subjugated by a social system that appeared to relegate women to a second-class status in society, particularly in the area of marriage and family, the women of the South were armed with a hidden power that was challenged at fatal risk.

It was trade and commerce and the market stall that gave the women this power. When the local authority decided to charge a stall fee in Calabar market to boost revenue, the District Officer found himself within an hour of the announcement confronted by a mob of angry women estimated at over three thousand. Armed police had to be called in; the riot act was read; rifle butts flailed; blood flowed. The fee was rescinded.

This threatened market tax was one source of annoyance in the south-east but Lugard's attempts to impose indirect rule on the region was of a much more serious affair. His intention to implement this rule through government-appointed warrant-chiefs caused deep and dangerous resentment. An imposed and autocratic rule was not acceptable in the South and particularly not so in the south-east. Warrant-chiefs were regarded as mere pawns of government, stooges of the colonial power. Even deeper resentment was felt against the local courts and particularly the court clerks. Their knowledge of the White-man's language and consequent ability to manipulate evidence and court rulings gave these clerks a power that was wide open to abuse. Many abused it.

When it was decided by central government under Lugard's successor to impose a system of direct taxation on the East, resentment flashed into open rebellion. The year was 1929. World recession was biting deeply into the Nigerian economy. Palm oil prices had dropped to starvation level. This threat of taxation was a match to a short fuse. A census was to take place to facilitate this taxation: the men were to be counted. Enumerators were met by silent opposition. The Warrant-Chief of Oloko, a village in Bende province, threatened the women with legal action for non-cooperation. Women were to be taxed as well! The rumour spread like wildfire. They rose from their market stalls, surging into Okugo's compound. They were met by brute force; women were injured. The District Officer arrived with a police detachment; order was restored. The Chief was taken into protective custody. To pacify the women, Okugo was tried and imprisoned for assault. The women had won.

The news spread quickly. The women were on the move, linking up in their thousands. The East was ablaze. Native courts were attacked and burned; court messengers were threatened, abused and disarmed; court clerks were harried and ousted, warrant-chiefs deposed. The town of Aba went wild, a frenzied mob surging through the streets, robbing, burning, looting, shops, stores and banks. The women marched on to Owerri, four thousand of them, burning and destroying government property as they went. Troops were called in; bayonets were drawn. It took three companies to restore a semblance of order. Complaints were made and listened to. Promises of compliance were given. The mob moved on.

Further south in the Rivers Area the violence was even less controlled. Stripped to the waist with leaves around their ankles as a sign they were prepared to resist and die, the mob surged forward on the government offices wielding not sticks and stones but sharpened machetes. The struggle had taken a deathly turn. The officer in charge confronted the mob with his two dozen men. The riot act was read. The mob yelled in return, machetes were brandished; the officer ordered his men to fire. They did so at point-blank range. Women in the front rank fell. The mob kept advancing. The Lewis gun was called up and opened fire with a controlled burst. More women fell. Still on they came. The gun fired again. Dead and dying littered the compound in front of the District Office. The women retreated in silent order. The battle was over.

The women had lost the battle but had won their campaign. A governor general was appointed, sympathetic to their demands. Sir Donald Campbell undertook vigorously the task of establishing a form of government more acceptable to the people. Firmly opposed to Lugard's system of indirect rule which he called a veritable monster of government, he endeavoured to set up a system which the people could call their own. By the time he retired in 1935, the Governor had established such a form of local government, flawed in many ways but basically sound and acceptable to the people. The women had not raised their voices, nor bared their breasts, nor shed their blood in vain.

8

Independence

A year had rolled by, a year of dry season and harmattan running into wet season and rainstorm, violent, flashing, thunderous rainstorms which left me open-mouthed at the ferocity of their power, blinding lightning, roll after roll of crackling thunder, wind-torn palm trees, streaming gutters, storm-hammered roofs. Then the rain stopped; the thunder rolled away; the wind from the north began to blow: it was dry season again and holiday time.

We went across to Lagos. A certain amount of business had to be enacted and a welcome break was included. I found myself on Tarkwa beach after an invigorating plunge in the surf, comfortably ensconced under a palm-frond shade with a cooling beer and an engrossing book, lost to the world and the bustle about me.

The books I had been reading filled in many of the gaps in my knowledge of the country, going far to explain the origin of things and the tangled web of Nigerian politics. As my gaze wandered over the beach, beyond the crashing surf to the open ocean, I could see in my mind the sails of the Africa Squadron billowing on the horizon, hear the boom of the ships' cannon roll across the bay, as they had indeed thundered in the days before Lagos became the sophisticated seat of national government with its bustling crowds, roaring traffic and the imposing administration buildings we had visited.

In the short century since its formal annexation under Palmerston, Lagos had developed into the capital of a mighty, modern African country under an African government. This struggle to achieve self-government had been long and had not been easy.

As early as 1920 the National Congress of West Africa had sent a delegation to London demanding a greater and more realistic say in the Legislative Council. The request was turned down but the Clifford Constitution of 1922 did allow for a number of representatives directly elected on the basis of a limited franchise.

Limited though the franchise was, it opened the floodgates of party politics, of a political press, of rhetoric, of impassioned party speeches. The fight for independence had taken a new turn; the protagonists were the same, the weapons were different: it was no longer a question of spear and musket against Maxim gun and howitzer; it was government edict against informed rhetoric, the diplomat and administrator against the journalist and politician. Macaulay's party was in the vanguard and he rode triumphant at its head; the three Lagos seats were swept up by members of his Nigerian National Democratic Party. Other parties sprang into being and battled their way to success. In 1938 the Nigerian Youth Movement with men like Awolowo and Azikiwe at its head overtook Macaulay's party in the Assembly election.

Then war broke out. The Second World War effected yet another paradigm shift in Nigerian life: it opened the country to the world and the world came to its doors. Nigeria was a staging post on the route to the East: servicemen and shipping, aircraft and crews. Thousands of Nigerians volunteered for the forces, serving in East Africa and North Africa, the Middle East and Far East. They came back from the war with a different view of the world and their place in it.

Even before the war ended, Azikiwe was active in the struggle for greater autonomy. The Labour element in the British parliament was sympathetic towards colonial demands. The lessons of recent uprisings in the West Indies had not been lost; the statutes of the Atlantic Charter proclaiming the rights of all people to representative government were heeded. Winston Churchill, however, had no intention, he let it be known, of presiding over the break-up of the British Empire.

Azikiwe's representation was summarily dismissed. His influence in the home political scene was also weakening whilst that of Awolowo's was growing. Azikiwe left the party and with him an important element of Easterners. The party system became fragmented with a consequent loss of impetus and influence. Azikiwe worked at co-ordinating these disparate elements and in 1944 there came into being the National Council for Nigeria and the Cameroons, with the grand old man of Nigerian Nationalism, Herbert Macaulay, as its titular head. Zik was secretary, active on the executive level. The NCNC had entered the arena.

The rising tide of nationalism was not unnoticed by the Governor General, Sir Arthur Richards. His post-war constitution had a conciliatory and positive element that went some way towards answering demands: an enlarged central legislature and a more representative involvement of local authorities in the day-to-day running of their own affairs.

It was, however, the tone of its introduction as well as the overall shortcomings of the blueprint that upset the Nationalists: Richards did not appear to realise how deep the tide was rushing nor how fast. No longer was it possible for a benign government to pacify nationalist agitators with a paternalistic gesture. Rage and fury blazed on the pages of the Southern nationalist press. Were they not to be consulted? Were they mere spectators at the process of devolution? And as for the proposals: mere whitewash! The South was to be divided against itself, the West separated from Lagos, the East marginalised, the megalithic North untouched. Surely the Government recognised the anomaly of this imbalance, this blueprint for disaster. The ghost of Lugard appeared to be at the helm. And look at the farcical system of representation! Legislature? Still no more than four elected representatives out of a total of forty-four. The executive council? European to a man. Not an African among them.

This constitutional outrage was coupled with serious unrest within the country where towns and villages were bristling with unemployed ex-servicemen. Prices had rocketed, the wartime demand for local produce had diminished, wages were static. Strikes broke out: ports and railways were closed, telecommunications were cut.

Azikiwe's newspapers threw their weight behind the strikers. *The Pilot* and *The Comet* might be regarded with contempt by the Establishment, but they were read by the people. Editorials and leading articles highlighted the plight of the workers, adding strength to their demands. Their editor became the hero of the day. The government became concerned. Zik's papers were banned.

Azikiwe's action went beyond the printed page; he toured the country seeking a mandate and funds to carry the war to Westminster. He received both in abundance. His visit, however, though received with sympathy in certain quarters, achieved little. His delegation was told to go back and give the new constitution a chance.

There was much to commend the reforms and development accompanying the Richards Constitution. The ten-year development plan financed by the newly established Colonial Development Fund afforded much change. Despite the cruel hardship of the European post-war situation, the strangling repayment of war loans and the cruel winter of 1947, an, at that time, enormous sum of £23 million of British taxpayers' money was allocated to the Nigerian development programme. Urban and rural projects went on apace; water schemes were implemented; electricity lines extended; hospitals and schools were built; Ibadan University with its modern teaching hospital was opened. It was a heady time of progress. The school in which I was teaching was a product of that development fund.

The new governor, Sir John McPherson, was a man well suited to the task of guiding Nigeria towards self-government. With his able First Secretary, Hugh Foot, he recognised the dynamism of the situation in which he had been thrust. He proposed a new constitution and announced plans for the fullest possible consultation before the drawing up of the final version. Everybody was consulted: village council through to General Council. Whilst consultation was going ahead, the Governor set about the task of handing over the administration of the country to the people of the country, appointing Nigerians to the Executive Council and to administrative posts.

The draft constitution presented to the Colonial Secretary contained much that was to set the pattern for an independent Nigeria. A federal form of government was accepted with a strong central legislature and executive counterbalanced by greater powers delegated to the regions. The demand by the South, however, for the break-up of the North into regions commensurate in size with the West and East was refused. The North was left as it was in the beginning and was given representatives to the House of Assembly equal in numbers to that of the Southern regions combined. The Southern regions were not happy.

This demand for greater regional autonomy on ethnic lines had deep implications. With the weakening of the colonial authority, tribal differences were beginning to increase. The Igbos banded themselves under Azikiwe in the Pan Igbo Union; the Yoruba, led by Awolowo, retaliated with the formation of the Oduduwa Society; whilst the Northern People's Congress (the NPC), founded by Tafawa Balewa, was established to look after the interests of the Hausa and Fulani.

The maverick beyond the herd was the Zikist movement, intent upon disrupting the orderly progress of the official political bodies, urging direct action, strikes, non-payment of taxes, sabotage. It was a difficult situation for the Governor when implementing legitimate reform and his Secretary, who was responsible for law and order.

Unrest flared into active violence. A critical point was reached with the strike of the Enugu miners. Here were no vociferous market traders demanding better prices nor passionate politicians demanding speedier reform but strong men armed, potentially, with explosives. The dynamite store was vulnerable. Mobile police were rushed in. The miners confronted them in force. Rifles were levelled; a warning was yelled. The strikers surged forward. The police opened fire; dead and dying lay everywhere; some thirty miners were killed.

The East erupted: rioting broke out in the townships; the life of the Secretary, Hugh Foot, was threatened; demands were made for the arrest of the police officer responsible for the Enugu shooting. The Zikist firebrands were everywhere, urging more violent action. Arrests were made, the movement was proscribed. Gradually order was restored; legitimate progress resumed.

In 1952 the first Federal elections took place. The major parties in the North and in the East were triumphant in their respective regions, but the Western party, the Action Group, found itself sharing spoils with the Eastern-dominated NCNC. Azikiwe had won the Lagos seat.

The first aim of the Federal Assembly was the achievement of independence. All parties were agreed on this but not on the timing. Whilst the Action Group and the NCNC were intent on achievement as soon as practicable, the Northern party was less enthusiastic. When a Western representative in a speech in the House moved that complete independence be granted within four years, the Northerners objected strongly. They knew they were not ready. In all of the North there were to be found no more than five indigenous university graduates. Key administrative posts would be staffed by Southerners. Time was needed. They moved for postponement. Tempers flared; angry words were exchanged. The members of the two Southern parties marched out of the House in dramatic protest. An impasse had been reached. The North found itself in isolated opposition. Members withdrew to their constituencies. The Northern House of Chiefs demanded dissolution of the Federation. Resentment flared. Angry words turned to angrier blows. The ghettos in the Northern cities were attacked. In Kano alone over three hundred Easterners were killed, many more wounded by an enraged Northern mob. Central government intervened. The warring political parties were called to London.

Oliver Lyttleton, the Colonial Secretary, found himself with the difficult task of breaking down prejudice and intransigence. Compromise was eventually reached, the North agreeing in principle to independence and accepting a federal form of government but insisting upon much greater power being accorded to the regions. The South agreed to waive their demand for independence within four years on condition that the regions be granted self-regulation.

Differences lingered, however. The Action Group were opposed to the Easterners' demand that Lagos should remain autonomous Federal territory. The East refused to accede to the West's demand that the regions should be accorded the right of unilateral secession from the Federation if and when desired. These differences were eventually smoothed over; a formula was drawn up: the Lyttleton Constitution of 1954. The representatives returned home and set about the task of working out the details of the proposals, preparing for that which was now seen as inevitable: complete independence.

The 1954 elections resulted in an overall victory for the NCNC in the West as well as its heartland in the East. The NPC swept the boards in the North and, having twice as many representatives as the Southern states combined, found itself in a strong majority position in the Federal House. There was, however, a major difficulty arising from the NCNC victory in the West: since each of the Regions had the right to send a limit of four members to the Central Executive, the Southern regions under NCNC fielded eight ministers whilst the North had only four. The Northern Party was forced into alliance with that of the East; the Action Party went into formal opposition.

Thorny questions still remained unanswered: the achievement of independence was beyond question but the timing was far from settled. The Action Group's demand was for independence as soon as possible; the North still did not feel itself ready; the NCNC brokered a compromise date.

Who was to lead the House as Prime Minister? In a coalition government this was obviously a delicate question. Given the deep-seated regional differences that existed it was more than delicate yet such a degree of unanimity had been formed over the months of debate that the appointment of the Northerner, Tafawa Balewa, met with scant dissent.

Alhaji Sir Abubakar Tafawa Balewa was an obvious choice: a Northerner yet not of the dominant Hausa-Fulani group, relatively well educated, a former schoolteacher, loyal to Northern interests yet broad-minded enough to realise the necessity for co-operation with the other regions. The NCNC were given to understand that their co-operation would be rewarded. Azikiwe was seen as the Governor General's heir presumptive.

A commission had been appointed to look at the possibility of the creation of more states, the break-up of the regions. The South were determined that the North be reduced in size, the East siding openly with Middle Belt opposition to Hausa-Fulani domination. The West wanted the break-off of the Ilorin-Kabba area. The North, however, would have none of it. The struggle was not just between North and South. Inter-regional differences began to appear. The East demanded the secession of the minority Mid-Western Region. The West were prepared to agree on condition that the Rivers Area be granted independence from the East. The question of the status of Lagos came up again and again. The Willink Commission, fearing Balkanisation, sided with the North: there was to be no change. The West insisted; the North threatened to delay the date for independence. The West acceded. The way seemed open to the granting of full independence. The first day of October 1960 was the date proposed for the formal handing over of power. All parties agreed. Nigeria had come of age.

9

Cracks in the Foundation

With the granting of Independence, the story of Nigeria stepped from the pages of history to the reality of life around me. I had arrived in the country a mere three months after those euphoric days of fireworks and dancing, speech-making and ceremony: the dawn of the new Nigeria. The spell of it was still in the air, the joy, the exhilaration, the novelty of it experienced by a people responsible at last for their own affairs.

And that responsibility was undertaken with enthusiasm and with gravitas. Despite a warning and threat by the Nigerian Federal Government, France had had the temerity to conduct an atomic-bomb test in the Sahara desert: Nigeria broke off diplomatic relations. There was trouble in the Congo, fierce, post-independence tribal war. The United Nations stepped in. Armed intervention was needed. A contingent of the Nigerian army under Major-General Aguiyi-Ironsi was dispatched to restore order.

Britain was inordinately proud of Nigeria. Potentially the richest, certainly the largest country in Central West Africa, composed of peoples entirely disparate in language, culture and religion yet within sixty short years welded together into a success story that was a model for the continent. The random shots that were fired along the road to Independence, the political imprisonments, were conveniently forgotten. Relationships were cordial and mutually advantageous.

Despite the heavy gloss, however, within a very short time, cracks began to appear in the structure. The basis of that structure, the formation of the regions, had been flawed from the beginning, and had been seen to be flawed. Lugard's policy, continued by his successors, of refusing to take into account the finer points of tribal differences, was leading to direful consequences. The East claimed the Mid-West, populated by non-Yoruba peoples, predominantly Igbo. The Western government would have none of it: land west of the Niger was land of the Western Region. They were prepared to bargain, trading the Mid-West for the independence of the River Provinces. The East was not prepared to bargain; there was no need; they shared a parliamentary majority which enabled them to impose their will on the government of the West. A Mid-West referendum was ordered; the NCNC, sure of their support in the province, were certain that the result would be in their favour.

Within the Mid-West province itself political power was shared between the NCNC and the Action Group, but it was becoming increasingly obvious that power was sliding away from the NCNC. Immediate action was required

52

before the political situation became critical. The action took the form of violent intimidation. NCNC 'party-thugs', so-called, roamed the countryside terrorising political opponents. The West retaliated by establishing a corps of 'party-stewards', armed and prepared to use their arms. An impasse was reached; the referendum was postponed.

Meanwhile, within the Action Group itself a split began to appear. Languishing in impotent opposition was not an inviting prospect for active politicians. The Premier of the West, Akintola, was tempted to side with the Northern Party of the coalition government as a means of breaking the deadlock. His Federal counterpart, Awolowo, favoured the NCNC camp. Clandestine overtures were made by both parties. It was Akintola who first came out into the open, approaching the leader of the Northern Party directly and openly, thus decisively splitting his own party. The move met with stout opposition from within his own party. A motion of no confidence in him as Premier was tabled.

When Akintola's support was officially accepted by the leader of the Northern Party, the Action Group members opposed to the liaison called for his dismissal as Premier. The motion was ratified by the Governor of the West and clearly defined lines of division were established. Crisis loomed. Violence was growing. Both factions were summoned to debate.

Even as the House assembled, tension was in evidence. Riot police were stationed in and about the House. The two factions faced each other across the floor in battle array and debate began. The formal opening gave way to angry words, to threatening gestures. Control was lost in the fury of debate. Members crossed the floor, fists flew, blood flowed, missiles were hurled about the Chamber, the mace was smashed. Riot police leapt into the fray. Truncheons flailed, members were ejected. Eventually a semblance of order was restored.

Higher authority was called in. The Inspector of Police took control; the House was reconvened. The Speaker spoke sternly to the opposing parties; debate recommenced. Uproar broke out: banging desks, yelling abuse, hurling papers, stamping feet, crossing the floor. Violence appeared to be getting beyond control. Tear-gas grenades were lobbed into the melee. The House was cleared, the doors were locked. Parliamentary government was suspended in the West.

Violence flared beyond the House of Assembly; the whole of the Western Region was aflame. Highway robbery was becoming endemic, murder, mugging, arson. The army was put on alert. The Federal Prime Minister, Tafawa Balewa, intervened; he declared a state of emergency in the Western Region.

It became increasingly clear that Balewa was on the side of Akintola and his Northern-looking faction. The West's Federal representative, Chief Awolowo, with his supporters was being sidelined. The Emergency gave the Federal government wide powers of control and they were used to effect;

Awolowo was arrested. Charges of complicity with Nkrumah's Ghana were made; accusations of an attempt to take over the government of the Federation with armed foreign support were laid before the hapless leader of the Opposition. He was exiled to the Creeks, sentenced to ten years' imprisonment.

Awolowo's deputy, Anthony Enahoro, made good his escape out of the country, reaching the relative safety of Accra. From there he flew to Dublin and, officially on family business, on to London where he was arrested, imprisoned and eventually deported back to Nigeria. There he was tried on charges of conspiracy and treason and given a fifteen-year prison sentence. The opposition of the West had been crushed.

Despite the turmoil in the West, material progress in Nigeria continued apace. After a brief period of leave in England during the bitterly cold winter of 1963, the changes I saw on my return were dramatic. Oil was flowing in abundance. The first tentative steps of British Petroleum and Shell were rewarded by an ever-increasing flow of high-grade petroleum gushing from the wells in the East and more abundantly in the Rivers Area, generating a revenue fuelling the flame of progress. Foreign investment was pouring into the country, fanning to fever pitch the confidence of businessmen and politicians alike. Manufacturing was fast developing, markets were expanding, townships were booming. Everywhere building work was in progress. In Enugu, the Ministry Layout and Presidential Hotel with its marble and terrazzo, crystal and gold brought a dignity to the town in keeping with its new-found confidence. And all the while bulldozers and dumper trucks, rollers and tar spreaders were everywhere, clawing at bush and forest, pounding laterite and spraying bitumen as rivers were bridged and roads were widened.

Even the quiet bush around Orlu was affected: we were to get piped water. The Public Works Department involved asked permission to use the machinery in the school's technical department. We seemed in the very heart of the vanguard of progress as lathe and saw and drills whined and roared. A huge storage tank was built on the compound, pipes were laid, pumps were installed. The engine was switched on, valves were opened and water, cool, clear and abundant, flowed in gushing streams. The boys in the school were pleased; the children in the village went wild with delight. Water that they had struggled for, day after parching day in the dry season was now bubbling before their eyes in limitless abandon, gushing and flowing unheeded down the dusty track. Little terrier dogs yapped with delight and lapped at the clear running water. Then electricity was promised: pylons were being erected, wires slung from pole to pole. The days of the generator were numbered; we were to be linked to the national grid. Progress seemed beyond limit. Nigeria was on the move.

Beneath the sparkling surface of progress, however, a seething tide of social unrest was beginning to flow. It was not only the heightening tension of political struggle, the polarisation of regional forces, the violence at the polls, there was beyond the posturing a more sinister, more widespread, deeper cause for alarm. The people were unhappy. While rich men flaunted their riches, the poor were becoming poorer. The cost of living was rising every day; import duties were reaching critical level. Taxes were increasing; incomes remained the same. The disparity between the haves and the have-nots was glaringly obvious. The poor village-mama shuffling her way to market bowed beneath her head-load, coughing in the dust of the stretched limousine sweeping by with its ministerial passenger, epitomised the suffering of the people.

The people were vividly aware of the injustices acted out nationwide by the opportunists in politics and business: politicians siphoning off foreign aid, individuals using party funds for their own ends, small men from the bush becoming big men overnight, building ostentatious houses, selling contracts, channelling grants to their advantage, sending sons and daughters to the best schools overseas.

Corruption was rife, bribery was a way of life. A new term was beginning; funds were needed for school fees. We were stopped at a roadblock; the police were extracting on-the-spot fines. They waved us on. I had been told on arrival never to offer a bribe, never. The rule was sacrosanct. The police knew it. The people were caught in the web. An English language class I had were dealing with a passage on traffic and transport. The question was asked: "What is the speed limit in town?" "Thirty miles per hour." "What happens if you exceed that limit?" "Police will stop you." "Then?" "You give dash." Dash, fine, present, bribe: words interchangeable.

On a much larger scale, however, than petty fines was the corruption in the country as a whole. Resentment was growing against this bribery and corruption, against nepotism, tribal discrimination, injustice, greed, vested interest and arrogant, open dishonesty. Unscrupulous entrepreneurs borrowed big money from their banks with the minimum of security, financing property development, the property then let to migrants pouring into the towns looking for work. The wages offered were of the lowest level; the rent for accommodation was as high as could be extracted.

Resentment boiled over into action. Trade unions formed a joint action committee; sporadic strike action was taken, threats of a general strike were made. They could no longer be ignored. A commission was set up to look into workers' demands and conditions. The report issued by Chief Justice Morgan favoured an immediate rise in the minimum wage. The Government, whilst accepting the recommendations of the commission, was niggardly in their implementation. The country already seething with discontent called for immediate all-out strike action.

By strange coincidence I found myself flung into the vortex of the struggle. It was the dry-season break and we were on the hill ranch of Obudu in the foothills of the Cameroon mountains, a welcome change after the steaming wet season of the lowland forest. The ranch had horses for hire, but the groom was disconsolate when I went along on the first morning: they had been all booked out. There was one horse but she was 'woman horse'. I assured him I had no objection to women, equine or otherwise. She had not been ridden for some time. Good, she would be happy with an outing. She must not go near the men-horses. I assured the groom I would keep to the track he indicated. He brought Savannah ready tacked into the stable yard, a beautiful sorrel mare, all of sixteen hands, standing quiet and willing. I climbed aboard. The groom opened the gate and Savannah walked daintily through into the tree-lined track leading some distance off through a further gate to the open countryside. Savannah walked calmly on then broke into a gentle trot. I refrained from checking her. She loped into a canter. Still no restraint, I was enjoying the swift smooth rhythm. Savannah bolted, headlong into a mad gallop. I hauled on the reins; too late, the mare had the bit. The gate loomed large. Would she jump? I could see the barbed wire entangled on the top bar. I crouched over her neck, gathered mane and reins in preparation for the jump when Savannah stopped, forelegs planted firmly on the ground. I went over her head face-first into the gate.

I found myself in the deep grass looking through a film of blood into the eyes of the groom. Savannah's reins were still in my bleeding hand. The groom shook his head sadly: "Ooman horse! Much palaver."

The local clinic could do little for me save ease the pain. The doctor at the hospital tried but the complexity of dealing with the crushed septum was beyond his skill and I was referred to the University Hospital in Ibadan.

The road to Ibadan was blocked by armed banditry. Highway robbery was the order of the day, hijacking, mugging and murder. I flew down and landed

Obudu Ranch

in a cauldron of trouble. Ibadan was in turmoil: demonstrations, marches, public gatherings, inflammatory speeches highlighted the unrest reaching fever pitch. I made my way from the taxi park to the hospital past mobs of chanting, placard-bearing demonstrators. It was an unnerving experience. The hospital was deserted save for a lone porter who accosted me and was surprised I did not know of the situation. "Not just Ibadan, my friend. The whole country is on strike. Na dis be war."

I found a room in a nearby hotel and went down with fever. The next day I struggled up and tried the hospital again; the gates were locked. A taxi took me back to the outskirts of the city centre but refused to go further. The mob appeared to have taken over. There was a mass demonstration. Cyclists and pedestrians were making their hurried way to the scene, wide-eyed in their intensity. I was confronted by a group chanting incomprehensible slogans. Still chanting, dancing, waving placards they formed a circle about me. I was trapped. Anything could happen. I smiled disarmingly. The chanting, dancing group opened and I passed through wearing my brave conciliatory smile till I was clear.

The manager of the hotel was amazed to see me back. "You must leave now. This is no place for you. There is a plane for the East leaving this afternoon. You must go." He arranged transport. I paid my bill and went. The plane touched down on its way from Lagos. The pilot warned us it had not been serviced for some time and we were required to sign a disclaimer. I did so, settled in and found myself after a bumpy flight back in the relative calm of the East.

Savannah had thrown me bodily into the turmoil. What I had seen augured badly for the peace and calm of the country.

10

Coup

The Premier of the East was to visit our school.

The CID arrived. They interviewed individuals and made a general check on security. The mobile police, accompanied by a military detachment, were more thorough in their survey. They were not happy. The officer in charge said so. The school was built on the edge of a narrow valley. The steep sides and dense foliage made security difficult if not impossible. No matter how many of his men he deployed, he could not guarantee safety. The concealed flank was too vulnerable to infiltration. The visit was cancelled.

How casual, by contrast, I was told, had been the visit of the previous Prime Minister ten years before. What was this talk of exposed flanks and enemy infiltration? It sounded like war. Indeed it was. Things had changed dramatically in the ten years since Azikiwe's visit.

The census had precipitated trouble. With party loyalty depending strongly on regional division, population figures were of paramount importance. The result of the 1962 census gave the combined South a decisive majority over the North. The Northern Premier refused to accept the figures. He demanded a fresh census.

Despite all the efforts on the part of the South's party campaigners and the assiduity of the electorate in standing up and being counted again and, sometimes, again, the North won the census contest by five million. Their returning officers had gone to all lengths. They had even counted the women.

The census was but a prelude to the election battle. Lines were drawn; alliances were built up; no effort was spared to ensure victory at the polls. The Premier of the North drew the disaffected Akintola into his camp as part of his formidable North-West Nigerian National Alliance. It was a deft move. Ahmadu Bello, he of the house of Usman Dan Fodio, surveyed his ranks with pride. The Northern jihad, crushed at the gates of Ilorin by the guns of Taubman Goldie, was once again, now under an electoral banner, on the move south.

This mighty alliance brought the remaining factions of the South together: NCNC, along with the minority opposition parties in the West, North and Middle Belt, joined the Action Group. The new party called itself the United Progressive Grand Alliance. UPGA had launched itself into the fray.

It was a bloody fray: Premier Ahmadu Bello, the Lion of the North, would brook no opposition. Aminu Kanu's Northern opposition party was attacked with methodical violence; villages were sacked, meetings broken up, individuals arrested and imprisoned; executions, murder and mayhem became the order of the day. Abdulahi, Kanu's friend and party organiser, was thrown into a police cell, beaten and killed, as Aminu later said, "In the night, like a dog." Opposition was crushed before a vote had been cast.

The chances of the major political opponents campaigning in the North were wiped out in the violence of the campaign. One such hardy candidate did venture to the North only to find himself attacked not with the acceptable weapons of political rejoinder, heckling or even verbal abuse but sticks and stones and sharpened machetes. The UPGA member and his supporters dashed for their cars. Revving engines shot off south in a cloud of dust. The candidate's car, leading the flight skidded on the mountain road, its off-side wheels spinning dangerously over the edge of the precipice. "Luckily," he told me when recalling the event with grim unconscious humour over a glass of palm wine, "my thugs were just behind me and got us back on the road."

Similar intimidation was carried out in the West. Returning officers were spirited away before the UPGA member could file the required application; even in cases where conditions were fulfilled, forms and deposits could mysteriously disappear. Officials were bribed, cajoled, threatened, kidnapped, murdered. Candidates and supporters were terrorised into inactivity.

UPGA members complained bitterly to the Electoral Commission which had been established by President Azikiwe. They had an official candidate for every seat in the West yet over sixty of their opponents were returned 'unopposed'. They demanded action from the Commission: postponement of the election, investigation of unopposed seats, and external monitoring. Their demands were unanswered. There was talk of boycotting the December election. There was even talk of Eastern secession from the Federation.

Azikiwe summoned Balewa and suggested a six-month moratorium and the possibility of United Nations supervision. Balewa refused. The President asked the Attorney General what constitutional rights he had to enable him to postpone the election and appoint an interim government. He was told he had no such rights.

The election took place. The Northern party won with a resounding, unbelievable majority. Sir Abubakar Tafawa Balewa presented himself with constitutional nicety before the President and requested his permission to form a government. Azikiwe refused. He had read the small print. The election had not been conducted in a free and fair manner; it was null and void. Balewa protested; the President stood firm, he was prepared to resign rather than give way.

The legal experts were called in, the Attorney General, the regional chief justices joining the Prime Minister-elect, and the President. Discussion took place against a frightening background of violence and murder in the West, violence that had little or nothing to do with political gain. Law and order were breaking down; anarchy was rising. The police were stretched beyond their limits; the army was kept securely garrisoned. A caretaker government was appointed under Balewa. It was a compromise government with members from all shades of political allegiance and none, a government with neither bark nor bite. The Constitutional Committee called for a regional election in the West. This, it was thought, without Northern or Eastern interference would clear the air. Such thoughts and aspirations were doomed from the beginning.

All semblance of legality was thrown overboard; the decks were cleared for action. Total commitment to outright victory at the polls was called for. Violence erupted in the West beyond the scale of even the Federal elections. It was warfare, bloody and unrestrained. Armed thugs posing as political agents roamed the countryside. No one was safe. The highways were death traps; few ventured forth. Marauding gangs at roadblocks demanded to know political allegiance; the wrong answer could and often did mean death. Lorries were hijacked, passengers robbed, raped, murdered. Villages were attacked, party offices set on fire, agents run down, beaten, murdered. The innocent suffered with the guilty, the committed with the uncommitted. The stories crossing the Niger were frightening in their nightmarish detail. We were watching the break-up of a region, Freedom in its death throes.

The election was held in October. Akintola's party won. The opposition went wild with anger. The total lack of credibility was glaring. Even the Federal Prime Minister acknowledged it and with it, Akintola's responsibility; yet what was the Federal Government doing? Why did not Balewa declare a state of emergency and bring out the army? His hands were tied. Ahmadu Bello of the North was the power behind the throne. Disorder mounted on disorder.

Chaos reigned. Robbery, murder, and pillage increased with no longer any semblance of political motive. The police were unable to cope. The army, stationed at flashpoints, limited in numbers, were hard-pressed to maintain order. Private armies were springing up; politicians went about with heavily armed guards; warlords and political barons were setting up their fiefdoms.

It was December 1965, I was in Enugu shopping. There was a commotion at the store entrance. Uniformed, armed men hustled in and took up positions at strategic points, automatics at the ready. Shoppers froze. A whisper went round: "Mbadiwe!" The Federal Minister for Transport strode in, chequebook in hand. He had come to do his Christmas shopping. The scene had about it the elements of comic opera but it was not comic; it was deep tragedy.

It was the Christmas break, the dry season. Mark had been unwell, struck down by a violent attack of gastric malaria; he had been ordered a complete rest and a change of climate. With no hesitation I accepted the invitation to accompany him to the hill station at Obudu.

It was the Saturday morning after our arrival. I was setting out on an amble over the hills with my little Arab horse, Bende, when I met Mark at the gate, transistor radio to his ear. He held up his hand. I stopped.

"What is it?"

Mark continued listening then he looked up. "There's been a coup. The army's taken over. Enugu's off the air. This is Lagos: Balewa is missing."

"Missing?"

"Suspected dead. This is worse than we feared."

"What do we do?"

"The ranch are trying to contact Enugu on shortwave. I suggest we pack and set off now."

I took Bende back to his stable in a thoughtful mood. Mark still had the radio to his ear when I got back.

"Somebody's speaking from Kaduna; a major called Nzeogwu. Claims to be in control."

Before we left, Lagos was back on the air: a dissident section of the army had staged a coup. The Federal Prime Minister and the Minister of Finance had been abducted. Their whereabouts were unknown. The Commanding Officer, Major-General Aguiyi-Ironsi, with the bulk of the army loyal to the Federal government was moving against the dissidents. Order was being restored. Everybody was to remain calm. Further announcements would be made.

The journey back was a journey into a nightmare. A deathly calm seemed to prevail everywhere, a silence, a waiting. We stopped for something to eat. There was an unwonted restraint in the welcome but beneath it we detected an air of satisfaction. At last something had happened; somebody had taken action. The army might do what the politicians had failed to do; there might now be peace.

Enugu was in a state of shocked calm. Military patrols were in evidence. We were stopped at a roadblock. Where were we coming from? Where were we going? This was serious; the usual banter and light-heartedness were absent. We were glad to get back to the school. They were very pleased we were back. Then began the job of piecing together our bits of information to get a picture of what was happening. It was a tortuous task.

11

Counter-Coup

The hard facts behind the news reports and rumours were a long time coming out but eventually the pieces of the jigsaw began to interlock.

One version we heard concerned a Major Emmanuel Ifeajuna, a noted athlete, Commonwealth Games high-jump record holder, university graduate, and Sandhurst-trained officer. He had accepted a key role among the group of young officers who had set themselves the task of wiping out the political iniquities of the country, restoring law and order. He went about his assigned task with method and determination.

In the early hours of the morning of Saturday, the 15th of January the Major led a detachment of armed men out of Abeokuta barracks along the Lagos road to the residence of the Prime Minister. With machine pistols drawn, they brushed aside the armed guard, burst into Balewa's private apartment, arrested him in the name of the armed forces of the Federal Republic, bundled him into the car and sped off in the direction of the Ikoye Hotel.

On the way to the hotel the convoy was flagged down by an army officer standing at the side of the road. It was Brigadier Maimalari, hatless and breathing heavily. He had escaped a hit squad, it transpired, sent to assassinate him, had broken out of his house, raced across the adjacent golf course, and, by good luck, he must have thought, encountered the army patrol speeding up the road towards him. Ifeajuna signalled the vehicles to stop, got out of his car, walked towards his senior officer and shot him.

Having arrived at the Ikoye Hotel, the patrol summoned Lieutenant-Colonel Largema from his room, killed him, dumped his body in a truck and then sped on along the Abeokuta road. The murder of Lieutenant-Colonel Largema, commanding officer of the Northern Fourth Battalion, had dire repercussions when, later, the men of the Fourth exacted wild revenge.

Approaching the Eastern junction, Ifeajuna stopped the convoy, ordered the Prime Minister to get out, walked him at gunpoint to the bush at the side of the road, allowed him some moments to pray and shot him. The body was lightly buried and the convoy moved off, Ifeajuna taking the road to Enugu. The rest of the convoy was ordered to make for Lagos barracks. On the way the officer in charge stopped the vehicles and ordered his men to remove the bodies of the murdered officers. It was then he noticed a prisoner arrested along with Balewa shivering in the shadows of the interior.

"Who is this man?"

He was told: Ekotie-Eboh, Chief Federal Minister of Finance, one whose name had become synonymous with gross corruption.

"Shoot him."

The body was slung to the side of the road.

In the Western Region, events occurred with the same lightning speed. The artillery commander at Abeokuta was detailed to take out the regional Premier. Given the signal late on the Friday night, he summoned his men, armed them and dashed off for Ibadan, surrounded the Prime Minister's lodge and, under cover of machine-gun fire, charged the main door and raced upstairs. They were met by a hail of gunfire. Akintola was waiting for them. Nwobosi was wounded and ordered his men back. Akintola came after them, firing into the darkness until his magazine emptied. He was ordered to come down with his arms raised, which he did and was shot where he stood.

The takeover in the North, centred on Kaduna, was engineered by Nzeogwu, he of broadcasting fame. Ahmadu Bello, the Northern Premier was in residence. Nzeogwu organised a squad of Northern troops, loaded up a heavy anti-tank gun along with a variety of other weapons and sped off for Ahmadu's dwelling. The guard was quickly overcome and positions were established on the perimeter. The bazooka was ordered to open up and, under cover of the deafening noise, Nzeogwu rushed the building, forced his way into the Sardauna's bedroom, ordered him up against the wall and shot him. The Lion of the North, Sardauna of Sokoto, Premier Ahmadu Bello, was dead.

It was the morning of Saturday, the 15th of January 1966. Nzeogwu made his way to Kaduna radio station, established full control and triumphantly declared the assumption of command of the country by the Nigerian army. The brief message we listened to reflected the confidence of the young officers who had initiated the coup. Their confidence, however, we soon learned, was misplaced. It was far from full command.

If Kaduna was under rebel control, further north in Kano, legitimate authority in the hands of the regular army under Lieutenant-Colonel Ojukwu was very much in control. With the Emir of Kano representing civil authority, the army commander broadcast over the radio his loyalty to the legitimate Nigerian Government and his determination to stamp out any opposition to that authority. He had the men and the means to do so.

Major-General Aguiyi-Ironsi, supreme commander of the Nigerian armed forces, veteran of the Congo campaign, was at a Lagos party on the night of the coup. An urgent phone call warned him of the revolt of the junior officers. They had taken over the central police station. Ironsi armed himself with a sub-machine gun, called up his car, roared round to the police headquarters, confronted the rebels and ordered them back to barracks. They went.

Having re-established police control, he raced on through the night and the roadblocks, brandishing his automatic at the soldiers manning the barriers and reached Ikeja barracks where he hastily reorganised soldiers loyal to the government. He then set about the daunting task of quashing the revolt.

By dawn of that same day, loyalist opposition to the revolt was beginning to exert itself. Mobile patrols were sent out to confront rebel strongpoints; arrests were made; men were marched back under guard to barracks. Ifeajuna's squad, racing into Lagos to link up with the rebels, was stopped at a military roadblock and disarmed. Nwobosi and his men were captured on their way from Ibadan to Ikeja.

Pockets of resistance held out. Northern troops in Ibadan were in a state verging on mutiny. Their popular commander, Largema, had been assassinated. They wanted to know why. In Kaduna, Nzeogwu still held command. Enugu was in an ambivalent position.

Despite the pockets of resistance, however, the coup was beginning to crumble. Ironsi's authority was quickly recognised throughout the regions.

The plotters in Enugu had been thwarted: the planned attempt to assassinate the Premier had failed. The Premier of the East, Michael Okpara, was host to Archbishop Makarios returning through Enugu to Greece after the Lagos Commonwealth Conference. The junior officer sent to assassinate his Premier hesitated in the presence of the foreign guest. When the opportunity to carry out the execution did arise, loyalist authority had been restored.

The Northern element in the Enugu garrison was restless. With consummate skill the acting commander took control of the situation, retrieved the keys of the armoury, set up a guard and made it quite clear that he demanded unequivocal loyalty to legitimate authority both civil and military. He obtained the submission and held the fort in control until the arrival of Lieutenant-Colonel Ejoor, dispatched by Ironsi to take over command in the East.

In Lagos, Ironsi continued to regain and increase military control, allowing a semblance of legitimate government to take place. The Federal Parliament, depleted in numbers, debated the situation. The Prime Minister of the Federation was missing, presumed dead; the Premiers of the North and West were known to be dead. Michael Okpara of the East was under arrest charged with corruption. Successors needed to be found. Debate went on. Ironsi listened with growing impatience. The country was falling apart and all these people could do was talk, arguing over the nicer points of political procedure. Nzeogwu was still defiant in Kaduna; indeed there was talk of a march on the South and a link-up with Ibadan. Counteraction, firm action, untrammelled action was needed. Ironsi demanded authority, full, plenipotentiary authority to be vested in him and through him in the army, without compromise, else he could not guarantee the strength needed to restore order and control. Debate came to an end. The Cabinet conceded the obvious.

The President, Dr Azikiwe Governor General, Azikiwe, was, by coincidence, in Sussex undergoing a health cure. The acting Governor, Ogundipe, assumed constitutional power and with the full backing of the Federal Cabinet, formally invested Major-General Aguiyi-Ironsi with the plenipotentiary power of Supreme Military Governor of Nigeria. Parliament then dissolved itself sine die. Ogundipe spoke over the radio, formally announcing the Government's decision to the country and to the world.

We listened with bated breath. The Supreme Military Governor was introduced. Ironsi spoke firmly, stressing the interim nature of the military government but making it abundantly plain that, temporary though it was, there was no question of weakness or compromise. Full constitutional power, legislative and executive, had been vested in the military and he intended using that power, first of all in restoring peace and order, and in the long term in setting about the rectification of the iniquities of the previous regime.

If coup and counter-coup had been planned together, things could have hardly worked more smoothly. In one grim, bloody weekend the old order had been abolished and Ironsi, his hands unstained by blood, had, with due and constitutional formality, been handed the reins of Government.

The British High Commissioner, Sir Francis Cumming-Bruce, who had been present at the Cabinet meetings, duly reported the proceedings back to the British Government. Mr Arthur Bottomley, the Commonwealth Secretary, speaking in Parliament, accepted the de facto situation, making it quite clear that in view of the constitutional nature of Ironsi's appointment there was no need for formal recognition by Her Majesty's Government. The transference of power by Parliament to the military was an internal matter in a sovereign state conducted in accord with constitutional requirements. Acceptance by Britain of the situation was a formality. The BBC External Services reported and confirmed the situation.

Nigeria rejoiced. There was singing and dancing in the streets of the South. The corruption and the bloodshed, the disorder and injustice of the recent years were being wiped out. The country had a rider in the saddle with the reins of government, it was hoped, securely in his hands.

Yet along with the rejoicing was a feeling of apprehension and of awe: what was the nature of this new power that was in the land? Within the week, news of the assassinations was announced. Beneath the euphoria, questions were being asked: who were these people who with blood-chilling force and apparent ease had destroyed all that had been held sacred and inviolable? Who was it who could take the gentle-faced Balewa, fresh from the Lagos Commonwealth Conference where he had hosted the mightiest of many lands, could drag him from his bed in the dead of night, throw him in some wayside bush, shoot him in the back of the head and leave his body to rot? Who were they who could take the Warlord of the North, scion of the House of Usman Dan Fodio, the power behind the throne throughout the land and shoot him in his bed? Lines which the students had chanted with academic detachment suddenly took on a dark and sinister reality. 'Confusion now hath made his masterpiece; most sacrilegious murder hath broke ope the Lord's anointed temple'. Men walked in silent, wondering trepidation. The country seemed enveloped in dark night, yet with that night there came a silence and a calm. The burst of gunfire on the steps of the Western Premier's Lodge had brought an end to three years of political intrigue, infighting, violence and disorder. Ironsi promised that that peace would be consolidated throughout the land. The people breathed more freely; we settled down under military command.

Military Governors were appointed to the Regions; Ojukwu was transferred from the North to the East; Katsina took his place. Nzeogwu accepted the situation, surrendered to the military authority and was imprisoned. The remnants of rebel activity faded.

The military governors of the regions took up their appointed tasks with energy and zeal. We were given a series of directives from the office of the Military Governor, Eastern Command. They were short, sharp, to-the-point directives with a tinge of 'Let's-have-you-lot-standing-straight' colour about them; not forthright barrack-room command, after all our Governor was an Oxford man, but it was obvious from the tone who was in command.

The picture nationwide was even more clear-cut: civil servants turned up at their offices in the dawn of the coup to find the military waiting. "You are late. You are twenty-three minutes late. Whose car is that? Who pays for the fuel? Who is that person in the car? Who gave you permission to carry passengers? What is her function in this office?"

Dismissals were rife. The military were prepared to work with the civil service but on military lines: 'Jump to it, you horrible little man! Let's have you!' Politicians fared much harder. Many were dismissed. Quite a few, particularly in the East, were imprisoned. Charges of corruption were rife; charges of nepotism, fraud, embezzlement, and inefficiency were hurled right, left and centre. Cabinet ministers, senior ministers, junior ministers, ministers with portfolio, ministers without portfolio were dismissed and jailed. Ministers apparently set up for life with their bodyguards and Pontiacs were flung out of office. The old order indeed was changing, yielding place to new.

The great scaffolding in bright lights dominating Enugu's commercial centre proclaiming NCNC majority rule was torn down. Pictures of the Eastern Premier and his entourage were ripped off walls. Major-General Aguiyi-Ironsi's image took their place. The populace was delighted. A great sense of justice fulfilled was in the air.

"Mai mai today, okra tomorrow, na so de world de be." Nathaniel carpenter sang with a chuckle as he ripped away at his length of iroko wood: "Big man today, small tomorrow, na so de world de be."

Hospitals were visited, patients were questioned, fingers were pointed, staff were dismissed. Local government offices were put under the same scrutiny. Even market places were subject to military visitation; weights and measures were checked, quality was examined. Arrangements were made for school inspections. The whole country was sitting up in a position of bright-eyed expectation. Clear consciences held heads high; guilty cowered in corners. The wind of change, albeit from a new direction, was blowing fresh and strong.

12

Unity Decree

Market weights and measures and hospital bedpans were not the only concerns of the newly installed military government. Ironsi had his eyes focused on a much wider horizon: the creation, no less, of a new Nigeria.

Ironsi was a military man through and through: from the ranks, to Sandhurst, through the Congo to Supreme Command of the Nigerian Armed Forces. He was a professional professional. The bungling inefficiency, vested interest and nepotism of the politicians was to him anathema. He saw the effects of the problem; he examined the roots of the problem and he saw the cause: Regionalism. The duplication of effort and office that this entailed, the bureaucracy, the red tape, to say nothing of the political infighting and regional violence which this had produced filled him with dismay and frustration. Used to the clean-cut, monolithic structure of army command, the amateurish fumbling of civilian rule, the shambles that was the legacy of the colonial order, as he saw it, was the root of the evil that had beset his country. Having identified the cause of the problem, he set about destroying it: the regional system of government must go. The answer to the corruption and the turmoil and the bloodshed lay in the creation of a united country: the United Provinces of Nigeria. Such was Ironsi's dream. He set about fulfilling that dream.

There were many who sympathised with the Military Governor's aspirations. Not only was the break-up of the country into regions seen as a recipe for disaster but far worse was the imbalance in size of those regions: the mighty North opposed to the South broken in two on the principle of divide and rule; the North, Lugard's North, an ethnic mixture, with a Hausa-Fulani majority, left intact. Administrative division of such a mighty landmass as Nigeria, yes, of necessity; Azikiwe had urged the creation of eight divisions, creating a geographically balanced group of provinces without the domination of any. Ironsi was prepared to go along with this idea in principle but his main preoccupation was establishing an uncompromised unity among those provinces controlled by a strong central government, not a federation, certainly not a confederation but one united country.

He set about the task of unification with a certain degree of constitutional niceness: he established a commission to examine the matter, to listen to various points of view, to consider those points of view, to report to the Military Governor.

There were many points of view and not all of them favourable. Gatherings of students expressed strong feelings; letters to the press warned of increased tension; academics at the Eastern University of Nsukka voiced misgivings. In the North, opinions were held and expressed much more forcibly, resentment boiling not only against the threatened loss of regional power but more acutely at Ironsi's high-handed way in brushing aside any suggestion of opposition.

His ear was open to one opinion, that of the Chief Commissioner, Francis Nwokedi, and Nwokedi was prepared to tell Ironsi what he wanted to hear. The fact that the Commissioner was Igbo was not helpful.

By the end of May, Ironsi felt that his subjects had had plenty of time and opportunity to express their opinions and air their points of view. He was aware that opposition to his plans did exist but, military man that he was, he gave the civil dissent no more attention than he would to that of barrack-room grumbling. My will be done. And so, on the 8th of May 1966, from the Office of the Supreme Military Governor of Nigeria, Major-General Aguiyi-Ironsi proclaimed Decree Number 34: Nigeria was One. What Lugard had done out of vested interest, what Governor Clifford had perpetuated in his post-war constitution: the division of the country into semi-autonomous regions, all was swept away with the stroke of a pen.

Opponents of Unification were appalled. The North seethed: not only was government to be unified, the legislative power of the Regions was to be taken over by central government; not only was the North to lose, in effect, its executive power, but the civil service of the three Regions was to be absorbed into the control of central government. The Northern civil service saw the danger immediately: they were to be swamped by Southerners, particularly the deeply resented, over-qualified Igbos. The barriers were down; the country was theirs. The whole significance of the January coup became glaringly obvious: it was an Igbo takeover. Why else had Ahmadu Bello of the North died? Why had Akintola of the West been shot down, why had Balewa been brutally murdered when Okpara of the East lived? Who were the perpetrators of the coup? Nzeogwu, Ifeajuna, Nwobosi: men of the East.

Initially the coup had been welcomed in the North. The Northern People's Congress hailed the military regime as a means out of the impasse of political violence that had strangled the country since Independence. Even the death of the Sardauna had been accepted with a degree of equanimity; his assumption of personal power had been seen as a rising threat. Resentment deep down, however, went beyond the death of individuals. The Northerners recognised the part that the Easterners had played in the coup and the advantages they had reaped. Ironsi on his mother's side was of Igbo stock, born in the East; his own brand of nepotism was becoming apparent. Silent anger swelled.

It was an anger that was inflamed to white heat by the attitude of the Easterners in their midst and the Igbos who poked fun at the hapless Northerners among whom they lived: "Where is your Warlord now? Where is your Federal Prime Minister? Where is your Western ally?" Magazine articles, cartoons and jokes, songs and placards were a constant reminder of the Northern debacle, and the Eastern triumph.

The Northerners were not only humiliated, they were threatened: Were the Easterners to take over the region, now no longer a region but borderless provinces open to the Igboman armed with paper qualifications, backed by the military regime? Were they, the Northerners, to be ousted by their Eastern rivals?

Their opposition to western education and the limited academic scope of the Koranic schools had left the Hausa and Fulani inadequately prepared for open competition. They seethed and squirmed beneath the boasting triumphalism of their tormentors. They bore the insults until the embers of their anger glowed white hot. The Unity Decree of May 1966 caused that anger to burst into violent flame. The worm turned. The worm became a fiery serpent, a serpent that lashed out at its tormentors with violence and with venomous fury.

The Easterners were taken by surprise. Their mindless arrogance had made them blind to the risks that they were courting. Dragged from the high horse of their assumed superiority they found themselves victims of frenzied attack; hundreds died in the outburst of anti-Eastern violence. Rampaging mobs ran screaming through the streets of Kano and Kaduna, Zaria and other Northern towns, hunting down the fleeing Igbo; they hacked them to death, burned them out of house and home, ransacked their market stalls, looted, pillaged, murdered at will.

We could see the aftermath vividly on the streets of the East. Refugees began to pour in, dazed and shocked, beaten, wounded, wandering, homeless. I was in Enugu, at the time, as the lorries came rumbling back from the North. John was visiting the General Hospital to offer assistance. I went with him. Wounded and dying littered the wards. A little child, head swathed in bandages made a pathetic attempt to smile. Beside her on the ground, staring unseeing at the ceiling was an old man. A nurse explained: "Her grandfather. He brought her. Machete cut." John enquired about the child's parents. The nurse shook her head.

The tale repeated itself with frightening regularity. Victim after victim arrived back, by train, by lorry and on foot with tales of horror, of burning, looting, pillage, rape and murder. The dream of unity was over.

Reports had been sent to the Military Governor; Ironsi was appalled. Rioting was not permitted; they, the other ranks, the people, were not allowed to riot. This was in direct contravention of army regulations and dictates of the Military Governor's office. This must stop forthwith. Firm commands were sent to the North. Katsina ordered his troops on to the streets. A degree of calm was established.

It was too late, however. The Lion of the North had growled and bared its teeth; it had loosened its claws with deadly effect. The people had spoken. The Council of Emirs sent Ironsi a strongly worded memorandum advocating a moratorium on Unification and the eventual repeal of Decree 34. Ironsi listened. The shock of the news of the uprising, clearer reports of the devastation and carnage were having a salutary effect. He promised in reply that his Government would be prepared to take account of the opinions of the traditional rulers; that his Office would be prepared to listen to official words of advice reflecting the feelings of the people. On the ultimate point, however, the essential point, the Decree of Unification, Ironsi stood firm. Decree 34 was to remain inviolate on the statute books.

Ojukwu in the East heard his master's voice. He listened: the decree had gone forth from the Governor's office that the whole country should be united and united it should be; the people must return to the place whence they had fled. Anti-Igbo riots in the North had taken place before. In the early fifties during a violent pogrom many had been killed yet peace had been restored. Threads were picked up again; the dead were buried; homes were repaired; businesses re-established. So now, the violence having abated, the people must return to the land of their adoption, the land that was now, by decree, their land. And they returned.

They had little choice. The overcrowding in the East was compelling; competition for posts among over-qualified applicants was fierce; markets had many sellers but there were few buyers: mains-electric refrigerators had little appeal in a village-market. Compounds overflowed with refugees, many mouths to feed but little in the pot. The hardship of the East forced many to face again the terrors of the North. The return trek began.

The darkened atmosphere lightened in June. The Military Governor of the East invited his friend, the Emir of Kano, to take up the Chancellorship of Nsukka University. It was a profound and public act of reconciliation. The Emir responded with generosity; deep regret was felt. Strong resolutions were made that the outburst all had witnessed was never to happen again.

Ironsi on his part announced that he was to tour the country to seek out for himself the real feelings of the people. A referendum was talked about; a calmer, more realistic, political approach to unity was considered. Ironsi's fact-finding mission started with high and positive hopes. It was to end in deepest tragedy.

13

Massacre

I was in Paris following a course at the Alliance Française when we had news of the second military coup. It was late July 1966. I made my way through the leafy boulevards from Raspail to the Community House at Denfert Rochereau to be greeted by the old cook, Frère Michel, with a late lunch and a worried look. He had news of the coup, of much trouble in Nigeria; he was concerned: "You will go back?"

The evening news gave weight to his concern. There had been a massacre of Eastern army personnel. Northerner troops were on the rampage. Civilians, particularly the Igbo, were not safe. Again they were being hunted down, chased and harried. The television had pictures of a family fleeing with their goods stacked on a handcart. Naked terror was in their eyes.

The following morning I picked up a paper to find further details. Reports spoke of massacres of Easterners in the three major garrisons of the West. More details came out in the following days until I was able to form a picture of the disaster that had yet again befallen the hapless Easterners. The exact details were longer coming out.

Shortly before midnight on the 28th of July the conviviality of the officers' mess at Abeokuta barracks was suddenly silenced by the appearance of a Hausa captain accompanied by a group of men with automatics levelled. With calm deliberation the commanding officer was singled out, then a major and a lieutenant. They were shot where they stood. All were Igbos.

The shots that exploded in the mess that night were the signal for the uprising. The Igbos in the battalion, taken completely off-guard, were rounded up, led out to the barrack square and shot. The Northern coup had begun.

Ikeja barracks was the scene of even more horror. A telephone call alerted the waiting Northerners. They sprang upon Eastern personnel in their midst, dragged them from their beds, manacled them, and drove them at gunpoint to the barrack square. There they stripped and flogged them, tortured them further and slit their throats. By dawn sixty crumpled corpses lay in their blood on the parade ground.

A squad of troops from the same barracks commandeered a vehicle and raced round to the airport. A VC10 was on the tarmac ready to take off for London. They stormed the plane and took control. On the passenger list was a Captain Okafor, an Igbo. He was picked out, dragged off the plane and taken prisoner in triumph back to barracks, stripped, beaten, tied to a cross, scourged and left to bleed to death. Vengeance was afoot, red in tooth and claw.

The main prize was Ironsi. He was at Government Lodge, Ibadan, a guest of Lieutenant-Colonel Fajui. In the early hours of the morning of the 29th of July news of the Ikeja mutiny was phoned through to the Lodge. A detachment of troops was stationed nearby; Ironsi ordered them to the Ibadan barracks to maintain or restore order. As they left, Danjuma arrived. He had a squad of Northerners with him and quickly overtook the light guard at the Lodge, forced his way in and took command of the ground floor. Ironsi and his host were ordered down, manacled, stripped, beaten, forced into the waiting van, driven out of town, tortured and shot. The bodies were dumped at the side of the road; the detachment drove on to barracks.

The garrison at Ibadan where Njokwu had been ordered to restore order was a scene of wild carnage. Acting on the agreed signal, the Northern element struck with dire force, rounding up officers and men of Eastern origin, they lashed them into line and forced them into the tailor-shop. Doors and shutters were slammed against the captives and grenades were lobbed in through an opening; explosions tore the flimsy building apart. Some actually escaped the carnage only to be met by a hail of gunfire.

Tales of similar horror and retribution were reported from around the country. Even in the East itself there was trouble. Northerners in Enugu took over the armoury and for some very tense moments it looked as if they were to take over the garrison. Common sense prevailed, however, in view of the numbers involved. Keys were handed over, a joint guard was established and discipline was restored.

News of Ironsi's death reached headquarters in Lagos. Ogundipe, second in command, took over, declared martial law in the affected areas and dispatched troops to quell the rioting in Ikeja. They were wiped out before they reached the barracks. A second detachment was ordered out but refused the command. Their officer's insistence was met by sullen refusal. The situation was tense. Ogundipe was after all a Yoruba; this was a Northern affair. Threats were muttered. Ogundipe retired, changed into civilian clothes and left, seeking refuge on an offshore naval vessel. The last remnant of legitimate constitutional rule had gone.

Who was to take over supreme command? Ojukwu in the East was next in rank and line. He was, however, too far away from the centre of things and in no position to exert extra-territorial authority. This, as Ogundipe had been informed, was a Northern affair. Already the new-sewn flag of the Northern republic was flying at the gates of Ikeja barracks. The word was going round: destroy Lagos and pull out. Civilians were already trekking north; busloads were on the move. The cry of "Araba" was in the air: Independence for the North.

Ikeja was seen as the heart of the rebellion. A Northern officer had assumed de facto command, a capable but unpredictable lieutenant-colonel, Murtalla Mohammed. A section of the men were solidly behind him but, in the anarchic atmosphere, not all.

Ironsi's Chief of Staff presented himself at Ikeja barracks. It was a brave act. The killer dogs were unmuzzled. There was no selection committee, no consideration of qualifications. Gowon was in a particularly vulnerable position: although a Northerner, he belonged to a minority tribe, the Angas. Also, he was a Christian. It was his courage and the force of his gentle, firm personality that won the day. He gained the confidence of the cabal of junior officers, convincing them of the impracticality of Northern secession. With this support gradually over-riding Murtalla's pretensions, he won over the rank and file, emerging as the leader of the leaderless. His was not an enviable task, one akin to taking hold of a short rope tethered to the snout of a raging bull. His grip was firm, however, and uncompromising, demanding an end to the killings, threatening execution of any who disobeyed. His position as military commander was acclaimed. His position as political supremo was assumed. He informed the governors of the North and Mid-west who offered him their firm support. Ojukwu in the East was not consulted; he was not even informed. The fabric of the new Nigeria was built upon very loose constitutional foundations.

Killings or no killings, my time in Paris was drawing to a close. I was given a touching send-off by the Brothers of the Community. The *econome* produced a bottle of champagne. This was indeed an occasion, a double occasion in effect: England had just won the World Cup. With Gallic courtesy they toasted England's success and, with deep feeling, toasted my return to West Africa. I replied in kind. It was an entente most cordiale. There were speeches and more speeches. The celebration came to an end; a short prayer was offered for the safety of the Brothers caught in the crisis of Nigeria.

The following day I flew back to London and then on to Lagos and Nigeria.

14

Pogrom

The Nigeria to which I returned was indeed in crisis; its extent was apparent the moment I stepped off the plane. We were surrounded by armed guards. The airport was ringed with troops. The lounge bristled with men fully armed and threatening. My passport was examined with hostile intensity; my letter of employment was read and reread. Documents were stamped, customs were cleared and I was through. There was a flight to Enugu, I was pleasantly surprised to hear but not surprised to learn that there was to be a delay. I made my way to the lounge and found a seat by the window.

The steward brought me a beer. I thanked him: *"Dalu."* It was a gamble. His hand stopped in mid-motion. He was Igbo. He looked at me and smiled. *"Kedu?"* I told him I was well and asked how things were. He poured the beer slowly and placed the glass on the table. He told me in an undertone that things were not good. There had been much trouble and still there was danger. He had, however, managed to get his family back to the East. He was holding on meantime. I could feel in his whispered words the stark danger of the situation. I watched him taking orders, moving smoothly between bar and tables, all with apparently unruffled efficiency and no sign of the anguish that was in his heart.

Our plane was called. We were led under guard to an exit gate and told to wait. I took a seat among silent fellow passengers and waited. The tension was palpable. A baby cried. Its mother quietened it with nervous haste. Her little boy was at her side staring at nothing. The guard stood above us, impassive. A stewardess appeared. We followed her quietly to the plane, found our places and buckled ourselves in. The engines whined into life, there was a brief cackle over the loudspeaker and we were off, above the rain clouds into the bright sunlight. There was a gentle lessening of tension. We droned on high above the lagoons, over the rainforest, the Niger glistening in the noon sun, and on to the East. We lost height rapidly, palm trees flashed past our windows. There was a distinct bump, a roar of reverse thrust and we were home. A cheer went up in the cabin; there were handshakes and smiles all round. The doors were opened and we stepped out into another world.

A mind-numbing sense of despair had settled on the region. The joy, the cheerfulness, the optimism that had greeted me on my first arrival, had vanished. There was an unwonted silence, a sadness in the air. It was small wonder why: the rioting against the Unification decree in May, the looting and killing that had gone on in the North had caused deep shock and anguish. The hopes and aspirations that had accompanied Ironsi's attempt to unite the country had been drowned in a bloodbath. The memories of the horror and the terror and the misery that the Northern massacres had produced were still sharp in people's minds.

Ojukwu had told the people to go back, to pick up the threads, to mend fences, to keep Nigeria One. They had done so. Life began to take on again the semblance of normality. Then July: the Night of the Knives, ripping apart the thin veil of peace that had covered the festering sore of Northern resentment.

Although aimed at the military, they were not the only Easterners to suffer. The story briefly told by the steward in Lagos airport was repeated many times. I saw the effects of those days of bloodshed in the overcrowded hospitals, in the overcrowded compounds, in the crowded school. "Sir, I have no chair." "The carpenters are making more." "I have no paper." "Go to the market and buy a slate." "I have no money."

Life had to go on. Highly qualified staff abounded, returnees, refugees. They were absorbed into the police with more traffic to control, into the hospitals with more sick and wounded, into schools with more pupils than we could cope with. The marketplace was crowded with sellers; not a few traders had escaped with their stock. There were few buyers.

On the political scene, some degree of control began to revive. In August it was decreed by a committee of regional representatives that army personnel should be repatriated. The injunction was fulfilled by the East: Northern troops, based in Enugu, paraded fully equipped before their commanding officer. Ogunewe addressed his men. Farewells were exchanged and the men marched in full strength to the railway station where they entrained for the North. The tattered remnant of Easterners straggling back from the West and North were a sorry contrast. Even as troops were regrouping, the killing was still going on. Twenty-two men held captive in Ikeja, in response to Ojukwu's request for their release, were summarily executed. January-coup plotters held in Benin were slaughtered in their cells. The aftershocks of the earthquake continued to rock the land.

Something had to be done. In September, Gowon in his assumed role as Military Governor summoned regional representatives to a Constitutional Conference in Benin. The question raised was: what form the governing of the country should take? The North had no doubt: a confederation, a loose association on the lines of a common market, the looser the better. They had had enough of Southerners competing with them according to a set of colonial rules. The Northerners were a different people, born into a different culture, brought up in a tradition which went back long before Lugard and his Gatling guns had imposed foreign rule at the end of the previous century. The edicts arising from 'recent accidents of history', as the Northern memorandum referred to colonial intrusion, were no longer binding.

The delegates from the East concurred. It was not what they wanted. Theirs was the dream that Ironsi had had, that of a united Nigeria where they could travel at will in a land that they could call their own. But the harsh reality of the situation bore down upon them, the glaringly obvious fact that they were not welcome throughout the land. They had been forced back to the East; they would stay there but they must have the right and the power to defend themselves.

Then the Northern delegates changed their minds. There had been some behind-the-scene consultation. The exaltation inspired by 'Araba', Northern Independence, was tempered by economic realities: they did not like the southern regions but they needed them; where else were Northern development funds to come from if not from the more affluent South with its cash crops and oil? Who was to pay for the Kainje dam, the Bornu railway extension? What guarantee would there be for access to the sea? Northern traditional rulers might look towards Mecca and the East, but the businessmen looked towards Lagos and the South. Proposals for a confederation were withdrawn.

The September meeting was not over before all the proposals and counter-proposals, agreements and amendments were blown up in the face of the delegates. The rumbling and the trembling that had shaken the country over the preceding months erupted in a great cataclysm of violence. The killing of Easterners had started again, this time in real and deadly earnest. "Get the Igbos," was the call and the Northerners went for them with knives drawn in manic fury.

Soldiers led many of the attacks. Maddened by looted drink and drugs they were unbridled. The Fourth Batallion, Largema's men, broke out of barracks and ran amok. Other troops followed. The police were powerless, the Igbos among them gunned down or in flight. Looting, rape and murder were once again rampant, this time armed not only with clubs and swords but with sub-machine guns and bandoliers of lead.

The Fifth Batallion based at Kano attacked the Southern ghetto. The people were defenceless against the armed might of the marauding soldiers. Men, women and children were butchered with mindless ferocity.

Still maddened with drink and bloodlust the soldiers charged out to the airport. The quiet airport where I had first touched down on Nigerian soil six years before, where the windsock had flapped lazily in the harmattan breeze and egrets swept white over the tarmac. Kano airport now turned into a bloodbath. Reception staff cowering behind desks were dragged out and bayoneted, passengers of Eastern origin hoping to escape the mayhem of the North, were gunned down on the spot. Igbos who had already boarded their plane were singled out, dragged back to the lounge and shot. Transit passengers, foreign individuals, ran screaming from the chaos. Gunfire hammered around the building mingling with the screams of the injured and dying. A *Time* correspondent was present; the matter was reported in detail.

Little else was reported yet the reality of the situation stared us in the face. Refugees began pouring back into the East and with them their stories piling horror on horror, building up what has been called the mythology of the events. There is nothing mythological about blood dripping through the floorboards of a wagon standing in Enugu lorry park; nothing mythological about the dead and dying laid out on the railway platform.

I was in the office of the British Deputy Commissioner. The husband of the secretary was an official on the railway. He had taken a train north, she told me, to rescue beleaguered Easterners clamouring to get out of the killing fields. The tales he had to tell were scarcely credible: rampaging mobs stopping the southbound train, dragging passengers out, hacking them to death before his eyes. He remonstrated violently: they were pulling a young girl through a carriage window, stabbing her as she was dragged down. He yelled, "Leave her. Leave her. She is only a little girl." Their response: "She is Igbo." The stories were multiplied.

I was called into the inner office. There was an exchange of pleasantries then the burning question: "What are we doing about this? What is our Government doing? The people ask us: what is the Queen doing about this? Are we not her children? they say. How can we stand by and watch these people slaughtered and do nothing? It is unreal."

The diplomat shrugged: "We send messages to Lagos; we inform them of the facts of the situation. The Deputy Commissioner is in Lagos at this very moment reporting on the matter himself but there is nothing we can do to make them act. Policy is dictated by the High Commissioner himself."

The British High Commissioner was obviously no friend of the East. Safely ensconced in the West away from the turmoil and the carnage, why should he be involved? There was also, of course, the question of the oil gushing with ever-increasing abundance in the East. One had to be extremely diplomatic in handling the question of ownership of that commodity. If the North were to go it alone, they would lose the oil. Presumably diplomatic advice had been given on that point. The strong central government advocated, demanded by the Northerners, would enable them to keep tight control of the oil revenue. The question of constitutional rights and precedence, de jure as opposed to de facto, were obviously not allowed to interfere with the workings of realpolitik.

The nicer points of constitutional precedence were not uppermost in our minds in the face of the tragedy that was increasingly evident about us. I was in Enugu and called into the house for lunch. John and Norbert were returning for a brief break from their work with the Red Cross; the tabards they were wearing were spattered with blood.

A little boy accompanied Norbert. "Sleeping rough on the station," he explained. "You might take him down to Uturu when you're going tonight, Jim."

15

Panic

It was dark when we reached Uturu, the Marist novitiate nestling in the Okigwi hills. The genial Californian, Brother James, welcomed us with a meal and arranged a bed for little Joe. My explanation of the boy's presence was cut short: explanations were unnecessary.

After supper I was sitting on the veranda in the darkness. James was in the novitiate house. I was alone. The night silence was broken only by the shrill cry of crickets. The smell of bougainvillea trailing over the veranda was heavy in the air. Suddenly I was aware of a shadow standing near me.

"Joe."

"Sir Brother."

"Why aren't you in your bed, Joe, asleep?"

"Myself I no fit sleep. I dey fear too much."

"Joe, there is no need to fear in this place; here all are friends."

He had sat down beside me on the bench. "In the dark when no one is there I dey fear. I think of my place in the North."

"Tell me, Joe. Tell me what happened."

"When I dey for Kaduna? When Hausaman come for we?"

"Tell me. From the beginning."

"From the beginning my father was electrician." Joe's tale was breathless, told in his peculiar articulate brand of pidgin. "Very early he leave for work. My mother she dey for house; myself I dey for house. Mama say make I no go for school. After there be some palaver for road. Plenty people shouting. People running. My mother dey fear. At night my father never come back. We wait.

The genial Californian, Brother James, deeply involved in the housing and care of refugees and, along with Francis, the establishment of the rehabilitation centre, 'Hopeville'

He never come back for evening chop. We wait more; he never come back for dark. Night-time be dark-dark. No light for house. We hear people moving for roadway. People shouting. Some time they scream. We never go bed. After when there be small light mama say make she go look for father. Make I stay home, no move, no go for out. Make no noise. After she say she go come with father she bring chop. I wait. All day I wait. Mama she never come back. Noise dey plenty for street, people running, people shouting. I dey fear. I dey cry. After dark come, Mama no dey. Papa no dey. There be quiet for street. One woman dey come. She open door. She say: 'Come quickly. Come with me.' I follow this woman into dark. She take my hand. We run. Some people come. They shout. We run fast. Myself I no get breath. Na dis woman be crying, be running, be holding my hand. We reach railway station. One big person come from dark. He stand in front of we. He has long knife, machete. Na dis kind woman drop my hand. She shout, 'Run! Run!' Myself I run for inside station. I never see this woman again. Only I hear her scream like pig when my father dey stick-am for knife."

In the shadows Joe's eyes gleamed white. His story poured out in a steady stream from the darkness of his memories.

"What of yourself, Joe?"

"Train dey for station. Many people dey for train. Myself I dey push-push. Many people get sick too much. Many people get cut. People cry. They dey moan. They dey pray for God. After, train dey move small-small. People they dey say, 'Tank God'. Train stop. Wicked people come with machete and stick. People get pulled from train. Many people get cut with machete, get beat with stick. They dey cry; they dey shout. I dey fear too much. I hide small-small. After, train move. Long time e dey go. People pray for God make him no let Hausaman come for train one more time. Long time train move tackety-tackety-tackety-tackety. I dey feel hunger for belly. Many people cry for water. Food no dey; water no dey. After, e be dark. Train be dark. After, I sleep small-small. When I wake e be day. Train be moving quick-quick then e dey stop. People cry for fear. People come for train. They dey open door. They be good people. They dey pass water for we to drink. They give orange plenty, banan. After train dey move we come for Enugu. I wait long time. I sleep for station. After, I go inside town. I beg food. Then I come for station for sleep. One day, two day. After, Brother take me to his house. He be kind too much. After, you bring me here."

"Your mother, Joe? Your father?"

Joe said nothing. He shook his lowered head slowly. A large tear fell on to his knee. I took his hand. "After this palaver, Joe, we go look for your father, your mother for North, eh?"

He looked up, his eyes glistening with tears. "We go try."

Fear was all around us, an almost tangible fear. A feeling of insecurity, of vulnerability, a fear of what next. It was late at night. I had returned to Orlu alone. There was a hammering on the door. A dormitory prefect was standing there. "Come quickly, Brother. There has been an accident. Bring first aid." I grabbed the box and followed. By the light of a smoking oil lamp I saw the nature of the accident, many accidents, broken, bleeding shins. Water was brought, antiseptic, gauze, bandages, sticking plaster. Wounds were patched up. A degree of calm was restored.

"What happened?" The prefect had followed me outside.

"You know that Augustine is dead; in Kano, murdered."

I nodded. Augustine had been our senior prefect the previous year. News of his murder had sent shock waves through the school.

"This was his dormitory. One of the young boys woke up screaming that Augustine was standing at the foot of his bed. It caused panic. The iron beds caused the cuts and lacerations. Thank you for your help, Brother."

Nerves were frayed to shreds. It was Sunday evening a couple of days later. Lewis was to return from Enugu. I was in the common room reading when he came in. "Where are the boys?"

"In the dining hall."

"They're not. They're nowhere. The place is deserted. Completely."

I followed him out. The compound was still and quiet and empty. We went over to the school; it was deserted. A car drove up followed by a truck. A police sergeant got out and came towards us: "Where are your students?"

"They are coming." I could see figures emerging from the surrounding bush, returning in groups. "What's going on?"

The policeman turned to the car. He indicated the driver and passenger. "You see how these people are dressed, like Northerners. They are from the North but they are Igbo, refugees. They were passing the school and stopped the car on the road to look. The boys saw them. They saw the Northern dress. They panicked and ran. All of them. These two gentlemen drove to the station and reported the matter. They apologise."

A roll-call was taken. The matter was explained. Apologies were again offered. The police and the unwitting cause of the excitement left. The boys went into supper.

We were inclined to make light of the incident. There was an element of humour in it. To some of the boys returned from the North there was nothing remotely humorous. I met one of them a few evenings later, crossing the football field. We dropped into conversation. He told me where he was from in the North. "Did you have much trouble getting here?"

"Much." He was at a mission school along with a host of others Igbo boys. The rejoicing at the January coup had given way to the horror of the May killings, but they survived and stayed. The July massacres had filled them with even greater fear but most had stayed on; their parents' jobs, their own education was at stake. Then came the September pogrom and terror was brought home to them. A truckload of Northern soldiers burst into the school compound yelling for the Igbos. Most of the boys ran to the Principal's house.

"And yourself?"

"There were four of us, or five. We cut for bush."

They had lain there in the undergrowth hardly daring to breathe. Yelling and screaming could be heard from the school and the rattle of gunfire. Darkness fell. Intermittent firing shattered the silence of the night, an occasional yell and prolonged scream. They lay trembling with fear. Throughout the long next day they lay listening to confused noises, the revving of trucks and the barked orders of command. When evening came there was silence. In the silence and in the darkness they made their way with infinite caution to the Principal's house, scarcely breathing as they did so, stopping stock still at the slightest noise, creeping from shadow to shadow until they reached the house. With terror in their hearts they roused the Principal. He took them in and the following day, with the assistance of the British Consul, got them under safe conduct to the airport and on to a plane for Ghana. From there with similar assistance they were able to return to the East.

The story of the Priest and the Consul was repeated time and time again, stories of courage in the face of naked terror, rescuing the victims of the pogrom from the hands of their assailants, from the very jaws of death. Not only missionaries and expatriate consular officials were involved: Hausa, Fulani, Idoma, Tiv risked life and limb and reputation in a bid to save lives. Despite the mayhem, many refugees returned unscathed to the East with the help of many a good Samaritan. A million and a half, it was estimated, poured into the region from North and from West. Nobody knows how many died: ten thousand, thirty thousand, fifty thousand? Countless numbers.

16

Secession

Something had to be done. The military coup in January had been carried out with feelings of righteous, military indignation against the corruption and ineptitude of the civilian government. Ironsi, whilst reclaiming constitutional authority, had swept away the remnants of that government. His high-handed reforms, however, had provoked bitter and bloody reaction, throwing the country into chaos and bloodshed. It was up to the military to re-establish order.

A meeting of the Governors was called for. Everybody realised the dire necessity for consultation and dialogue but the problem was: where to meet? Where in Nigeria was safe haven for the Eastern delegation? Various venues were considered and turned down until General Ankra of Ghana offered a place of refuge in the hills above Accra, Nkrumah's palace-retreat, Aburi. There the Governors of the four regions met with their staff.

Ojukwu of the East came fully prepared. Consultation with his Leaders of Thought, his Assembly, his military chiefs had given him a clear idea of what was expected and the remit to implement those ideas. He approached the meeting with all the seriousness he considered the gravity of the situation demanded. As in a military campaign his objectives were clear, his tactics were planned.

Gowon's attitude was different: Aburi was a friendly get-together of top military to discuss and clear up the problems of disunity that were besetting the country. Officers were gentlemen, not politicians, far less lawyers. They could meet on gentlemanly terms, talk over their differences, seek a mutually acceptable compromise and part on the best of terms. Gowon was neither a smoker nor a drinking man but a good cigar and a vintage port would have well accompanied his approach to Aburi.

Ojukwu was appalled: this was not an officers' reunion; this was deadly serious, not a game. If it was a game, it was a game to be won and Ojukwu knew about winning. He had played rugby at Oxford. He had also for a period studied law; he was doubly equipped to score points and he intended doing so.

Gowon was taken off guard; he had not come prepared for a diplomatic onslaught, indeed he had hardly come prepared at all. He obviously did not appreciate the depth of feeling in the East. Lagos was a world apart from Enugu. Refugees escaping leave little trace; refugees pouring into a region bring every trace of injury, bloodshed, loss. Ojukwu was surrounded by the signs of bloodshed and deprivation every day in every part of the region.

Gowon and Ojukwu faced each other across the table, the one a dreamer of soft dreams, the other tormented by the nightmare of the East.

General Ankra had made arrangements to have the discussions recorded. They were, in detail, point after cogent point, hammered out with remorseless clarity. Nigeria's army was broken and fragmented, the assassins of Ikeja and Ibadan had seen to that. The army must be divided on a regional basis. The proposal was accepted. Nigeria did not have a legitimate, constitutional government; Gowon held command by might rather than right; there was more than one officer higher in military rank. This point was supported by others present and accepted. A Military Council consisting of the four Governors, each with the power of veto, was established. Gowon was accepted as titular head.

Other points were made, less fundamental but important to the beleaguered officer who insisted on their acceptance: compensation for the Easterners ousted from their posts; more help for the countless streams of refugees clinging to life in the East. The undertaking was accepted.

The committee broke up with a feeling of a job well done; Gowon must have had more than a suspicion that certain jobs had been left undone. Ojukwu returned to the East in triumph presenting the Aburi Accord to his Assembly with a flourish and a feeling of deep satisfaction. Gowon and his aides had little to show in the way of constitutional gain from the meeting. His hands were tied behind his back.

Gowon's lawyers were aghast. They set about the task of untying the knots. Regional control of armed forces was ruled out; all military were under central command, Lagos Command; the power of the proposed supreme Military Council was severely curtailed. The right of veto by any one region was rescinded. The right of the Federal Government to intervene militarily in any region where law and order were breaking down was firmly stipulated. Furthermore the consent of only three of the four regions would be considered necessary. Federal financial responsibility for dispossessed civil servants was repudiated; they had left of their own free will; let them fend for themselves. A proposal was put forward for the break-up of the regions by the creation of more states within a firmly united federal republic. The tragic irony of the proposal appeared to go unnoticed.

The Benin meeting at which Ojukwu was neither present nor represented, codified and published these directives as Decree Number 8 of the Supreme Federal Government issued on the 10th of March 1967.

Ojukwu repudiated them out of hand. One clause alone, proclaiming the right of Federal military intervention, obviously aimed at the East, justified his repudiation. The Aburi Accord was the first and last and only constitutional agreement reached since the death of the last constitutional ruler, Major-General Aguiyi-Ironsi. 'On Aburi We Stand'. The declaration became a watchword.

The Benin Agreement, the Aburi Accord: words, words, words, shouted, yelled, declaimed, broadcast, promulgated on both sides of the Niger. Neither side would move. Compromise was beyond consideration.

Rhetoric gave way to action: Ojukwu began the move. Compensation was not forthcoming, he authorised the confiscation of Federal property within the Eastern Region. Gowon replied with the imposition of a partial blockade: post, telephone, air flights.

Massacre, pogrom, sanctions: the writing was on the wall. What had been unthinkable from the Easterners' point of view, what was the antithesis of what they had striven for, the negation of the unity for which Ironsi had died, began to be whispered till the whisper became audible, became a clamour: Secession! Crowds paraded with banners aloft demanding secession; letters appeared in the press spelling out the logical imperative of secession. The voice of the people was loud and clear: On Aburi we stand or else we stand alone.

Ojukwu summoned his Consultative Assembly. With unemotional, remorseless logic he addressed the members: The Federation did not want the East; this had been made abundantly, bloodily clear time and time again. In May the previous year when Easterners had been hacked to death in the North and harried, raped and driven from their homes back into the East, he, Ojukwu, had taken upon himself to mend that broken bridge. He had sent his people back. He had sent them to further bloodshed, massacre and death. In the West, at Ikeja, Lagos and Ibadan, military there had been gunned down, tortured to death, the lucky ones forced to flee. They were men of the East. The pogrom in September was still fresh in the minds of all, the sight of it fresh before their eyes: refugees, harried in the land they knew as home, wounded in mind and body, penniless, starving, driven homeless to the East while the rest of the country looked on with cold contempt. Was this Brotherhood? What help was offered? While the East was striving with every resource stretched to breaking point to care for, to house and feed the thousands and thousands of refugees pouring in day after day, what help had the Federal government offered? Less than a pound for each displaced person, far, far less than a pound. And now, while the East were succouring their starving, homeless, jobless, wounded, dying brothers and sisters, the Federal Government, Lagos, was threatening military intervention; the same soldiers that had harried them from their homes were to follow across their borders and harry them further still. It must not be. The Region had a right, the Region had a duty to defend itself. The word had been given, Gowon had been informed: the Eastern Region must take upon itself the right to self-existence in order to ensure to itself the right of self-preservation.

The Consultative Assembly, the Leaders of Thought, the Military did more than applaud, they insisted. Ojukwu was given no alternative but to carry out his threat: Secession it must be.

Gowon reacted strongly: a state of emergency was declared. Troops were mobilised. The Aburi Accord had been forgotten; the Benin Agreement was rescinded; the blockade was tightened; the regions were abolished. Gowon, in a deft move, he must have thought, had pulled the carpet from under Ojukwu's feet: by replacing the regions with a multiplicity of states, he had divided the East and its internal loyalties.

It was too late, however. The wild horses of secession, bits clamped firmly in their teeth, were careering headlong towards complete independence. Decrees from Lagos were an irrelevance.

In the early morning of the 30th of May 1967, Colonel Odumegwu Ojukwu, addressing the nation through a radio broadcast, solemnly declared that the territory and region hitherto known as Eastern Nigeria, together with her continental shelf and territorial waters, was, henceforth, to be regarded by all as an independent sovereign state bearing the name and title of Biafra.

We were at breakfast when we heard the broadcast, the solemn measured tones of Ojukwu, the solemn, breathtaking import of his declaration. There was a pause then an equally solemn roll of music. I looked over at Lewis.

He explained: "That's our new national anthem. Copies of the words came to the school yesterday."

"The music's familiar."

"Sibelius, *Finlandia*."

"And 'Biafra'?"

"Apparently the name the Portuguese gave to this area centuries ago – as in the 'Bight of'."

"So! It has come." I raised my glass of orange juice: "To Biafra."

Lewis raised his glass in response: "And all who dwell therein."

We looked at each other and smiled a grim and solemn smile.

17

Threat of War

The upper-school English class was quietly restrained. Drums might beat in the townships, bands might squeal, crowds might march, but away from the euphoria there was some deep thinking to be done. Lagos would not take this declaration of independence without deep demur. Too much was at stake: would the defection of one region lead to the break-up of the country? Would the Northern military stand by and let the hated Igbos dictate policy? And the oil! Reserves, refinery and terminal were all in the Eastern Region and on its continental shelf. Secession would not be permitted without a fight. The senior boys knew this and they knew they would be involved.

They were quiet when I walked into the classroom, quiet but respectful. We exchanged greetings and I congratulated them on their newfound state of nationhood, it seemed the proper thing to do. They thanked me solemnly. We talked about the situation and the implications. So much, it was agreed, depended on recognition. Would Britain recognise Biafra? If not, why not? Was it not obvious that the East had no choice: secession or strangulation, servitude and death? Did not Britain realise how they had suffered, that they were fighting for their very existence, for their very lives? The massacres had spelled an end to Nigeria as it had been created by colonial power. It had proved defective; now they must restructure. What was 'Nigeria' in any case? Had not the name been coined by Lady Lugard over her tea and toast and her letter to *The Times*? Biafra was a name with more history. "A rose by any name can smell as sweet." The speaker sat to quiet applause.

The essays waxed eloquent. Israel would recognise them. A great deal of store was put on Israeli recognition, the little land surrounded by hostile Arab states. The Jews had suffered as the Easterners had: ghettos and genocide and death camps. Even as they wrote, the state of Israel was threatened with attack from the south, Egypt poised with tanks and planes and infantry. The jubilation when Israel counter-attacked, cut the Egyptian supply lines and destroyed tanks and infantry from the air was ecstatic. 'Here was a Caesar. Whence comes such another?' Victory gave great heart and eloquence to our upper-school essayists: here was their shining star, their David in the desert, Goliath prone on desert sands. Were they not as David? Were they not threatened by a Goliath? But their slings were loaded, their feet set firmly on the ground, their heads held high. With a little help, with recognition of their position they would succeed; victory would be theirs.

Israel never did recognise Biafra. It was long before any state ever did: Gabon, Tanzania, Ivory Coast, Haiti, but not Israel, and not Britain.

It was a puzzling situation. Britain has a record of siding with the underdog: the Guerillas of the Peninsula against the might of Napoleon's army, Belgium threatened by the Kaiser, Poland against Hitler's panzer divisions. And why not now? The logic of it was laid before me with passion and indignation. A people who had fled in terror from the wrath of those with whom they had lived, killed and maimed and forced to flee, lucky to escape with their lives into the overcrowded East where they had sought refuge, had barred the gates against the oppressor and now that oppressor, breathing fire, was at the gates. And what was Britain doing? What was Harold Wilson doing? Aiding and abetting, offering advice and arms to the oppressors.

The Federals had the ear of the British High Commission. The British High Commissioner made no secret of his preference for the Federal cause. Biafra had no friend at court.

To us on the ground the situation was a simple one: stand up for a people beaten to their knees, send in a brigade of Ghurkas and a flotilla of gunboats, save the East from threatened brutality and genocide, establish a demilitarised zone and gain the everlasting gratitude of a people thus saved – and their oil. Britain might be prepared to forego the gratitude but desperately needed the oil. The Suez Canal was closed.

It is the prerogative of the layman to see politics in such simple terms. On reflection, however, and in reality, as far as politics is concerned, save in the eyes of peasants and prophets, there are no such things as simple terms. Among others, we were aware that the Russian Bear was beginning to cast a hungry eye on West Africa. England had no prophet in Government, no one to stand up for the right of the oppressed against the might of the oppressor. Certainly not in Lagos. Biafra was left to defend its injured and its homeless without help or succour.

Biafra was not unprepared. We were at Enugu airport seeing off a member of staff when an army officer walked over and greeted us warmly. He was a past pupil. There was the usual small talk with guarded mention of the political situation. One of the party made reference to a black-painted DC4 standing on the runway. Our friend was reticent. He was, we gathered, in charge of the offloading. The cargo, we further gathered, was not corned beef. The officer gave us a grim smile: "Biafra will defend herself," and he went back to his job.

Already troops were mustering in the townships. In Enugu, soldiers marched in parade along the roads accompanied by stirring military music. Guards stood armed and vigilant at public buildings. Recruiting drives were in force bringing out starry-eyed youths and wary veterans. Expatriates were leaving by the carload. We knew there would be war.

The blockade was beginning to bite. Shelves in the stores were emptying. With the closing of the Onitsha Bridge, trade with the West was reduced to a trickle; Port Harcourt was strangled by the blockade of the Bonny River. To the East, Northern troops were blocking the way to Cameroon. Isolation was becoming a reality.

June passed, however, without incident. Ojukwu, we thought, may have been gambling with the weather when he declared Independence. It was the beginning of the wet season. The Federal forces, in order to penetrate Biafra, would have to advance many miles from bases north and west. The difficulty of maintaining supply lines in the wet season was obvious. Maybe there would be no attempt to do so. Maybe there would be no fighting; maybe army command was waiting for the diplomats to make one further effort; maybe Aburi would be resurrected. Maybe the wolf would lie down with the lamb. It was not to be.

The first shots rang out on the north-east frontier. It was Saturday, the 6th of July 1967. The Ogoja front, lightly defended, crumbled before the Federal advance. We heard the news on the radio. Obudu fell. The war had come home to us. The Nsukka front was still holding. Biafran forces were preparing to counter-attack.

Morning meal and chores finished, the boys were making their way to the chapel. It was my turn to lead the service. As I approached, whispered conversations stopped. I felt a rigid formality in the replies to my greetings. There was a coldness. I knew why: I was English. Sir David Hunt, our man in Lagos, was English and he was opposed to Biafra; his predecessor, Cumming-Bruce had worked actively with the Federals. I shrugged inwardly: na so de world de be.

In the chapel there was the same tense silence. This was their war. Those who are not with us are against us. I opened the bible I had brought with me. I asked the boys to be seated. They sat in the same audible silence.

"This morning we will not use the normal form of Saturday prayer. This morning, as you know, is one which will mark a turning point in your lives, in all our lives, for this morning, this country is at war. Therefore, this morning we will use the prayers that Jesus used, the prayers of the people of Israel. We will take our prayers from the Book of Psalms."

I had chosen the passages carefully, selectively. I read them thoughtfully, solemnly, before a congregation silent in rapt attention: "We have so many enemies, Lord, so many who turn against us. They talk about us and say: their God will not help them . . . The Lord listens to the sound of our pleading. He listens to our cry for help. He will not turn away. Our enemies will know the bitter shame of defeat; in sudden confusion they will be driven away."

The boys were sitting up and listening; this was no ritualistic reading from the Good Book; this was alive; this was reality; this was their prayer.

"See the sufferings our enemies cause us, Oh Lord. Rescue us from death . . . The enemy has invaded the land, they have desecrated our holy places. They have left the bodies of your servants to the vultures, the bodies of your people to wild animals. They shed your people's blood like water. Blood flows through the land and no one is left to bury the dead. Now I know that the Lord gives victory to the one he has chosen. He answers him from high heaven and by his power gives him great victory. Some trust in war chariots, some in horses but we trust in the power of God. Such people will stumble and fall but we will stand firm. Give victory to him who leads us, Lord; answer when we call."

The service over, I left the chapel in silence; heads were bowed in silent prayer. It was indeed a solemn moment in their lives, in our lives.

18

Harassment

The coldness I had experienced, the rigid politeness apparent in the exchange of greetings, had sprung, I surmised, from the presumption that we, as expatriates, were about to leave the country. The ironic aspect was that our Principal was at that time in London trying to obtain an entry permit to allow him to return to school at the end of his leave. The Federal government was not willing to grant the permit, so Harry was making arrangements to come in through Cameroon. Hundreds of others had left, however; certain of our own expatriate staff among them. We were sad to see them go but with family commitments they had little choice. In the end we urged them.

I had a journey to make to Uturu. There were arrangements and decisions to be made with the staff of the novitiate. The journey was a nightmare.

"White-man, get out!" Vigilantes armed with sticks and machetes swarmed around the car. "Open your bonnet. Open your boot." I did so. The search began. There was nothing in the boot. It was hard to see what they were looking for under the bonnet. "Pigeonhole!" I opened the glove compartment. They found a map. Ah, this was interesting: White-man carrying a map hidden in the pigeonhole. "Na what ting you use-am? I tink you go show-am to Harold Wilson. No be true?"

"I am going to Uturu; Harold Wilson is in London."

"Show passport." It was snatched from my hand. I snatched it back. Suddenly the stakes changed. Their rifles may have been made of wood but their machetes had very sharp edges. "Give." I gave. The leader of the mob took the passport with forceful dignity, opened it and scrutinized the writing. When he turned the page and recognised the photograph he discreetly turned the booklet the right-way up.

"I think this man is saboteer." The muttering in the group became more threatening. "Sach car."

"I am teacher at Bishop Shanahan College. I pass by this way many times. Why this palaver?"

"Shut your mouth."

By this time the back seat had been removed and an intensive search was being conducted under the front seats.

"What are you looking for?"

"Bombs."

"There are no bombs there."

"Na you say so. You be British man. You go for UK. You go tell Harold Wilson all."

"I am going to Uturu, Okigwi. I go see my Brothers there. After, I return for BSC. If to say I go for UK where are my loads? You see-am? Nothing. No loads, no money."

"Go well."

I held out my hand for the passport. It was returned. "Make you put back seat." They replaced it unbolted. I left it so. The next roadblock would have it out. Bonnet and boot were slammed shut. I got in and revved the engine. The crowd made way and I drove through. I was concerned. I had kept my dignity but lost my sense of humour. Without a sense of humour it is very difficult to have rapport with the Igboman.

Around a bend in the road I was stopped again, and again and again: bonnet, boot, pigeonhole, pockets, passport. "British man. Harold Wilson's spy. Saboteur." I was making for Lagos. I was Gowon's spy. I was Federal sympathiser. "What of this map now?"

"Keep the bloody thing."

Out of the bush on the main tarred road, matters were more serious. There was the occasional khaki uniform among the tattered guardians of the way, dane guns, even a Lee Enfield. Passport was checked, details copied at the desk by the side of the road. Less was said but the menace grew grimmer. I passed a lorry, driving me off the tar into the laterite verge. The driver's hand was displayed to view, fingers and thumb well spread. He was indicating, I gathered afterwards, that my ancestors had been illegitimate for the preceding five generations.

I was a traitor. That was why I was leaving the country. That was why I was going back to UK to see Harold Wilson and tell him all. White-man bastard!

When I reached the house at Uturu I was drained. Frank and James, Irish and American, were attentive and sympathetic.

"Sure, Jimmy, you're not going to let a few idiots from the bush with their toy guns bother you. What do they know? How many of them know what went on in the West or up in the North? They're just out for a bit of fun."

"Twenty-three roadblocks, Frank, between here and Orlu. I counted them. That wasn't much fun. It'll be the same on the way back."

"Well, you know what they say, Jimmy: 'Nil carborundum . . .'. Have a beer. There's chop on the way."

Over a late lunch we discussed intensely the implications of the situation: refugees, orphans, the blockade, the growing hunger, the possibility of a Federal breakthrough, Biafran resistance, the future of the schools, our own situation.

It was late afternoon when I left and well after dark when I got back to the school. The roadblocks in the dim shadows were doubly menacing and dangerous. Some miles from home I left the main laterite road and took a short cut through the bush hoping to avoid the harassment. It was a mistake. The bamboo pole across the path was as effective as the oil drums that had barred my way on the main road.

"White-man, come down! Come down!" I got out. Shadowy figures mingled round the car. In the dipped headlights other figures emerged from the surrounding bush. Here was a prize indeed. Here was a prize that justified the watch in the night.

"Passport!" And a British-man to boot! Spy, saboteer! Why was I driving through the bush at night, under cover of darkness, I had something to hide. The car was searched from bonnet to boot. Disappointment. My pockets were turned out. I was searched. The car was searched again. Eventually the bamboo pole was raised and I edged through. "Go well." I went.

It was near midnight when I reached the school. Lewis was waiting for me. He produced the remains of a bottle of whisky and poured two drams.
"How did it go?"
"Sit down and I'll tell you."
We sat and talked into the early hours of the morning.

It had been raining heavily. Thunder and distant lightning growled and flashed. As I stood on the veranda watching the ragged storm clouds being torn apart by the wind, the lightning faded, the thunder rolled away, the wind and rain dropped. I stood and listened to the water dripping from the eaves and, in the silence, the moon rose in the wind-swept sky and silvered the palm forest across the valley.

It had been a hard day, an emotional, draining day. How many more such days stretched ahead. It would be easy to take the car and slip into the convoy heading south. There was a naval vessel at Port Harcourt waiting; the launch across to Calabar was still plying. It was a tempting thought. I stood there and let my thoughts drift and my gaze was caught by a shaft of moonlight glinting in the valley. A cross stood there, planted on a mound, and the figure of Christ hanging in agony was touched by the light of the moon. My gaze lingered, my thoughts turned to the words of the gospel: 'He came unto his own and his own received him not'. I knew that I would stay.

19

Exodus

The vigilante fiasco soon came to an end. Common sense, with a little persuasion sparked off by Sister Clara, prevailed. She had been stopped at a roadblock on the way back to her convent. One of the self-appointed guardians, presumably misunderstanding his instructions to examine boot and bonnet, ordered her to take off her veil. He had not reckoned on Clara's Celtic temper. Throwing herself back into the car, she slammed the door, roared off through the barrier and drove straight to police headquarters. The Chief of Police was equally irate when he heard the story, followed her back to the offending roadblock, leapt out of his vehicle, kicked over the barrels, threw the barrier into the bush and let the amazed and subdued guardians of the highway know exactly what he thought of them and their interfering ways. Security after that took on a more professional aspect. The barriers, fewer in numbers, were manned by regular police.

Internal security was firm but the border was under severe threat. Ogoja had fallen, the Federals were pressing south; the battle for the Nsukka sector above Enugu was still raging. Twice the Federals broke through; twice they were repelled. Though severely under-armed in comparison to their opponents, the Biafrans fought desperately, sharing a gun and a pocketful of bullets with a companion in arms. I heard a story of recruits facing the enemy armed with nothing but machetes. The story seemed hardly credible. "A sharp cutlass is better than an empty rifle," was the riposte.

Some of our own boys had been drafted into the army. There had been an air raid on Owerri town. The Convent school was hit. Areas of concentrated population were an obvious danger. The order went out for the closure of all schools. Our pupils left, but the senior students were told to stay. A short time later a message arrived that they were to stand by. Army transport would arrive the following day to take them to their basic-training camp.

It was a wet evening, dark and windy. The boys had finished supper and congregated in the library, the only room, having blinds, where light was permitted. I had set up the projector and together we watched slides of school life, slides going back to the early days of the school showing the construction of the building in which we were seated, showing the bush and the forest giving way to axe and saw and hoe to form the magnificent playing fields which stretched in front of the school. There were slides of more recent years, sports days and high days and holidays, days of sunshine and laughter, much laughter when they caught sight of their own much younger faces wreathed in smiles, blissfully unaware of what was before them. They were good lads; it was good to be with them.

The slide show came to an end. The projector with its noisy fan was switched off. The distant puttering of the generator died, a candle was lit. The rain beat steadily on the roof. Conversation was low and serious: what would the morrow bring? They were in the hands of the Lord. A prayer was said, a prayer for safety and protection and an end to bloodshed and violence, a prayer for peace and comfort. A hymn was sung, one from the Scottish hymnal chosen as the anthem for Biafra, the words asking protection from the Lord; the tune: *Finlandia*. The evening ended with the intoning of the 'Salve Regina', the ancient plainchant melody to the Mother of God, sung with such earnestness by those young lads against the beating of the rain on windowpane and iron roof. As the sound of their voices died, the rain stopped and there was silence. The candle was blown out and in darkness they went to their beds.

In the morning an army truck came to take them away, all of them to brief basic training, many of them to the Nsukka front, some of them to their death.

Biafra, born in agony, was baptised in blood. The blood shed on the Ogoja front desperately trying to hold on to positions, the blood spilt in attack and counter-attack on the Nsukka front, the blood spilt in defence of Bonny Island.

The tide of battle was flowing strongly against the Biafrans. It was small wonder: raw recruits, ill-trained, under-armed, a poor match for the professional Federal soldiers whose numerical strength was virtually intact, whose arsenal, apart from the bullets used to kill the Easterners, was at pre-war level and greatly increased by a constant flow from overseas: British armoured cars, Belgian guns, Italian mortars.

The Biafrans suffered heavy losses in those first few days. We heard of some of our own boys killed at Nsukka. Christopher Okigbo, the poet, died there. We had read his work with its mystic premonition of death and now his premonition was fulfilled, leading his men into battle with guileless gallantry. Nzeogwu died also, the hero of the first military coup. The Federals buried him with honour. An army chaplain was killed at Bonny. We attended his funeral. Bishop Anyogu spoke in moving terms. It was a sombre moment. A dark cloud seemed to hang over all.

Suddenly the news changed. The Biafrans had attacked on the Western front; swarming over the Niger Bridge, they had advanced virtually unopposed through the Mid-West. Linking up with sympathisers they pushed on with speed into the West itself.

Reports were coming through, recounted with intense jubilation. We were cynical; there had been many false reports, much wishful thinking. But this was different, reports confirmed by foreign correspondents, chief among them Frederick Forsyth, the redoubtable BBC reporter who had lost his job because of his refusal to toe the party line and doctor his reports. He had told the story as it was and it was a sad story in the telling. The British High Commission in Lagos did not like his attitude: "The damned fellow is telling the truth, for God's sake; get him out." He was dismissed and reported freelance. His report of the Federal advance was thrilling: "Standing on a bridgehead at Ore." The sound of intense gunfire was around him.

Ore was the bridgehead for Ibadan and Lagos and victory. It seemed unbelievable. The Federal Guard had put up a resistance and had been pushed back over the river. Reinforced, they counter-attacked and again were pushed back. The Biafran advance seemed unstoppable. Then it was stopped. Why, how, was a mystery. What had been an advance became a retreat. What was a retreat became a rout. The Biafrans came streaming over the Niger Bridge; the dream of victory shattered.

One explanation we heard was the threat of entrapment by Murtalla's brigade moving to the north, counter to the Biafran advance. Under threat of being cut off from base, the main Biafran force pulled back to Benin. Understandable. Less understandable and justifiable was the continued retreat from Benin over the Niger Bridge, the collapse of the Biafran initiative and defeat. Murtalla walked into an undefended Mid-West.

Treachery was spoken of, collusion between the senior officers and the West. The name of Awolowo was mentioned. The Chief of Staff was arrested and tried for treason. The fact that he was a Yoruba did not help his cause. Along with him was Ifeajuna, the gunman of the January coup. Both were executed.

The country was thrown into the depths of despair. Even talk of advances on the northern front did little to lighten the gloom. Stories coming from the West and Mid-West told of unspeakable slaughter. Murtalla's men were on the rampage; no one was spared. In Asaba alone over a thousand victims, we heard, men and boys were machine-gunned and thrown into a bulldozed grave, dead and dying together. No one was safe; civilians joined in the fray. Whole families were set upon by neighbours, harried from their homes and slaughtered.

I was in Enugu. A Sunday evening service was being held. The Cathedral was packed. A red and angry sun glared through the leaded windows, reflecting the mood of desperation of the congregation deep in silent prayer. Suddenly a jet screamed low overhead. A moan went up from the people. There was a terrifying moment of stillness then panic broke. There was a rush for the door, the congregation bursting out into evening darkness, weeping, holding on to each other, despairing. Was there no place of safety?

I had come up to Enugu to obtain an entry permit for the headmaster of the school attempting to return to his post after home leave. He had got as far as Cameroon but could go no further without the permit. I obtained one with little difficulty from the police countersigned by a friendly army officer. My own papers were checked, stamped and signed. Everything seemed in order. It was arranged that I should travel into Cameroon to deliver the permit.

I got as far as Oron and was about to board the launch for Calabar when I was stopped. The soldier checking papers called over an officer. Together they examined my passport.

"Come with me."

"Where?"

"You are British."

I was bundled into a Land Rover and driven round to headquarters.

The Camp Commander, Lieutenant Bassey, saw me when he returned from guard inspection. He was not a happy man. Oron was exposed to sea-borne attack. Security had been found less secure than he demanded. His anger was obvious as he stormed into the room, threw his hat on the desk and slumped into a chair.

"Who is this man?"

He was informed: I was a suspect saboteur; I was Harold Wilson's spy; informants had revealed that I had a secret transmitter; I was in contact with Lagos.

Bassey was examining my papers with a fierce frown.

"Who is this man Gillan?"

"He is the headmaster of Bishop Shanahan College in Orlu. I am a teacher there. He is in Cameroon. I am taking him an entry permit to allow him to return to Biafra."

"Where is your exit permit?"

"I am returning within one week. The police in Enugu told me I did not need one."

"So you are leaving the country without permission. You will go to Lagos, you will go to London, and you will tell them all you know. Do you know what your British Government is doing to us? Do you know that there are British gunboats offshore waiting to attack. Have we not suffered enough? Do not think it was only the Igbo people who were killed and turned into refugees. Our people also suffered and suffer and it is your people who are helping the Nigerians and you are helping them."

I sat in silence until he had finished. Bassey looked levelly at me, waiting for a reply.

"I have been in this country for six years. I also have seen the suffering of your people. We are not spies. We are not informants. I am not leaving. In one week I will return with our Principal. You have his entry permit on your desk. We will continue to help as we can."

Bassey got up. "Has this man been searched?"

"Yes, sah. Myself I dey sach-am."

"Search him again." He left the room.

I was searched. Bassey returned, a bottle of brandy in his hand.

He sat. He told me to sit. "You are British?"

I nodded.

"You are a member of the Roman Catholic Mission?"

I said I was.

"You are going to Cameroon to bring back your Principal?"

"Yes."

"I believe you. Have a brandy."

He poured two generous measures. We raised our glasses. It was early morning. The brandy was Spanish, I felt its warmth.

Bassey stood up. "You will not be allowed on the launch without an exit permit. That you must obtain in Enugu. Go well." He left.

I went back to Enugu.

The paper I received with some difficulty. Few officers were happy about giving expatriates permission to leave the country. When I showed my re-entry permit and spoke of Lieutenant Bassey's insistence I was eventually granted the permit, sealed and signed.

I was by no means the only one leaving. The Federals had broken through on the Nsukka front. They were advancing on Enugu. Already the guns could be heard in the hills above the town. The consulates were closing.

I went with John to the sports club. A few members were assembled. We knew it was the last night. Most had left. Some redoubtable souls were holding on to company assets knowing soon there would be nothing left to hold on to. Consulate staff, American and British, were there also; they had planned to leave the following day. It was a farewell. Blinds had been drawn. A lone oil lamp gave light. The beer was warm but plentiful. A committee member told the staff they could go. He would lock up. They went and we knew it would be long before they would return. The crump of guns was closer.

"Who's got a song?"

The mood suddenly changed. The quiet, intense, serious talk gave way to a rousing chorus inviting the landlord to fill the flowing bowl. "For tonight we'll merry, merry be, for tonight we'll merry, merry be, for tonight we'll merry, merry beeeee! Tomorrow we'll be sober." The chorus ended in glorious soulful harmony. John sang of the maiden he met, yet again, by the lochside. The fate of the pussy killed by the crow, was sung in doleful Scots. The English contingent sang sweetly in close harmony a tale of unrequited love, restoring order where chaos had threatened. The American Consul was on his feet, a big man with a big voice, singing with lusty abandon the ringing notes of an operatic aria. It sounded like an Italian aria but not of Verdi, Puccini or any other Italian. The shadows dancing around the room quivered to his ear-splitting fortissimo, drooped to his pathetic pianissimo, lingered over his dying rallentando. Then the whole company burst into a cheerful, meaningless, ersatz Italian chorus: ringing tenori, quavering falsetti, gravel-voiced bassi profundissimi pouring forth their hearts with a passion that would have paled the principal chorus of La Scala, Milan. We were a merry crowd with heavy hearts.

The party ended on a quiet note. A verse of 'Cwm Rhondda' was remembered and a lone Scots voice sang 'Crimond' to a silent, thoughtful audience. The lamp was blown out, we trooped into the star-lit night, stood and listened for a while to the guns echoing in the hills, shook hands and wished each other well with quiet sincerity. The doors were locked and we went our different ways.

20

Cameroon

I had little trouble joining the launch at Oron; a glance at my passport with the exit permit, I was on board and we were away, swishing past the mangrove trees, through the muddy waters of the Cross River, up the channel and on to Calabar. The gangway was crowded as we waited to disembark. A friendly deckhand suggested we use the forward exit; he showed us the way, undid the chain, ushered us down the gangplank and into the arms of the military police. We were bundled into their waiting Land Rover and whisked round to headquarters.

I was getting used to this. There were now six of us in the party: an elderly couple, a young couple, myself and a lad called Bruce who, backpacking through West Africa, had stumbled into the Biafran conflict, found he could not get out, had appealed to the British Commission and had been handed over to me for safe keeping into Cameroon. My own track record did little to commend me for the task.

We were taken singly into the Provost's office for questioning. I was the last. The interrogation was a repeat performance of that conducted by Lieutenant Bassey. I answered all the questions and offered all my papers. I had had them countersigned by an officer high up in internal matters, and expressed surprise that his name and signature should be so questioned. Name dropping was a risky business but it worked.

"Who can vouch for your identity?"

"The Fathers at the Catholic Mission."

The same Land Rover drove us round to the Cathedral. The Fathers there, Vincentians who on occasion had visited us at Enugu, did not hesitate to vouch for us. They took us under their wing, gave us a meal and accommodation, arranged transport into Cameroon and, the following morning, saw us off.

The road to Mamfe was a bumpy one. As the minibus emptied of local passengers, the road became bumpier. It was a tense journey, never knowing round which corner we would run into a Federal roadblock. But we made it to the border unhindered. The guard there ordered us out, examined our papers and spoke briefly and firmly to our driver who got back into his cab, reversed and drove off in the direction of Calabar.

"Hey look at! This man, we dey hire him for Mamfe. Why he go for Calabar? You tell him so?" The soldier was non-committal, shrugged his shoulders and ambled back to the guard-hut. I followed him. "What thing we go do now? Transport no dey." He turned and gave me a look reserved for rats abandoning a doomed ship. Again he shrugged his shoulders and pointed up the road. We took our cases and walked in the shade of the forest canopy, in the silence of the afternoon towards the next roadblock.

It was manned by soldiers, professional looking but no more concerned. One of them detached himself from the shade at the side of the road and opened the steel barrier sufficiently to allow us through.

Another barrier blocked our way. He stood there. We stood there.

"Na which side we dey go now?" There was no flicker of comprehension. *"Monsieur, s'il vous plaît, nous allons a Mamfe. On peut passer?"*

One of the soldiers pointed to a path up the hill. *"Douane. Passeport."*

The commanding officer was English speaking and courteous, asked us to be seated at a table under a flame-of-the-forest tree and excused himself. Moments later an orderly appeared bearing a tray rattling with bottles of Guinness and Fanta. The customs officer came, flipped through our papers and told us that we must be hungry; his wife was preparing a meal for us. The commander rejoined us; asked if all was well. They were interested, very interested and concerned; they had seen the refugees pouring through, battered, crippled, and bleeding. They knew there was desperate hunger and hardship. Enugu was under heavy bombardment. There were internal refugees. They were astonished to learn I was planning to go back. I explained the situation. The meal appeared, peppered meat with mounds of fluffy rice. A Land Rover drove into the compound. It was a French official on his way to Douala. Yes, he would give us all a lift to Mamfe. Blessings were raining down. We left a discreet gift for the food and drinks, joined the diplomat and driver in their vehicle and arrived, shaken but heart-warmed, in Mamfe.

We were stopped in the town centre. A group of soldiers ambled over; our papers were checked; the Frenchman was escorted into a nearby office; his Igbo driver was ordered out of the vehicle and beaten up, quietly, brutally, methodically, pushed from man to man, slapped, punched, kicked and told to go. He limped back to his vehicle, bruised, bleeding, dignified. We looked on silent in deep shame. The French official reappeared, joined his driver and left.

Yes, there was a lorry for Douala leaving shortly. We made our farewells and my companions went on their way south. Transport for Bamenda would leave the next day at noon. There was a rest-house I could try. I bought bread and sardines in olive oil, a couple of beers and made my way to the log cabin by the lakeside. I was offered a room for the night, left off my backpack and went down to the lakeside, glass calm in the evening stillness. I sat there and slowly sipped my beer. It had been a long day.

Harry was overjoyed to see me the next day armed with his entry visa. "When do we start?" We sat up late that night. There were many questions to ask: The boys? The Brothers? The school? The people? Chief Patrick? "You heard about Enugu?"

"Under bombardment."

" It's gone. Fallen. The Feds are in."

"Gone? What about the Brothers?"

"No news. It was a fierce bombardment. They'll have been lucky to get out alive, if, that is they get out at all."

There was a silence. My thoughts were on my Brothers: Norbert and John with their blood-stained Red Cross tabards, striving night and day to alleviate the suffering, now they themselves could very well be victims. It was a solemn moment.

"We can still get in without touching Enugu."

"When?"

We set off early next morning for Mamfe. It rained, heavily. The Land Rover leaked, badly. We were soaked to the skin. The skies cleared as we drove off the hills and late afternoon in Mamfe was bliss. We made a meal of fresh bread and bananas with ice-cold beer. A Land Rover pulled up outside the store and a White-man got out. We exchanged greetings.

Harry, Principal of Bishop Shanahan College, with his genial vice-principal.

Straying behind enemy lines on one of his missions of mercy, Harry was captured by Federal troops spending the rest of his tour working with refugees in 'liberated' Biafra

"Going far?"

"Orlu, Owerri."

"I can get you as far as Calabar."

We thanked him, loaded our goods, climbed on board the truck and set off at speed.

Our driver explained: "Curfew in Calabar. Got to be there before dark. Hold tight. Road's a bit bumpy."

The Reverend Cairns, Principal of Hope Waddell High School, was obviously used to the route and the road, his vehicle touching the surface on occasions. Daylight was already fading into dusk as we sped along, deeper and deeper into the forest.

"There's a short cut over the river that will save a bit of time, the Dunlop Bridge. I've a pass; it's a military zone."

The checkpoint at the entrance to the bridge was courteous and efficient, examining papers briefly by the dim light of a torch. "Hurry now. Curfew for Calabar."

The Reverend Cairns stamped on the throttle. The vehicle roared over the bridge, planking rattling beneath us. We hit the second barrier at top speed, sending the iron pole flying, colliding with the trestles, scattering the sentries.

"Heads down!" We crouched; round a bend in the road, full speed into the thickening forest and out of range.

"Sorry. Forgot about the second barrier. All right?"

Calabar was still open. The Cairns's home provided a warm welcome, a filling supper and a heartfelt prayer of thanksgiving. We slept well.

Early next morning we caught the launch for Oron. It was a tense crossing. Gunboats were seen stationed in mid-channel. Were they friendly? We stared into the river mist. Harry sidled up: "Got your passport handy?"

I nodded. "Expecting a boarding party?"

"Never know."

We anchored without incident and made our way through the surging throng waiting to board.

"We seem to be going against the tide."

We were met by an astonished Brother James. He had brought down John from Uturu.

"John!" There was a joyful, brief reunion. "What about Norbert and Martin?"

"Safe. In Uturu." John was on the gangplank ready to join the ferry, on his way to Calabar, Cameroon and Scotland for his long-overdue leave. We watched him board.

James slowly shook his head as he watched. "A lucky man. They had a dreadful time under that shellfire. Waited until the very last minute; got out with the last of the refugees." He turned. "And you are coming into the country!"

We nodded. James shrugged. "Get in; let's go."

With Norbert and Martin, John endured the intense shelling of Enugu until the last minute when word eventually was given for evacuation, causing them to leave with the last of the refugees

21

Evacuation

With the fall of Enugu thousands of refugees came flocking into the interior, almost a hundred thousand it was estimated, hungry, wild-eyed, desperate; more mouths to feed, more bodies to cram into overcrowded compounds. The breakaway state of Eastern Nigeria, as the BBC invariably referred to the enclave, was a disaster area. Enugu had absorbed many of the refugees from the North, now they were on the run again, many of them in our direction.

The blockade was beginning to bite. Calabar fell shortly after we came through. Adekunle with the Third Marine Commando in a seaborne attack took the town and pushed north linking up with the Federals in Ikom and cutting off Biafra's last link with the outside world. With the fall of Bonny Island to the south, Port Harcourt was blockaded and the staple protein supply of Scandinavian stockfish came to an end. Cattle no longer came from the North. With Federal possession of large parts of the land-rich Eastern area, even local food supplies, maize, cassava and yam, were diminishing. Norbert, who had established himself in Orlu with its hordes of refugees, had to travel farther and deeper to supply his growing number of feeding stations. The New Year of 1968 ushered in a time of famine.

A committee meeting was called. Local government officers were at their wits' end. Norbert had a word of consolation. Shipments of supplies, he had learned, were on their way from Europe heading for the Island of Sao Tomé, some three hundred miles offshore in the Atlantic. Port Harcourt airport was still open; food could be flown in; already the churches were organising space on government planes.

It was cheering news, a spark of light in the blackness about us. The blackness, however, was intensified by the continuing news of military reverses, each reverse sending more refugees pouring into the ever-diminishing enclave.

Onitsha was under attack. Murtalla, having established a firm bridgehead at Asaba, launched a fierce artillery bombardment. The market went up in flames and with it all the fun and laughter I remembered. The people fled. The Federals came over the river and took a virtually undefended town. They went wild, pillaging and burning, looting and drinking.

Achuzie was in command of the Biafran defence. Recognising his vastly inferior strength in men and arms he had delayed a counter-attack until the optimum moment and then struck with devastating effect, taking the Federal troops by surprise, sending them scattering for their boats and picking them off as they desperately made for the Asaba shore. Many never made it. Achuzie took possession of the town and collected the arms and ammunition left by the retreating Federal troops. Murtalla re-established his western bridgehead and signalled Lagos for more supplies.

During the bombardment of Onitsha, the newly built Borromeo hospital had been evacuated, staff and patients pulling back to an already overcrowded Ihiala. I was asked to help in rescuing equipment.

The District Office supplied transport, a large rambling bus. The driver was not a happy man. "What of my passengers now?"

The soldier who had requisitioned the vehicles laughed. "Passengers no dey."

"What of diesel?" He was given a full tank.

"Which side we dey go?"

"Onitsha."

He did a double take: "Onitsha. I think you know Onitsha be war zone. There be Federal attack. How you say Onitsha?"

"Outside Onitsha. Borromeo hospital."

His mood did not improve as we approached the town. The sentries at the roadblock were adamant that we could not go through. I showed them my pass from the District Officer.

"You know this is danger zone." We knew.

Onitsha was deserted. It was an eerie experience growling our way through the empty streets. The blackened pillars of the market stood gaunt and bare like defoliated trees.

The Holy Rosary Sisters met us at the market square: a change of plan. We would take the bus down to Waterside, the clinic there still had valuable equipment; we could make a start; they would join us shortly.

The driver's mood deepened as he ground the gears and edged his way down the narrow road to the river and its Waterside clinic. Halfway down a soldier barred our path.

"Driver, quench engine now." The engine shuddered into silence. The soldier motioned me to come down. I did so and followed him up the embankment into a command post. An officer was standing at a blackboard surrounded by a group of soldiers. All were watching my approach.

The officer spoke: "Sir, that is your vehicle?" His voice was quiet and calm. I said that it was, more or less.

"Could you explain, sir, what you are doing in this area? Do you not know that this is a war zone; that already this morning we have been under bombardment? That already this morning I have lost two of my men killed by the vandals. And now you bring this, this bus into the area." His voice was rising. "The Federals are watching; they think you are reinforcement and soon the bombardment will start again."

I began to speak. The officer gestured with his arm. "Go. Go now. Take your vehicle and go."

I went. I could feel eyes following me as I retreated in disarray, the bungling amateur among professionals. The driver who had been spoken to by the sentry, snapped on the engine, revved the bus in high-speed reverse up the hill, switched off the engine, gently laid his head on his arms on the wheel and sighed deeply.

A green Peugeot raced into the square. A nun jumped out. "We've a pass for Waterside. Follow on!" She jumped back in the car and raced off down the forbidden road. I yelled after her but it was too late.

I looked at the driver; he stared straight ahead. I pointed to the key. The driver shook his head slowly. "White-man!" He turned the key. The engine barked into life. A jeep roared round the corner. An officer leapt out. This, I thought, was pure situation comedy, brilliant timing. But it was not comedy.

"Quench that bloody engine. Quench-am, I say, you bloody fool, you!"

Something gave way in the driver's reserves of strength; he snapped off the ignition and jumped down from the cab. "What ting I go do now? Dis Whiteyman say make I go down for Waterside. Soldier say go back one time. Sister say make we go down. Na what ting now?"

The officer was taken aback. I intervened: "Excuse me, sir, I can explain."

He swung round: "Explain! Explain! How can you explain? This is a war, my friend, not a market. What is this bloody bus doing here? Take your vehicle and go. Go! Go!"

The noise of a car engine was heard behind us. The officer turned in sharp disbelief. The green Peugeot was reversing at speed up the Waterside road. It stopped beside us. Inside were three nuns and an African driver. The officer stared for a while in silent amazement then walked back to his jeep. His shoulders were slumped. He got in and drove away.

The following day the Sisters had a pass from the army and Waterside clinic was cleared. There was a limit to what the Biafran armed forces could withstand.

They were a redoubtable lot, the Sisters of the Holy Rosary Congregation. Founded in the twenties by Bishop Shanahan who recognised the need for women on the Mission field, schooled in the strict discipline of the Dominican Order, they came out to work in schools, hospitals, clinics and leper settlements in West Africa, East Africa and beyond. I met them first in our local hospital at Amaigbo. Marcellus introduced me, a young Marist fresh to the Coast. They made me immediately and warmly welcome, inviting us

Holy Rosary Sister.

to join them as they sat there in the cool of the evening on the veranda of their house above the hospital. A young nun, tall and elegant in her starched white habit, scapular and veil brought iced lemonade. We were introduced. She also was newly arrived. Her name was Sister Clara, later renowned for her destruction of highway barricades.

The Borromeo hospital was the pride and joy of the Rosary Congregation. All of their resources had gone into the building of it. They were not going to lose their precious asset, Federals or no Federals.

We worked feverishly, transporting beds, linen, trolleys, medicines, surgical equipment. Harry came over with a second truck and more help. Our driver had reconciled himself to his lot and worked with a will, load after load being driven into what we hoped was a safe zone, away from the threat of invasion and the gunfire which occasionally erupted from the opposite bank of the Niger.

After three days we had more or less finished the operation. I was sitting with Harry in the shade of the courtyard, hot and tired after the frantic work but satisfied, waiting for the lorry to return for the last load all packed and ready. Sister Charles appeared carrying a cardboard box. "Look what I found in the medicine store. You missed it." She opened the box. "It's for maternity patients but I think we can stretch a point in the circumstances." We saw the writing on the side of the box and concurred wholeheartedly: 'A gift from Guinness of Ikeja. Not for retail'.

The crump of heavy artillery from across the Niger went unnoticed.

22

Famine

Hunger was turning to famine. As the Federal grip on the frontier tightened, access to food supplies diminished; as Federal troops pressed deeper inland, refugees continued to pour into the interior. It was frightening. With the fall of Enugu, Federal control of the North was complete. The Niger Bridge was closed, broken in a defensive move which cut off the western supply route. To the east, Adekunle had sealed off Calabar and the last link with Cameroon. The fall of Bonny Island along with the Federal gunboats completed the blockade of the South. Biafra was a concentration camp with millions of hungry and starving and dying prisoners.

Resistance was desperate. A fierce counter-attack on Bonny Island came within a degree of success. Federal firepower, however, with naval support,

A handful of garri

was overwhelming. The victorious Biafrans were dislodged. A seaborne attack on Calabar was no more successful. Mercenary troops were involved; they had seriously underestimated the capacity of their opponents. They were not facing tribesman with spears and muskets, as in days gone by, but heavily armed men led by officers trained in the art of modern warfare. The invasion was repulsed with heavy losses. Some half dozen French mercenaries were killed in the attack.

Biafran defence quickly turned into guerilla warfare. The troops learned the lessons well. Some had little to learn. Achuzie was one of them. A veteran of the Second World War and the Burma campaign, he proved a master of the ambush. His opponent in the field, the Federal commander, Murtalla, wary of a second seaborne attack on Onitsha, launched his campaign from Enugu, advancing his lengthy troop and supply lines down the narrow northern corridor. Achuzie was waiting for them. His attack on the exposed Federal flank was overwhelming. A mortar shell hit a leading petrol tanker setting off a devastating chain reaction. Vehicle after vehicle engulfed in the tide of searing heat, fuel tanks exploding, ammunition trucks bursting into flame, sending death and destruction the length of the convoy. The Biafran troops withdrew in wondering exaltation.

Successes were spasmodic, however, and limited. It was a defensive campaign holding back the Federal advance on front after front with arms and ammunition in pitiful supply, not always with success. Murtalla continued his push south, sending refugees deeper into the enclave. I was in Uturu when Awka fell, the town razed on command; refugees poured in. The job of feeding and housing them took our mind off the sound of gunfire thundering in the hills above Okigwi, but nothing could turn our minds from the stories of murder and mayhem we were hearing: dying and injured left to their fate, women and young girls raped and strangled, boys and old men bayoneted, families thrown still living down deep wells. The horror was beyond bearing and we knew we were in the line of attack. Night fell on a frightened people.

I returned to Orlu to find matters little better. Norbert was scouring the country to find food for his orphanages and medicines for his clinics. Orlu was considered a relatively safe area, deep in the enclave, remote from immediate attack. Refugees crowded in.

The army had taken over the school. Dormitories became barrack rooms; the library was converted into an administration centre; classrooms resounded to points of military instruction; tennis courts echoed to the bawling of drill sergeants; our metalwork block became a repair depot; the woodwork room was barred and shuttered and became, we guessed, the armoury. The chapel was locked and left untouched. A sturdily built fence divided our part of the compound from the military. We were left alone to continue the desperate task of feeding the ever-increasing number of homeless.

Supplies were coming in. Port Harcourt airport was open, though under regular attack. I was given powdered milk and took it to a nearby camp with a feeling of great satisfaction. The subsequent outbreak of diarrhoea taught me I had much to learn in the science of nutrition. Luckily Oxfam had sent in kaolin as well.

Norbert got his hands on a lorry load of cornmeal. This was indeed a bonanza. I was surprised at the reaction of more than one old mother with wide-eyed starving children: "Sir, what of salt?" "Salt!" Salt was a condiment one kept on the dining table to be sprinkled occasionally if cook had been too sparing. Little did I realise how desperate was its need in desiccating tropical heat; how tragic was its total absence. I appealed to Norbert. He arrived next day with a large sack of the precious commodity. "From where?" He smiled enigmatically. "There's something else in there might be of use." We had almost finished offloading supplies when I came across a crate of beer. I gathered Norbert had connections with cross-Niger traders working effectively under conditions of extreme danger. 'Attack marketeers' they were called. For a teetotal Scot he had a heart richer than gold. His ale in the midst of the misery was pure nectar. His salt proved more than a means of rehydration: it became something of a form of currency.

I was asked to go to Umuahia where medicines were available. Armed with a letter from our fatherly District Officer, I arrived to find the centre of the town in a state of trauma. I had narrowly missed an intense rocket attack, MiG 17s screaming out of the clouds, blasting the marketplace, leaving a trail of blood and destruction. Ojukwu had set up command headquarters in Umuahia. It was under regular attack. The medicine store was in operation, however; I returned to Orlu with a generous supply.

Orlu market had been hit. There were dead and injured. I picked up a young soldier bleeding at the side of the road. He was helped into the car and I raced on to the hospital six miles away. It was a race against time and I lost. He was dead when I arrived.

The Federals had Russian MiGs and Egyptian pilots. Enahoro had been busy in Moscow. He was playing off one superpower against another. Nigeria with its unmined wealth and flowing oilfields was a rich political prize. Whom should he favour? Russia had supplied fighter planes. And Britain? He had the Government at the end of a tickling stick and he must have loved it: Brixton prison had been cold and damp.

I sat down that night by candlelight and wrote a letter. I wrote it from a heart burning fiercely with indignation, addressed to a Member of Parliament with whom I had an acquaintance: Why? Why in God's good name was this happening? Defenceless people harried from the North, evicted with bloodshed from the West, crowding into this overcrowded enclave, now bombed and strafed, gunned down, knifed and bayoneted in their own homes and refuges by troops from far away in an attack led by armoured cars spraying death and destruction from the barrels of their guns, carving a way through defenceless villages. And these same armoured cars, Ferrets and Saladins supplied by Britain, a squadron of three hundred on the admission of the BBC 'for defensive purposes'.

The letter was taken to Port Harcourt; within days it was in the hands of the Member of Parliament to whom it was addressed; within hours it was on the desk of every MP in Westminster. But was it enough?

The airport was still open and in Biafran hands. Oxfam, the Churches, the Red Cross were hiring space on government planes and flying in supplies in increasing quantities. It was good but only a token. The need was limitless. Fleets of planes were needed; a land corridor; an end to the bombing and blockade. Peace. Why wasn't anybody saying anything? The BBC didn't seem to want to know. The papers that we managed to get appeared to entertain a conspiratorial silence. The Government was evasive, defensive, non-committal. Somebody has got to tell them what is happening.

"You tell them."

"Who?"

"You. You're next for leave. School's closed. Relief supplies don't justify the presence of all of us. Go home. Tell them as it is."

"But . . ."

"There aren't any buts. You know the story. Go home and tell it."

Harry was quite adamant. A plane was leaving from Port Harcourt. A flight could be arranged: "Go back to Orlu. Pack a bag. You got me in; I'll get you out."

We were in Uturu, at a council meeting. The debate went on: the pros and the cons, the ifs and the buts. A truly democratic meeting: say what you like and do what you're told. It was settled. I would go.

We returned to Orlu late. I stood, as I had stood, on the veranda and watched the moon silvering the palm fronds. My heart was heavy.

Early next morning the matter was taken out of our hands: Port Harcourt had fallen. The airport was under Federal control. The flight was cancelled.

A Volkswagen crunched up the drive. It was Father Jim from across the valley. "Are your bags ready?"

"No point. Have you not heard? PH is gone. The airport's closed."

"Uli's open."

"Uli?"

"Airstrip. Saint Teresa's. Check in at Awo Amama. Mike Frawley's, six o'clock sharp. They're expecting you. Sorry, can't stop. Few others to see."

The crunching of tyres, roar of the engine and he was off.

I turned to Harry. He shrugged. "Uli it is."

23

London

We stood at the window of Father Frawley's sitting room and watched the Super Constellation lumbering out of the rain clouds, its afterburners blue flame in the darkened sky.

"That's it. Let's get down."

The plane was unloading by the time we reached the airstrip, its engines rumbling. I stood and gazed in amazement: the Onitsha–Owerri highroad turned into a professional airport, complete with approach road, control tower, offloading bays, warehousing, alive with forklift trucks, lorries, bustling ground staff, ringed, I could see, with defensive gunnery and in the midst of all, shrouded in the darkness but vibrant with activity, the huge bulk of our Super Constellation.

Our flight was signalled, papers checked and we were on board. We flew in nervous darkness, three hundred miles into the South Atlantic. The coast had been cleared, the lights of Sao Tomé Island airport gleamed ahead. We landed with a rush and a sigh of relief.

The flight had been arranged by members of the Spiritan Congregation, men of limitless resource. We were met cheerfully by two of them. A meal was waiting: fresh, crispy bread, ham, cheese, tomatoes, coffee. It seemed untrue. Our onward flight was announced, we were on our way again, thirteen long hours, droning over desert and ocean, northwards into Lisbon airport. There we were met by yet another of the ubiquitous Spiritans and whisked round to a nearby convent. A meal was, yet again, waiting – set out in the cloistered peace of the vine-clad courtyard. Slowly the tension of the flight and the days gone by drained away. We sat and we ate, and we drank and talked and laughed.

I spent the night in the Lisbon Marist house, talked at length about the situation in Biafra and Portugal's ambivalent attitude and found myself next morning flying onward to Heathrow and our London house, where, by nightfall, in the heart of busy Islington, I was safely ensconced and full of plans for the fulfilment of my mission.

I wasted no time. I had been given a package for the Daily Express. It was Walter Partington's report on the situation in Biafra, current, accurate, urgent. I delivered it and impressed on the staff the absolute urgency of the report. It was in print by nightfall.

I called into a nearby Oxfam shop. They asked me what they could do for me. I told them they already had done much and went on to explain about the milk and medicines I had been distributing days before in the heart of beleaguered Biafra. They were intrigued; the manager was on the phone: a top-level emergency meeting on the Biafran situation was scheduled that afternoon in Oxford, could I join them?

The Oxford meeting was indeed top-level, tense and urgent. They were pleased to have me as part of the discussion, able to give them an up-to-date account of the situation. My report lost nothing in the telling. I was speaking to a group alive with energy and awareness of the urgency of the situation. Here were people who recognised suffering, who realised something had to be done, something gigantic had to be done, something now. Millions were displaced, on the move, starving. They had read the reports; they had seen the photographs; they listened to my telling of the reality. Resolutions were taken, demands were to be made: Government aid, massive government aid, Hercules aircraft, safe corridors. An emergency appeal was to be launched. I was asked to commit my report in writing. I did so. They asked me if I would get in touch with their London office in Crane Court. I was there the following morning.

The same sense of urgency permeated Crane Court. Emergency appeal posters were being organised. Meetings were being arranged. Lobbying of MPs was taking place. I had brought literature and photographs out with me which spared the reader nothing: a headless corpse on a railway station, skeletal babies, crowded relief stations. The staff were appalled. I made no apology for the horror of the graphic detail.

The phone had been ringing before I got back to Islington. Michael Barnes, Labour MP, wanted to speak to me. Nick Stacey of Oxfam joined us in a working lunch. The talk was heady, dynamic, and intense. The Government had to be made aware of the urgency of the situation, the inhumanity of the situation, the need for massive, immediate aid.

I was invited to a committee meeting that same evening. Barbara Castle was there, David Steele, Michael Barnes. It was a packed meeting, full of sound and eloquent fury, denunciation of the Government's supplying of arms, impassioned appeals for support and supplies, ingenious suggestions as to the means of getting the supplies to the starving. A memorandum was drawn up to be delivered to Lord Shepherd, Commonwealth Secretary, first thing in the morning. It was a lengthy meeting. We adjourned to the terrace. Discussion continued unabated.

Somebody handed me a drink, sat down and asked me what I thought. My enthusiasm, optimism, relief, hope, delight gushed forth in response. He listened quietly, smiled darkly and slowly shook his head: "That memorandum to Lord Shepherd?"

I nodded with enthusiasm.

"It'll be on his desk first thing tomorrow. By noon a copy will be with the general manager of Shell. By one minute past noon it'll be in his waste-paper basket." He drained his glass, shook his head again, got up and left. I sat wondering. I felt a cold breeze blowing up the river.

I had little time to wonder. Oxfam wanted me to speak here, to speak there. I found myself on the platform of Conway Hall in Red Lion Square, before a packed audience. I was introduced as one newly returned from the reality of the tragedy of Biafra. I got up and spoke with all the eloquence I could muster. I played shamelessly upon the emotions of the audience from the emotion of my own heart. I spoke of the horror of the massacre, sparing little of grim detail. I spoke of the flight to the homeland, the overcrowding, the hunger, the suffering. I spoke of the continued incursion of Federal troops, the continued flight of the refugees, the increasing hunger, the cruel shortage of food; I spoke of wide-eyed, skeletal, big-bellied children, empty bowls clutched in outstretched hands, hope in those wide eyes, the rejection and despair when turned away. I spoke of the shame of British statesmen siding with the aggressor, supporting, arming, aiding and abetting the aggressor. I spoke of England's history, her support of the oppressed against the might of the oppressor. I spoke as an Englishman proud to be an Englishman, of the shame that was England's in this perfidious union: British tanks supported by Russian jets pitted against a defenceless people. I quoted our wartime leader who rallied us to defiance against such aggression. I spoke as one for whom this Sceptred Isle stood for Right against Wrong, Justice against Oppression. And now the leaders of this same land of ours were prepared to sell our birthright of integrity for so many barrels of oil that might be grasp'ed thus. I would rather be a dog and bay the moon than such an Englishman.

I sat down with more than a suspicion that my Shakespearean allusions had been mixed, but with the hope my point had been made.

I went out to Barnes to speak to a girls' school. I spoke about salt. I spoke to a youth club in Kensington. Farm Street phoned and asked me to speak at the Sunday Masses. Westminster school wanted me. Canadian television wondered if I could do an interview in French. I did not hesitate. Oxfam were organising a rally in Trafalgar Square; they wanted me to speak.

Biafra was news. What had been a niggardly trickle of information suddenly became a torrent. Paper after paper, edition after edition had the news. Reporters were flying in, reports were pouring out. The Sunday Times devoted a supplement to Biafra with Don McCullin's pictures. The country was shocked into attention.

The news was not good. Umuahia had fallen. Thousands were on the run. Owerri was the next Federal objective. Ojukwu had established headquarters there. The Biafrans were putting up a fierce resistance on the Aba front but they were fighting against overwhelming odds. The activity in which I was involved kept my mind occupied, my feelings in control.

I was not working alone. A picture in one weekly paper caught my eye. It was the Cardinal's secretary at the wheel of an armoured car outside the Foreign Office. His protest against arming the Federals was eloquent. I rang him, Bruce Kent, recently appointed Chaplain to London University. He invited me to speak to his students, preparing a Westminster lobby in preparation for a forthcoming debate on the Nigerian question. Later we went to the offices of CAFOD, the newly established Catholic agency for overseas aid. It took little effort to persuade them to channel funds towards the relief programme. Oxfam were working flat out. The Bishop of Owerri was in Rome. They invited him over to talk. Their own Director went into Biafra to see for himself. He came back with startling reports of increasing hunger.

The Catholic Institute for International Affairs invited me for interview. Theirs was an ambivalent situation; there were Catholic bodies on both sides of the line. We talked long and earnestly. I persuaded their minds away from the niceties of constitutional probity to the reality of the situation. You don't look for a key to save a child from a burning house. Break the door down. They said they would think about it. I was hardly back in the Islington house before the phone rang. They had discussed the matter at length and decided to offer me access to their resources whilst allowing me freedom to work as I saw fit. I could have a desk and phone with secretarial help in the London office. Would I accept? Now things were indeed coming together. I accepted with a joyful heart.

The phone rang again. It was Glasgow on the line, Provincial headquarters: I was to report immediately. The next morning I was on the train north.

24

Scotland

I wondered, as the train clattered north, what the future had in store. There had been talk of my being called to the Generalate in Rome for debriefing. I realised the interruption of the work I was establishing and the contacts I was making must have been made for some strong reason. I had phoned Oxfam and the Catholic International Relations office tendering my apologies and asking them to cancel outstanding appointments.

When I got to Glasgow I was greeted with serious news: Harry was a prisoner of the Federals. The novitiate in Uturu had been for some time under serious threat. Federal troops were within striking distance. Heavy gunfire was drawing closer by the day. Harry, as he told me the story many months later, had been asked to go to Uturu and, backed by the Bishop's orders, instruct the Brothers to retire. Frank, in charge, had accepted the command with a heavy heart. A feverish couple of days were spent in organising transport, seeing to the sick and wounded, the refugees and orphans, planning the escape route and eventually setting out. They had hardly got as far as the first crossroads when they were stopped at a military roadblock. Frank's fiery Irish temper snapped. He leapt off the truck and

Brother Francis, founder of Hopeville with Mark and Norbert

ordered them to clear the road. "If you want to stop anybody get up to the front and stop the Federals." There was a moment of silence. A soldier detached himself from the group at the side of the road, ambled over, his sub-machine gun carelessly cradled in his arm and calmly confronted Frank: "We are Federals."

The trucks were ordered to turn. A dangerous situation arose. Escorted to command headquarters under trigger-happy guard, the situation looked grim in the extreme. On arrival there, however, matters improved dramatically. The commanding officer was more than understanding of the work that was being carried on at Uturu. Frank, with his companions, was allowed back to continue caring for the sick and crippled, housing the refugees, feeding the hungry, this work now under Federal command. Hopeville was established and flourished.

Harry became deeply involved in the work; he never did get back to Orlu. Norbert was on his own. Lewis, who had spent the latter part of his leave working in a school in the east end of Glasgow, desperately short of staff, was asked to go out to take Harry's place. I was instructed to take Lewis's place in Saint Mark's junior secondary school in Shettleston off the Gallowgate.

"But . . . but . . .!"

There were no buts; there were orders.

Saint Mark's, I was told, had once been a very fine school with a reputable band of past pupils proud to call it their alma mater. It had fallen on less fortunate days. The heart of Glasgow was being torn out. The broken tenements surrounding the school were mute witnesses to the social disaster. The movement of population had left behind a dispirited people. As the bulldozers drew nearer, the depression deepened. What had once been a proud part of a proud city was now the trysting place of warring gangs, their names scrawled everywhere: San Toi, Shamrock, Border. The school itself, in the heart of the desolation, was scheduled for demolition, the pupils to be absorbed into a fine modern comprehensive school already under construction. I was asked, meanwhile, to take part in the holding exercise.

I boarded the tram on a morning of drizzle and murk and gloom. The depression deepened as we trundled along the Gallowgate. The weather fitted well with my mood.

Work in Saint Mark's was unreal. Class 3E fifteen-year-olds had not the remotest intention of submitting to the new regime involved in the raising of the school-leaving age. Their resentment at being detained for another year was palpable. Academic prowess was low on the agenda. Discipline was a constant grind.

Things became pleasanter as we got to know each other. The previous headmaster, who had known the school in its heyday, had retired disillusioned. The new head was determined not only to cope but to raise standards. He did so with uncompromising determination: conform or go. He had the backing of the education authority and support, time, transport and finance.

There were positive aspects of the new regime. The Saturday morning hike became a feature of school life. Glasgow is surrounded by some of the most beautiful countryside in Britain: Loch Lomond, the Trossachs, the foothills of the Highlands; we saw it all. Sturdy boots and rucksacks, sixty happy Glaswegians tramping through the heather under a late summer sky, two bus loads of worn-out happy Glaswegians returning to the city as street lamps were lighting.

I came to know the countryside well. As winter approached and snows began to fall, the weekend bus trips were suspended. I continued to walk, alone. I walked with a heavy heart. News from Biafra worsened with every report. Federal troops continued to advance slowly: advancing, digging in, consolidating, slowly tightening the stranglehold on the enclave, sending more and more terrified refugees into an enclave incapable of sustaining its already overflowing refugee centres.

There was, however, some good news. The Churches had banded together and, working with the International Red Cross, had taken over the relief programme. No longer were they hiring space on Government planes but with strong financial aid, official and unofficial, the Churches were able to hire their own planes and crews and, using Sao Tomé as a base, were building up more and more supplies. DC4s, DC6s, Constellations, Globemasters flying in night after night under cover of darkness, offloading at speed, returning for a second shuttle. It was a grim battle against enemy fire and ever-increasing hunger but it was a battle being fought with courage and determination. And I was not there.

There was much to do on the home front. With the help of a local newspaper, *The Glasgow Observer*, we were organising fund-raising on a large scale. The word had gone abroad. Everybody was willing to give, to help. The Scots are a generous, warm-hearted people and it showed: schools and churches, youth clubs and social clubs joined in the campaign. A youth group from Edinburgh sent a cheque for a thousand pounds. A nurse from the Glasgow Royal hospital handed in her pay packet unopened. An elderly gentleman called in and donated his week's pension intact.

We were based in the Marist house in Townhead, Saint Mungo's, and the centre of intense activity. The doorbell was ringing continuously with people almost queuing to give. Little girls organised impromptu concerts at street corners, children danced and sang their little hearts out for suffering children far away. It was heart-warming.

The Glasgow City Council gave us permission and encouragement for a street collection. The response was overwhelming. Two little boys in particular stood out. They came in red-faced and breathless with two full cans, no time to wait to count the contents, two new cans and they were off, back again in double time. "How do you do it?" I asked. "Seasy. Clumb the multi's, chappit at the doors and asked and they gied." I gathered they had climbed the stairs of the multi-storeyed flats, knocked on the doors, asked and they were given.

A local medical outlet rang to ask if I would be interested in offcuts of sticking plasters they were packing. I said I was interested and they came pouring in. The guillotine operator must have been very heavy-handed, box loads of so-called offcuts arrived at the disused chapel in Partickhill we were using as a warehouse. Portuguese airlines offered to fly freight out free to the Lisbon staging post. We were inundated with offers: food, clothing, medicine. The medicines proved a difficulty until a retired chemist friend offered to screen and document them.

I maintained a lively interest in the political scene. There had been a number of debates on the Nigerian question. Arms supply was a recurring theme. The minister responsible was dismissive. Britain was supplying no more than fifteen percent and that in small arms only. I listened in wonder to the inanities of the government stance. Fifteen percent? Of what? How does one calculate such figures? The statement, it was later proved by the Federal government's own meticulous bookkeeping was innaccurate. That same fifteen percent including ammunition was capable of establishing the Federal army, according to one on-the-spot reporter, as the most effective defoliation agent known, and these troops were pitted against front-line troops sent forward with no more than five rounds per man.

And armoured cars? ". . . a few!" Had the Foreign Secretary ever seen an armoured car in action? Not one of a thousand pitted against thousands but a lone Salladin leading an infantry file, spitting death and destruction as it ground its way forward, carving a passage through forest and bush where in days gone by the horsemen of Usman Dan Fodio had failed to advance.

"The Russians are there in force, aircraft and crews, technicians and support staff. We cannot oppose them but we cannot be left out." The Foreign Secretary was unabashed in his self-justification.

Political peasant that I was, my vision unblurred by vested interest, I failed to see justification in the Government's vacillating compromise. If they believed in the validity of the Nigerian cause, why did they not go in lock, stock and barrel: helicopters, paratroopers, infantry, tanks, fighters – total war? They were not fighting terrorists. Both sides in the conflict had regular officers leading organised troops prepared to fight with determination and courage. But those same officers, as subsequent events proved, had the military sense to recognise defeat. The short, sharp surgical operation that Gowon had spoken of could have been effected in days, with order restored, peace established and the suffering civilians saved from strangling starvation. It was not to be. The patient was mangled during the operation over thirty remorseless months. "Fifteen percent . . . !" Fifteen percent of a hangman's noose.

And what about financial aid to the starving? There was no problem. The Foreign Secretary was on his feet in the House of Commons unctuously assuring honourable members that such aid was of the gravest concern to Her Majesty's Government; indeed some two hundred and fifty thousand pounds had been put aside for that very purpose. A quick calculation based on two million refugees would reduce the sum to half a crown per starving refugee, twelve and a half of the new pence that were coming into currency. The sum had the appearance of a calculated insult. I wrote to the Foreign Secretary and told him so. A secretary wrote back and said that once hostilities were over more financial aid would be available: once the fire is out we will rescue the hapless victims.

Despite the aid pouring in, hunger was increasing. Local food supply was becoming almost non-existent. Seed yam and seedcorn had been eaten. And more refugees were on the move. Aba and Owerri had fallen. Great swathes of land were depopulated as terrified villagers fled before advancing troops. Lesley Kirkley of Oxfam on a fact-finding mission spoke of the hundreds of tons of supplies needed to avert a cataclysmic famine. The Red Cross referred to the emergency as greater than any they had faced since the Second World War.

Newspapers, magazines, television and radio spared readers, listeners and viewers nothing in portraying the facts as they were.

I came in from school one evening, changed and joined the community. Dinner over, we gathered round the television for the evening news. A fresh and detailed report was available. It was grim news: lines were breaking on all fronts; once again there was mass movement of refugees. The report came from a camp near the fighting lines: mothers with skeletal babies sucking at dry breasts; children with staring eyes in skull-faces edging towards the camera, skin-covered bone-legs, arms raised in pitiful appeal, hands drooping limp.

Suddenly the scorching lump in my throat dissolved into tears that streamed uncontrollably, soundlessly down my face. I got up and left the room. I left the house, out into the darkness and the cold winter wind. The driving rain washed away the tears from my face but not from my heart. I trudged aimlessly on through the slush and fallen leaves and the darkness that was about me and in my soul.

The next morning, Saturday, I donned stout boots and haversack, took the bus to the shores of Loch Lomond and set off for Inversnaid. I had set myself a lengthy trek but there was determination in my soul.

It was a beautiful still morning. Winter sunshine glistened on the snows of Ben Bhreac. A light mist had risen on the glass-calm surface of the loch and a silence hung over all. A fish jumped, rippling the surface; a covey of wild duck clattered into the air as I passed. The glory of it all stirred my soul, a morning for laughter and loud, happy tramping song but there was no song in my heart, only my thoughts and they were sad.

The snow on the path was light and I reached Rowardennan and its lochside inn by early noon. Welcomed by a friendly host and a crackling log fire, I sat down to a hot Scotch pie and a glass of ale and rose with lighter heart, pulled my scarf tighter round my neck, bade good-day to my host and set out for the last leg.

It was a long trek but I reached Inversnaid with light to spare. Hopkins had been there before me, the mystical poet. I stood by his darksome burn, horseback brown still roaring down into the pitch-black pool in winter wildness where the ash still dripped.

Norbert had written. I had hesitated to read the letter. I took it out, opened it carefully and sat down. It was a lengthy account of affairs, worse than I had feared, a grim account of a grim situation. Reading it did little to lighten my heart. He had included a photograph, a little boy with a bloated belly holding out an empty bowl. His account of the kwashiorkor epidemic was heart-rending, the protein deficiency syndrome that reduces the limbs to skeletal size and fills the belly with fluid so that the child appears overfed and starving at the same time. I put the letter away and stared into the pitch-black pool.

The light was fading. I gathered up my rucksack, gripped my staff and set off for home. It was dark when I regained the loch. The sky had cleared and was full of stars, silent companions on the trail. I had missed the last bus. The walk to Drymen was wearisome and the chance of transport slight. I reached the Glasgow road as the lights of a little car flashed round the bend. I put out my hand forlornly. The car slithered to a halt.

"Where you going, Jimmy?"

"Glasgow."

"Hop in."

A young couple, used to tramping in the Highlands, dropped me almost at the door, dismissing my warm thanks. "Say nothing."

Luckily I had a key. It was almost midnight; the house was silent but a light was on in the kitchen. Old Brother Joseph was sitting there. His face crinkled into a warm smile when I came in.

"Welcome, Jimmy. Sit ye down; you must be frozen. Take this; it'll warm you. I've your dinner in the oven."

Two drams of whisky were on the kitchen table. We raised them:

"Slainte!"

"Slainte va! Tell me about your day, did you get far?"

I told him over a piping-hot roast dinner that had lost no taste in the reheating. I was hungry.

"There was a phone call for you this afternoon."

"Oh?"

"The Provincial. I took the message."

"What did he say?"

"Lewis has left Orlu; he's working at the Caritas depot. Norbert needs a break. He's coming home for a few weeks. The Provincial wants to know if you'd take his place."

"Me? Where? When?"

"Orlu. As soon as you can arrange it. Are you going to say yes? You know how dangerous it is out there."

"Joe, is there another wee dram in the bottle? I think a celebration's called for."

25

Return

Amsterdam airport was, for the lateness of the hour, a busy spot. A Boeing 707 stood waiting on the runway. Obviously the Christian Churches working together under the banner of JointChurchAid was an effective organisation. I could not help comparing the huge machine and its comfort with the empty aluminium crate that had brought us out. We were a merry crowd as we trooped on board: relief workers, aircrews, priests, nuns. Some of them I knew, some I was to get to know. I recognised Sister Clara's merry laugh; I found myself sitting next to an Icelandic flight-engineer. I was to recognise him again in the dark and the danger of Uli airstrip. We flew on effortlessly through the night.

It had been a hectic few days leave-taking. The Brothers of the community were sad to see me go. We had formed a deep and warm friendship. My brief visit to Newcastle was equally fraught. My sisters were worried: did I have to go? Didn't I realise the danger? My father, who lived alone after my mother's death, was quiet and understanding. He saw me off at the airport, gave me a brave smile and a gentle hug. London was busy: Biafra House for entry papers, hectic calls on some I knew from my previous stay, injections, last-minute letters and packages, out to Heathrow and on to Amsterdam.

We landed at dawn in Sao Tomé. Our onward flight, we were informed, would leave some time after six allowing us to cross the coast and danger zone in darkness. We were in a little tropical paradise, the water was blue and warm and inviting, the smell of the fish roasting on the charcoal fire, mouth-watering. We sat around on the beach with our grilled fish and Portuguese red wine and we laughed and we chatted, renewing old acquaintances, making new friends. The mood grew more sombre as the afternoon faded.

We went out to the airport, checked in and loaded our luggage. The normality of the procedure was incongruous in view of the flight ahead. We were travelling with Sterling; the flight captain was polite and correct, giving us the estimated time of arrival at Uli, the prevailing weather conditions and the probable intensity of the gunfire we would experience as we crossed the coast, assuring us that our height would enable us to fly above the danger.

It was dark as we approached land. The flashes we could see below us were, we guessed, gunfire from the blockading ships and shore batteries.

There was little said and that in whispers. The tension grew as we began to lose height; a brief cackle on the intercom, a sharp command to brace ourselves; we were dropping out of the sky; lights flashed on and we were down in a thunderous rush. I was back.

An arm grabbed me in the dark as I made my way down the ladder: "This way, Brother, quickly, come." I recognised Brother Gregory's voice. He turned and flashed me a magnificent smile: "Welcome. I'm sorry we must hurry. Tonight is very busy. This is your case?" I nodded. "Also this box." The medicine chest was carefully offloaded onto the waiting jeep and we roared up the perimeter road to reception. Norbert was waiting for me in the throng and grabbed my hand and my papers. "You're welcome, Jimmy. Throw your case in the car, the green Volks; I'll be with you. Gregory, make sure that medicine gets safe to Ihioma."

Godwin met us at the door of the Orlu house, lamp in hand shielding its glare. Godwin the little houseboy who had grown up with us, now, I gathered, the capable manager of store and feeding kitchen. His welcome was warm. A meal was waiting, flaked potatoes and meatballs with a delicious sauce. Donald cook came in to greet me; his wife came; their little boy came. Nicholas carpenter had heard I was coming back; he came with Nathaniel. A note of welcome and invitation was delivered from the Chief. I felt I was home.

I was wakened early the next morning: kitchen day. Already in the dawn-darkness the children were gathering, forming lines in the field at the back of the house. Fires were being lit, water poured into steel cauldrons. I met Norbert with Godwin in his storehouse doling out dried fish and rice. He looked up and smiled. "Feeding the five thousand. We'll need more salt, Goddy. In the upstairs store." He handed him the keys. "Gold dust," he explained.

I followed him to the field kitchen. The cooks were hard at work, machetting the wood-hard stockfish, measuring out the rice, sprinkling the salt. It was a huge operation. Norbert's eagle eye was everywhere.

We walked along the line of waiting children silent in their anticipation, Norbert with a cheerful word bending low to check their eyes, nodding now and then to the girl following with her plastic bag of pills.

"Iron," he explained. "Check behind the lower eyelid. You can gauge the blood count by the richness of the colour, or lack of it. Keep a check. Don't overdo it. The nurses know." I felt I was being instructed for takeover. "Linus, get that line in order; we'll be feeding soon." The children were kept under strict supervision. There was nothing sentimental about the operation.

By now the cooking was well under way. The cooks looked up briefly from behind the cloud of steam and smiled in welcome: "Welcome, Brother, nna. Come, eat food now; fine fish!"

"Smells good. You are fine cooks."

"Very fine." They laughed. I left them to their work, doling out the rice and stockfish to the hungry children.

Late in the afternoon the cooking pots were empty. Still there were children unfed. A cry of despair went up.

I met Godwin: "What do you do?"

"Brother Norbert is coming."

His truck roared up the drive and crunched to a halt. On board was a huge sack of garri, the dried and fried cassava root. "Quickly, Goddy, give this out to those who had nothing. Soon it will be dark. There must be no fires."

The children left rejoicing, clutching their supply of garri.

"That's it." Norbert seemed satisfied with the day's work. "Not ideal but we do our best. Should be more supplies in tomorrow. We've a kitchen three times a week. A shower now, and later we can have something to eat ourselves. We can go out to Ihioma then if you like to see the other side of the operation. Lewis is there in charge of stores."

It was dark before we sat down to eat and talk. I had much to ask; Norbert had much to tell me. Conversation suddenly stopped; he held up his finger for quiet: "Listen."

I listened, I heard the rasp of the grasshoppers, the croaking of the frogs then I heard what Norbert heard: the droning of a plane.

"The first of the shuttle." We could hear its engines moaning and whining as the plane circled over the airstrip.

"How many planes?"

"Caritas, World Council, International Red Cross, French Red Cross, Belgian Air Services; there could be twenty planes doing a double shuttle."

"Some brave men up there. Who pays for all this?"

"God knows."

We got out to Ihioma as the first convoy was arriving, great lumbering lorries packed high with cornmeal, milk powder, stockfish, flour, salt. Lewis was at the gate collecting manifests, supervising the offloading, checking amounts, noting, comparing. He looked over his clipboard, smiled briefly and nodded: "See you inside later for a beer."

There was a policy meeting going on in the mission-house. We were made warmly welcome, handed a drink and invited to take part. It was a gathering of the SCAPEGOATS, the Society of Caritas Airport Personnel, Executives, Ground Operators, and Transport Staff.

The talk was intense; the subject was agriculture: "We need seed: yam seed, maize, beans, we can't continue with this hand-to-mouth existence."

"We can't afford to give space on the planes."

"We can't afford not to. We need to think of the future. We need to sow; we can't continue to rely on handouts. How long is this going to go on for?"

"We have no time to sow and grow. A child could die of starvation while the father's maize is growing."

"A lot of children will die if the maize doesn't grow."

The argument went on, deadly earnest yet light-hearted, typical Irish debate. The agriculturists appeared to have won the day: land was subsequently dedicated, tractor and plough were brought in, seed was imported, a heavily guarded farm was established.

We visited the local mission hospital next day; Norbert had some patients from his first-aid clinic. Amaigbo was deadly quiet. Despite the crowd there was an uncanny silence. I had noticed it in the market, even in our own feeding centre where hundreds of children were gathered: they were listening, ears attuned to the sound of marauding MiGs, high-flying Ilyushins. Amaigbo hospital had been bombed. I had read about it in *The Times*, an article by Winston Churchill. He had been there; he had seen the damage caused despite the great red crosses painted on the hospital roofs. Word was whispered that the crosses were an invitation to some of the pilots.

Norbert was to leave; I was to take over. He introduced me to his outlying feeding centres and clinics, to his sources of supply, the refugee camps that he helped, his little orphanages, and his staff. His was a busy life. Back in Orlu he showed me his medicine store, the various medicaments, their proper use: those for general distribution, those to be administered by trained staff. I marvelled at his efficiency in the midst of the turmoil. I watched him in his clinic as he consoled and comforted, administered medicines for fever, linctus for colds, kaolin for dysentry, iron for anaemia. His nurses worked quietly and efficiently. It was going to be a hard act to follow but I knew the routine had been well established. He left within the week. I was alone.

And yet I was never alone. The house was surrounded by activity. There was a constant stream of visitors, every one a special case. Norbert had warned me strictly: give to one, give to all. There were exceptions I knew; I met one the morning after Norbert left. She was waiting for me in the dark as I opened the front door. She had a child in her arms wrapped in a tattered shawl, a skeleton child, round eyes staring from skull-face. I opened the store and gave her food. There was a sudden pattering of feet from the nearby bush. I was encircled by a host of mothers with starving babies in their arms. Silent. I looked at them in dismay; they stared back in mute appeal. Godwin pushed his way through the crowd: "Brother, you do not understand. Brother Norbert has a special feeding centre for these people in the orphanage. Later they will all receive food."

He ushered me out of the store and locked the door. The women were dispersing. I knew I had a lot to learn.

We had an excess of salt. The preceding night's supply flights had been extremely successful. For some reason there had been no harassment. Some of the planes squeezed in three flights. The lorries rolled into the compound with full loads, the storeroom was overflowing. We even had salt, lots of it, more than we would need for the kitchen. I decided to give some away. We were short of firewood.

"Godwin, send word to the village to say that tomorrow if they will bring one head load of firewood we will give one cup of salt." It seemed a good idea. The Romans had done no less.

Very early next morning, before a suggestion of dawn light, I was awakened by a strange shuffling, muffled murmuring. I looked over the balcony: vaguely visible in the misty darkness was a sea of firewood perched upon the heads of innumerable women concealed beneath their loads.

Godwin was waiting.

"Start distributing, Goddy. Get rid of these people as quick as we can. There could be an accident with that wood."

We had it arranged in streamlined order: firewood dumped on an ever-growing pile, salt doled out in an overflowing cup. The women were delighted; the queue shuffled forward in an unending procession, load after load of firewood, cup after cup of salt.

"There is no more salt." There was more but that we needed for the field kitchen and was safely locked away.

"Tell them, Goddy, there is no more salt."

He told them. There was no response. They had been promised salt. They had brought firewood. Where was their salt? They must have salt before they go away. There was more salt. We must open the store.

Things were turning nasty; the women were moving forward in an aggressive manner. Suddenly the military appeared, a column of men in smart order armed with sticks, ushering the women away from the storehouse, beyond the barrier fence, out of the compound. Peace was restored. We breathed a collective sigh of relief.

The patience of our neighbouring military was remarkable but there was a limit. The horde of women agitating on the drill yard was the limit.

Colonel Onwatiegbu, the camp commandant, had a quiet word with me. I had invited him for lunch. He appeared in smart military attire, cap and cane, the suggestion of a heel click. We shook hands and settled down to a pre-luncheon drink. My friendly Icelandic flight engineer had sent me in a special delivery box of manna. Conversation was amicable, polite and general. Onwatiegbu was the hero of the Owerri campaign, having with great military skill dislodged the Federals from the town and driven them back on their Aba front. Lack of supplies and ammunition had prevented further advance. We did not talk of such things; our civilian status was guarded and respected to a scrupulous degree. The Colonel did, however, mention the recent female incursion. He also expressed his grave concern about the feeding kitchen, the hundreds of children gathered in such a tight area. Both of us knew the risks. Awgu, Aguleri, Umuahia had been attacked from the air with grave loss of life. Even our own Orlu market had been rocketed. The risk was great but what could we do? Were the children to starve through fear of air raids?

The matter was resolved some time later. The incident coincided with the visit of the foreign-news editor of the *Morgunbladid* of Rekyavik. Bjorn Thors had been keenly aware of the starvation that had beset the West African enclave. He was aware that an essential element of the region's staple diet, their own Icelandic dried codfish, was getting through in only very limited quantities, and that thanks to the skill and daring of Icelandic and

Scandinavian airmen. He had decided to come and see for himself. I made him very welcome. After a supper of rice and Scandinavian cod we sat and chatted. Bjorn had brought in a bottle of vodka. We sat and chatted for a long time about many things: the fighting, the massacres, the hunger, the relief supplies.

We were up betimes the following morning to see the workings of the field kitchen and feeding centre. I showed him our store, the precious stockfish and rice and beans. He was impressed. He took photos of the hard-working, smiling cooks, the long lines of waiting, silent children, the efficiency, the good order, the need.

He noted with some surprise the silence of the children, the unnatural silence. I explained the reason for the silence, the constant, instinctive alertness. Suddenly, as if to bear out my words, a distant humming in the sky became a distinct roar: MiGs!

A groan went up from the lines of children as they scanned the skies and saw the silver bats dart out of the morning sunlight. They circled. The children stared in terror. Suddenly one of the planes dived. There was a shriek and the lines broke. Utter panic ensued, little ones clutching pannikins and smaller children, racing over the broken ground for the concealment of the nearby bush, the house, anywhere. Then there was silence. The planes had gone. The lines began to reform, the children limping back. The field we used was recently cleared bush; the jagged stumps and tree roots had caused much injury, bleeding and broken limbs.

Bjorn had stood his ground, snapping with his camera the chaos and the tragedy that he witnessed. He had turned to me when some degree of order had been restored; he tapped his camera: "I need see no more. I have the story here."

Shortly afterwards, the Chief and the Commandant ordered the relocation of the feeding centre. Cooking could continue on the compound but the feeding centres were to be distributed throughout the village. Orders were obeyed.

26

Desperation

Norbert was due back. He had left Scotland to visit family in Canada and had been caught up in something of a lecture tour. Valuable though this was in making people aware of the situation and in fund raising, it was not Norbert's scene. His was the hands-on approach.

There was concern for his health – he had hardly given himself time to recuperate from the ravages of the work he had been involved in, mental as well as physical. I was relieved, however, that he was coming back. Since the closing of the central feeding kitchen, the immediate workload had been cut down considerably. Norbert's system of supply and check ran like a well-oiled machine. His workers: drivers, cooks, nurses, orphanage staff, camp liaison were well versed in their tasks and efficient. I felt somewhat redundant. Lacking Norbert's enterprise and ability to conjure supplies from apparently nowhere, I was limited in my efforts.

Emergencies, however, continued their demands. I was visiting the orphanage when the MiGs came over. They came in low, almost at rooftop level, taking us completely by surprise with no time to make for the slit trenches. I watched helplessly as one of the planes barrelled over the valley

Playboy at the orphanage

and hit the school. In one frozen moment of time I had a clear view of the pilot intent on his controls as he roared past, unmindful of the wounded who lay in his trail. I saw them as soon as I reached the assembly area, spread-eagled like the petals of a bloodstained flower. A rocket had hit the group as they made for shelter. Already the medics were at work, staunching the blood, bandaging the wounds. I had brought over the car and helped to load the most seriously injured.

"They will need blood. At Amaigbo. You must be quick."

I was, the Peugeot bumping over the rutted laterite, my passengers groaning in agony. It was a nightmare drive. We were stopped at a checkpoint. The bored guardians slouched over. Their reaction when they saw the wounded was undisguised shock. No words were said. The barrier was pulled aside and we were through. The hospital appeared to be expecting us. Clara took over immediately, organising the transfusions. I went for the priest. He stood open-mouthed when he saw my bloodstained soutane. I assured him I was all right. He was needed at the hospital. One of the soldiers had died before we arrived.

I gave a report to the Commandant as soon as I got back. They buried the young lad that evening. As they lowered the body, the sun was sinking, fiery red behind the blackened palms. He had been a trumpeter in the regimental band. His colleagues played their anthem, the choral from *Finlandia*, a piece I was coming to know so well, the words a plea for comfort; the music haunting to this day.

Patient anticipation

Early the following morning I took the car out to a refugee centre near the fighting lines. It had been a difficult operation cleaning the vehicle. Godwin was hesitant about touching the bloodstained interior. I did the job myself. He was even more appalled at the idea of my taking the car so far afield into such dangerous territory. It had carried a corpse. I was jokingly dismissive: "Godwin, you are superstitious."

The journey south was fraught with difficulty. It had been raining heavily during the night. Spray flew high as I drove through the ruts. Eventually the car stopped. I got out, waded through the deep water, opened the bonnet, and dried the points as best I could, waited, restarted and continued on the journey deeper south.

Brother Paul in charge of the camp was overjoyed to see me. In their isolated position, supplies were low and visitors were few. I had salt and blankets and other goods. We offloaded and over a meal of rice and tinned meat we shared stories. Theirs were sorry tales of hunger beyond bearing before the relief operation was in full swing and supplies started arriving with some regularity. I saw their little graveyard. "Two hundred and seventy children are buried there," Paul told me. The rows of little crosses were mute testimony.

I prepared to leave next morning. The car refused to start. The coil was burnt out. A mechanic, skilled in the art of making-do, replaced it with one from a derelict Ford. I was on my way and, driving gingerly through the waterlogged ruts, eventually gained the main road. The car gathered speed. I was approaching a bridge and put my foot on the brake. Nothing happened. I rammed the car into first gear, drove onto the verge and stopped. This was getting serious. I found brake fluid in the boot, filled the empty reservoir and drove on.

Over the bridge the car stopped of its own accord. I suspected dirty petrol – a common fault with the locally cracked fuel we used – I cleaned the filter, closed the bonnet, got in, slipped into gear and started the engine. The car burst into flames. I leapt out. With the clutch disengaged the vehicle was juddering forward against its handbrake, short-circuiting, lights flashing, horn blaring. I stared in amazement. Soldiers in a passing army truck helped me try to douse the flames, but with only sand the task was impossible. We watched as the car burnt itself out. They gave me a lift back to Orlu. Godwin made no comment.

Clara asked me to get her some medical supplies. They had a patient in desperate need of a particular drug they could not hope to get through normal channels. We had funds and connections in Scotland; the doctor could give me details of the prescription.

I discussed the matter with Lewis and Father Jack, chief executive in charge of operations. No problem: over to Sao Tomé, plane to Amsterdam, London, Newcastle. See what Stan, our ever-resourceful pharmaceutical friend, can do, then over to Dublin. There was a DC6 due to come out within the week.

"When you're in Dublin call into Clery's; I've a list of things I want you to get." Jack gave me dollars for the trip and I was off.

Everything went according to plan. There was a hiccup at London airport while they examined the strange stamping on my passport but I was through.

I called to see Bruce Kent at Gower Street. I had a film I wanted him to see. We watched it with a group of his students: *Night Flight to Uli*. We watched it in silence. When it was over there was a continued silence. Bruce leaned over: "How can I get out there?" I said I'd make arrangements when I was in Dublin.

I visited my father in Newcastle, amazed and overjoyed to see me, and I went down to Whitley Bay to meet Stan, a past pupil of our school in Scotland, a pharmacist with a thriving business, many connections and a fund of goodwill. His goodwill was strained, however, when he read the list of required drugs I gave him.

"Do you know what these are?" I shook my head. "No idea."

He was due in Glasgow for an Old Boys' reunion. We agreed to meet there. Meantime he would see what he could do but . . .

The reunion took place in the Marist Club. It was a jovial affair, the minimum of business, the maximum of goodwill. I had been asked to speak. After the delightful meal and full-flowing wine, I did so. The laughter and the jollity died as I spoke.

The meeting had been scheduled as a fund-raising event. As I sat down the Chairman was on his feet: "Gentlemen, we have listened to a sad tale. We had planned a number of ploys for this evening to part you painlessly from the contents of your wallets. I suggest we forget the fun and games. The hat is coming round. Dig deep in those wallets." They did. The evening paid for an extra flight.

Stan called in to the chapel-warehouse with the drugs. He had a tea chest fully labelled, securely nailed down. "This is not to be opened under any circumstances." Stan was in earnest. "When you get to Dublin leave this in bond and see it on the plane yourself. Guard it." I did so.

Mark took me out to Glasgow airport. The box, when we had manhandled it onto the scales caused some stir. "This will be excess baggage. It'll cost the earth." The wee Scots lassie at reception was concerned. She had read the address label: "Medical supplies with care. Amaigbo Hospital, Biafra." She said she would see what she could do and came back with a smile. "The supervisor said a token payment will suffice." I opened my wallet and found a Biafran pound note. I handed it to her. "Will this do?" She looked at it, smiled broadly and nodded. "It'll do fine. Safe journey."

The box in Dublin caused not a stir. They were used to handling luggage with exotic hospital addresses: Ihiala, Emekuku, Azaraegbuellu. It was bonded, ticketed and stored and I went on into town.

The list for Clery's was long and complicated but we worked through it. The manager gave me a storeman to expedite things. He did so with skill and rich Dublin humour. "Make way for Biafrica. Stand back and let the man through; he's business on hand." The blankets caused no problem, the plastic dishes and kitchen implements were readily available. The mosquito netting gave pause.

"Now you moit have me there. There hasn't been a big demand in Dublin recently for mosquito netting, if you see what oi mean. Peggy, have you sould much in the loin of mosquito netting recently?"

Peggy, the lady in the drapery department, admitted that she hadn't but she produced a fine-meshed curtaining, which might serve. It did, ideally. The order was completed, the storeman assured me he'd have the goods out to the airport before you could say Barney O'Hare and I was off.

We flew in that night in the DC6 as arranged, refuelling in Casablanca and flying on to Niamey before the last leg to Libreville. We were to fly into Biafra in the early evening. Two Dublin reporters I met on the flight had expressed a concern: "The programme's suffering from overexposure. At least in Ireland it is. Everything that can be said has been said."

What a change, I thought, from the early days. "I'll give you an angle. Come with me."

We went to the back of the warehouse. I had seen it on the way in: a great white mound. I pointed to it. "That's it."

"What?"

"Salt." I explained the situation: the desperate need for salt. The acute shortage. The supplies waiting to be airlifted left lying off the runway while folk were dying.

"Why?"

"The planes are aluminium. Salt corrodes aluminium. Few owners are prepared to risk the cargo."

The reporter and his cameraman took the point and many photos from all angles. They even had me standing on the salt mound for dramatic effect. We retired to the bar for a lager and further discussion. A campaign was burgeoning and succeeded: a plane was dedicated totally to the salt run.

Bruce Kent came to visit us shortly after I got back. I showed him round our feeding centres and the refugee camps; I took him out to the hospital. We went down to Owerri, recently liberated. (No town was ever captured by either side; they were all 'liberated'.) We spoke with the bishop and I went on with Bruce to see the cathedral which had been in process of construction, now an empty, weed-grown shell, eerie and silent. The rain dripped and a light wind moaned in the place where voices should have been raised in happy song.

I became aware of a figure sitting in shadow, a young man in tattered army uniform. A movement on his part had attracted my attention. He had lost a leg. He raised the stump in mute appeal. I went over to him. He stared ahead sightless. I had coins to give him and a cigarette which he took in his outstretched trembling hand and put to his lips. I lit it. We were surrounded by other broken, limbless, sightless, silent young men. After the war the novitiate in Uturu was turned into a rehabilitation centre for such unfortunates. It was called Hopeville. At that time, in that shell-pocked cathedral there seemed little hope.

We went on to Okpuala, deep in frontier-land, over broken bridges, past mined roads till we came to what had once been a thriving seminary. Walter was there.

Walter was an Italian Marist. He had read reports in the press, seen the news on television, thrown himself vigorously into a fund-raising campaign and had come out with a confrère to see for himself. They had been with me in Orlu when Walter was arrested. Taking photographs in a military area was not done. My friend, the Commandant, was understanding but hinted firmly that Walter might be better employed in a less sensitive area. He had found himself in Okpuala near the fighting lines with a massive challenge, a refugee camp beyond the reach of normal supplies. We had some for him but too little too late. He took us into his makeshift clinic. Not in the depths of Hell would I fear to see such a sight: little children lying on matting on concrete flooring, in silent pain in their own vomit and urine and blood.

Walter looked on, tears streaming down his face. "We have no transport; we have no medicine, we have no food. We clean the children. Look." Walter accompanied us back to Ihioma. Bruce stayed to enforce his appeal. I went on to Orlu.

Later that night Bruce reappeared. They had had a long and serious discussion. Walter's case had been forcibly presented. Okpuala was put on the priority list. Walter had left with a truckload of supplies, a happier man.

"By the way, Jim, another point." I was listening. "They're short-staffed at the airport. Des McGlade is virtually alone; they need another man. I had a word with Lewis."

"Yes?"

"We suggested you. Hope you don't mind."

Norbert was due back within the week.

"Delighted."

27

The Airport

I went across to Ihioma the next day to verify my appointment and I met Jack, the organisation director. He outlined the relief operation over a cup of coffee, pulling no punches; it was a dangerous operation and a demanding one: alternate nights, six-thirty prompt report to Caritas base, Ihioma; lorries to assemble. At dusk, the convoy sets out for the airstrip and meets up with the trucks from Ihiala; the final approach to Uli is under cover of darkness, thus avoiding MiGs. "They've no night fighters – yet," he explained. On the airstrip the lorries disperse to the various loading bays. At seven-thirty the relief planes begin to stack over Uli. The airstrip lights flash on briefly to allow planes to land, one at a time.

"That's the danger point," Jack was emphatic. "The lights give the intruder his chance, a DC4 from Benin; usually carries seven or eight bombs. Circles with the stack of relief planes and picks them off, or tries to, as they land. There are slit trenches at the side of the runway; use them. Des McGlade is

Norbert visiting one of the orphanages

there, Bernard and three or four other African Marists, Colin also, he looks after transport generally; they know the routine. You'll pick it up. There are plenty of helpers, Caritas and air force fatigue boys. Two shuttles. Usually a break about midnight. Time for a quick cup of tea up at Joe Prendergast's place. Be on time for the second shuttle. The lorries will have unloaded by the time the second lot are back. You should be finished about three or four. It's heavy work. Good luck. God bless."

It was indeed heavy work. The following night I arrived at Ihioma as instructed, picked up the all-important airport pass and waited while the lorries fuelled up. Colin gave the signal to start and we were off. I was in the lead lorry sorting out problems at roadblocks: "This man no get proper pass. What of cigarette now?" Colin followed in case of breakdown. It was dark before we reached the airstrip.

"Off lights! Off lights!" We were stopped at the final barrier. The sidelights, with which we had groped our way down the approach road, were doused.

"Enemy plane dey for sky." The sentry was breathless, adamant. "Driver, quench engine. Quench engines all."

We were surrounded by darkness and whispering silence. Suddenly the airstrip lights were on. The earth erupted in an explosion of noise. The anti-aircraft guns opened up. The driver leapt out of the cab. A figure appeared at the door and grabbed me by the elbow. I jumped down and followed, bending low into a trench dug into the laterite bank. It was Brother Bernard, in dark habit, a shadow in the dark. The guns continued to hammer hysterically.

"Intruder. Plane is coming in."

Martin with confreres at the orphanage in Uturu.

Ihioma: Lewis and airport-worker

A black hulk thundered over us. There was a flash, a deafening explosion and the roar of a second bomb.

"The plane is at the top end. They'll need lorries. Take three, Brother. Quick. Bombs have fallen. You're safe."

"Caritas! Caritas! Lorries! One, two, three." I was back in the cab; we were making our way up the side approach road. The airstrip lights flashed on again. "Keep going, driver. Keep going." The guns were hammering into the sky; tracer bullets searching the darkness. A Constellation roared past us up the tarmac. It was trundling into position when we arrived.

"How many lorries? We'll need more. Walkie-talkie, more lorries from finger one." The intercom crackled against the roar of the reversing plane. "Two lorries up to top bay; they're unloading. Welcome, Jimmy. Don't worry, it gets worse."

It was Des McGlade, the redoubtable Des, parish priest and cargo handler. I had heard tales of his exploits. There were more to be told.

The DC6 in the first bay was offloading stockfish directly onto the tarmac. A lorry backed up, tailboard down. Brother Jude was already there: "Two in the lorry; two on the ground. Welcome, Brother. You have come to help. Keep lifting now."

The sacks were bulky, square and heavy. "Pack them well back. Pile them high. One, two, three, lift. One, two, three . . ." The old Bedford truck was groaning under the weight. "What of my tyres now!" The driver was concerned.

The landing lights flashed on. There was a scampering of feet, an insane hammering of gunfire. The relief plane was down, roaring up to bay one. Our plane had unloaded.

"Clear the props! Lorries move."

"Battery no 'gree start! Push-am!"

"Caritas! Caritas! Lorry! Push lorry! Push-am! Push-am!"

Shoulder to tailboard; stockfish dust in the throat. "Push! Push! Push!" The lorry kicked into life and drove away from the plane. Propellers whined higher; tongues of flame streaked aft; doors slammed shut. The huge bulk lumbered round on spindle-legs, engines building up to a deafening roar and the plane was off, thundering down the runway, up, up, wheeling over the tower of Uli church and away, up and away into the rain clouds.

I ran over to bay two; the DC6 had landed.

"Evening, Captain." He gave me the manifest. "Cornmeal." There was little time for small talk. Formula-two, fortified, basic relief. Already the cargo door was open, lorries backed up, roller chute in position, sacks clattering down. I climbed on board the lorry, showing the light from a shielded torch: "Keep them swinging. Pack them high." Down the chute, into the lorry, onto the pile.

"Off torch! Off torch!"

The airstrip lights were on. The relief plane was overhead. Guns were barking at the bomber waiting, circling overhead. We were under the truck. The roar of the landing plane was lost in the flash and the crack of the explosion, the whine of the falling bomb; another, closer still, a whistle of shrapnel singing overhead. The lights were off; the plane was down.

"Caritas! Lorries. Get this lot out of the way. Quick! Quick! Enemy dey for sky."

The pace was frantic, bend and throw, bend and throw. The lorry was packed, chute pulled aboard. "Clear props!" Lorries lumbering to the perimeter, aircraft engines bursting into life, smoke and flame, rattle and whine. The plane was turning, exhaust fumes and cornmeal grit flying into our faces. It was off.

Another was landing. The red light of the controller was beckoning him into our bay. "Not another one! Caritas! Caritas! Two lorries." The plane was in position, ladders down. I signed the manifest; it was salt. The co-pilot was already supervising the offloading. I was at the tail of the lorry. Salt was a difficult cargo, in big demand. Security was tight. We had airport guards watching the offloading, air force fatigue boys helping. The salt sacks were rattling down the chute. One fell, tipped. It burst on the tarmac. There was a scramble.

"Leave-am! Leave-am!" The sentry was among the scrabblers, stick flying, cracking unmercifully."

"Keep the sacks moving! Clear this bloody plane!" The loadmaster was frantic. The panic to get the plane off the ground with the bomber still above was acute. "Move! Move! Move!" The plane was cleared, loose salt frantically brushed out. They were off.

We had two truckloads of salt. Gregory was supervising their parking, back to back for tight security. He was one of a number of our African Marists at the airport. They were invaluable men: quiet, resourceful, faithful; night after Caritas-night on duty, organising transport, directing lorries, guarding supplies on the road back to base camp. They were there from the beginning; they were there at the end.

"I will take some of these lorries back to Ihioma to offload. We will need them for a second shuttle." Gregory climbed on board the lead lorry. A guard followed carrying a Madson sub-machine gun, strange company, I thought, for Gregory whose world had, a few months before, been bounded by the walls of his little primary school.

My reflection was cut short by a burst of gunfire signalling the arrival of another plane. The lights were on. There was a silent rush for the slit trench. The first bomb was very close; the flash of the second was blinding. The blast was breathtaking.

We were out of the trench. Father McGlade was beside me. "He's hit something." Through the dim light we could see a column of smoke rising at the bottom end of the airstrip. "Take a couple of lorries to bay one; I'll go and see."

The plane was down and trundling towards us, its landing lights blooming through the mist. They were late and anxious to fit in a second shuttle. The loadmaster was frantic. Sacks were tumbling down the chute into the lorry, piling up at the tailboard, onto the ground. "Give chance now!" The sacks kept coming.

"Move lorries. Clear the props. Move! Move! Move!" They were off.

Des was back: "What have you got?"

"Rice."

"Let's get this lot cleared and we can have a break. That should be our lot for first half."

"Anybody hurt at the bottom end?"

"Couple of lads, flesh wounds, shrapnel. They're taking them to Ihiala. Could have been worse. Missed the airstrip. They've been busy down at that end. Heavy night. How are you?"

"Shattered."

"We'll have a break after this."

The lorries were packed. The convoy was moving off. We were on our way. Father Joe was waiting for us in his little mission house off the airstrip with tea and rolls.

"Heavy night?"

"Very."

"Sounded like it with all the planes. Any damage?"

Couple of lads injured at finger one. A near miss."

The tea was hot; the rolls were fresh; the break was short.

"Is that a plane?"

"Sounds like the American, the Globemaster."

"They're early. Come on, Jim, back to work."

It was raining as we bounced our way along the track to the airstrip. Lightning flickered through the trees. The distant rumble of thunder was pierced by an ear-splitting crack immediately above us. Rain lashed down on the glistening tarmac. The plane had landed, a huge freighter offloading its cargo directly onto the runway. Brother Gregory was back with his lorries. Jude was to follow with the rest. Another plane was landing, its lights dazzling through the curtain of rain. The Globemaster was building up power for take-off.

"Caritas! Lorries!"

The bomber had left; the guns were silent; the atmosphere was more relaxed but the work was hard. It was after midnight. We were tiring and the rain was lashing down, lightning flashing, thunder rolling all around us.

"Keep them coming. Come on, lads; one, two, three, up."

It was back-breaking: bend and lift, down the chute, into the lorry. "Pile them high. Stack them well back. That's it. Close the tailboard. Lorries away. Thanks, Captain. Safe flight!"

Things became more frantic as the night wore on to early morning, planes desperate to get away before dawn brightened the coast and exposed them to patrolling MiG fighters.

"Quickly! Quickly! Quickly! Move! Move! Move!" The loadmaster at the hatch desperate as his plane emptied, engines roaring for take-off even as the hatches were slammed to.

Three a.m.; the rain had stopped, a fitful moon was glimmering through ragged clouds and a dense mist was beginning to form. We watched the flare of the relief plane circling over the church steeple and head off for the coast. The last.

"He'll need to be quick to get over the coast in time. God go with him." Father McGlade's blessing was heartfelt.

The lorries were loaded and were rattling into position.

"What's that?" There was a droning throb of an aircraft immediately above us. The silent scamper of feet. The airstrip lights were on.

"One of ours."

"Can't be. It's too late."

The plane was immediately above us now, roaring, invisible in the low mist cloud and off, up, up and higher into the cloud, turning, engine straining, coming in again, landing lights billowing through the mist. It was down, thundering up the runway, cockpit window open, a jubilant Scandinavian, head out, thumb up: "Ve try harder!"

"Leave the lorries." There was a mad dash for the plane, doors open, ladders down, stockfish bales thumping onto the runway, piling high, dragged out of the path of the tailplane. The hold was emptied, the engines were roaring.

"Clear the props!" We watched as the freighter backed and swivelled, edged out onto the runway and roared off, up into the mist.

Des handed me the manifest. "Stein. His third run. He'll do it. Have we lorries?"

There were two at the bottom bay. We loaded the stockfish onto the rear, up to the front. "Pile them high."

"Leave a couple of bales for the workers; Brother Bernard sees to the distribution. Let's get these going."

We joined the convoy at bottom bay and headed off into the rising mist. Lewis was waiting at the base camp. I handed him the manifests. "Heavy night?" I nodded. He smiled: "Not bad for a first. There's a coffee inside."

Dawn was breaking when I reached Orlu. Godwin was waiting. "Should I prepare breakfast now?" I shook my head: "First of all a long shower, Goddy. Then I think I will sleep." I stripped off the overall I had been wearing and handed it to him. "Have these boiled, Goddy. They'll make fine soup." He laughed.

I slept. It was late afternoon when I woke.

28

Aid

It was the arrival of the supply lorry that woke me. A load of rice and stockfish and cornmeal that we had scrabbled for in fire, rain and thunder and shouts unholy throughout the night was being offloaded for redistribution to the various feeding centres around us. Norbert's return had been delayed but the work was continuing.

I was not alone; along with the supplies was a note asking me to put up three nurses who had arrived; they were attached to Misereor, the German Catholic charity working with JointChurchAid. We had plenty of room; Godwin arranged accommodation and an evening meal. I went out to Ihioma to pick them up and thus Helga and her friends came into our lives.

We had a merry meal. The girls had been assigned to a camp and clinic some distance away, one near the ever-approaching fighting lines with difficult means of communication. They were given a couple of days to relax and acclimatise themselves. They had brought in supplies including a bottle

Norbert and African Brothers, intense discussion

of Brandtwein. We sat after supper when darkness had fallen and the shaded candle had been lit and we listened to the sound of the relief planes droning eerily in the distant rain-washed skies. We laughed and joked and sang songs about a Hofbrauhaus in Munich. They were brave girls.

There were French girls too, nurses working with Médecins Sans Frontières. I met one of them in the rush and the crush of 'State House' attached to the airstrip where entry papers were examined with meticulous efficiency. Her papers were not in order. The letter of introduction was missing. She could not pass. She would have to return to Libreville to obtain the necessary document. Marianne was distraught. Her companions had been cleared. What could she do? I took her aside, away from the crowded desk, asked her a few questions and discreetly wrote her a letter of introduction. It was accepted without demur.

We were invited some time later to her birthday party. Marianne was working in a clinic near the airstrip. Helga and her friends were also invited. They were on a few days' rest-leave from their work in the refugee camp and the demanding round involved in the clinics attached to the centre. Their director had come along, the elderly priest in charge of Misereor who was on a flying visit. He had brought wine. It mingled well with the smell of French cooking wafting from the little makeshift kitchen.

We were a happy band, French and English and German. The conversation was light-hearted, punctuated by laughter and an occasional burst of song but it suddenly took on a serious tone. We spoke of deeper things: their homes, their friends, their careers, their prospects, the war, the suffering, the misery, the hardship. I asked them why were they there; what motivated bright young girls to risk their all and their lives in this hell-hole? The question gave pause for thought. The answers were impersonal, non-committal, superficial, almost facetious. The conversation dwindled. It was interrupted by the arrival of the supper dish. The wine had been poured; the Gallic stew lay tempting on the table; our hostess was picking up her serving ladle when the priest interrupted: "Would you all mind indulging an old man before we begin? And together let us recollect our thoughts and offer a little prayer for each other, and for those for whom we work and for whom we care."

There was a profound silence around the table; a silence heightened by the noise about us: the constant shrill of the cicadas, the croaking of the frogs in the rain, the drone of the relief plane searching for the airstrip and in that attentive silence my question was answered.

Apart from the French and German organisations represented, there were others involved in the relief operation. The loss of the International Red Cross had been devastating. Continual harassment and the eventual shooting down of one of their planes flying in from Fernando Po had forced the organisation to pull out. Their work continued through national groups, the French Red Cross prominent in the relief programme flying in supplies night after night, building up their clinics and distribution centres with determination and significant success. The organisation to which our

French friends belonged, Médecins Sans Frontières, the medics who knew no bounds, were increasingly involved, risking limb and life in areas under constant attack. Austria and Germany were represented not only by Misereor but also most effectively by the Lutheran organisation which went under the impressive title of Diakonischewerk. We were indeed part of a massive international effort with everybody involved from Icelandic airmen to the Knights of Malta.

Politically it was a delicate situation, with very few governments prepared to allow official aid yet prepared to turn a blind eye on the work of independent organisations. Oxfam continued to channel in aid along with the recently founded Catholic Action for Overseas Development. The United Nations refused to be involved despite the fact that, ironically, 1969 was the Year of the Child. UNICEF refused to be deterred. Their food and medicine kept arriving in ever-increasing quantities. CONCERN of Ireland set up its own relief programme. American aid poured in night after night with their Catholic Relief Services very much to the fore. Various national CARITAS organisations were at work both within the enclave and offshore. Scandinavian aid was at the core of the operation.

My Icelandic reporter was not a lone voice nor my two merry friends from the *Dublin Herald*; newsmen and women arrived in a steady stream: journalists, photographers, television crews. I was alone one night in the house, reading by the light of a shaded candle when Godwin appeared: a gentleman wished to speak to me. The gentleman turned out to be a Japanese photographer working for *Life* magazine. He had just come back from the Owerri front and was wet and tired and hungry but jubilant. He tapped his camera. "Good pictures. Very good." He had been in the front lines for two weeks, scrounging food and drinking muddy water. He had suffered and he knew the reward was quality. "A spectator cannot take good pictures."

Godwin brought food. Our little photographer ate heartily, showered and slept and was on his way next morning armed with a tin of cigarettes, front-line currency.

I met Francis Wyndham of the *Sunday Times*. I had read his articles and recognised his stance. We had an interesting chat. He was on his way back to London. He had an urgent request: baby milk for the child of the attaché who had helped him.

Francis Wyndham was one of many I met for whom Biafra was not 'news'; it was a cause, doing much to counterbalance the British Establishment position. Frederick Forsyth saluted such newspeople in his book, *The Biafra Story*: William Norris, Walter Partington, Richard Hall and Norman Kirkham. The reporter Michael Leapman set *The Sun* ablaze with his story of starvation. Winston Churchill came out and reported at first hand the bombing of civilian targets. John Osman of the BBC managed to get himself expelled by Adekunle from the Port Harcourt sector. Susan Cronje of the *Financial Times* collaborated with Auberon Waugh to expose the situation.

John de St Jorre of *The Observer* was there gathering up facts which were later collated in his brilliant story of the Nigerian Civil War. And there were more, not only British but American, Irish, French, Scandinavian and Japanese.

But Britain was deeply involved and her reporters were there to find the truth behind the propaganda. A Foreign Office official in a fit of pique remarked that all the people sent out to report the situation came back pro-Biafran. He was not talking about cub reporters but hardbitten journalists who knew the difference between handouts and fact.

Frederick Forsyth was one of the first on the scene, long before *The Day of the Jackal* made him a household name. He came in before the fall of Enugu, threading his way through Cameroon and across the creeks. He recognised the position of Biafra and stayed to champion it, risking life and reputation and income in the process, and he it was who presented the accolade to his fellow reporters: "Whatever odium may have accrued to Britain through this policy, it was not the fault of the British press which had done its job and had done it well."

29

Fuel

Diesel was a continuing problem at the airstrip. Fuel for the lorries was available from government sources but at a price. The money paid by the relief organisation was said to be used to buy arms. This, it was argued, jeopardized our civilian status. Fuel would be shipped in. Belgian Air Services flew in a DC6 laden with 48-gallon drums of diesel. Offloading was difficult and dangerous.

"Where's the forklift?"

"Broken, out of action."

"How the hell . . .?"

A wooden chute had been contrived. The first barrel stuck halfway; the second hit it, tumbled over the side, crashed on to the tarmac and split open. A lake of diesel oil spread beneath the plane.

The loadmaster was not happy. He ripped the ropes from the chute, flung it aside with savage contempt, grabbed the plane's enormous spare tyre, dragged it to the rear, upended it and pushed it through the cargo hatch. It landed with a splash in the diesel pool.

Offloading continued, barrel after barrel of fuel crashing from the hatch. Some hit the tyre and rolled away; others hit the concrete; a few burst open and flooded the tarmac further. The plane was emptied; the barrels manhandled out of the way.

"Stand back, everybody, well back!"

We waited and watched with bated breath. The port outboard engine roared into life. A tongue of flame shot aft. We watched with mouths agape as it licked above the flood of diesel. Propellers whined and screamed. The plane swung on its spindled undercarriage and edged away from the pool of diesel. The starboard engine barked, smoke and flame streamed; propellers whined. The plane trundled forward out of the danger area on to the runway. Inboard engines were switched on, power built up in a deafening crescendo; the plane shuddered against chocks and brakes and then it was off, roaring down the runway, lumbering into the sky. We watched as it tilted over the steeple and vanished into cloud. There was a collective sigh of relief as we stood by the pool of diesel glinting in the moonlight.

Something had to be done. The skill and courage of the Belgian aircrew was beyond praise, but a less dangerous, more efficient method of bringing in fuel had to be devised.

How? The ever-resourceful members of the Spiritan Congregation set about the task. A Stratotanker, saved for a nominal sum from the scrapyards of the Nevada Desert, flew into service.

We were ready and waiting with a truck laden with empty drums. A fuel hose was attached, the pump started up and the diesel flowed fast and abundant. The trick was to switch the hose from one drum to the next with minimum loss while the pump was still in action. In the dark of the enclosed wagon the task was a difficult one; diesel splashed everywhere. We were drenched. Triple-headed hoses were introduced. The problem increased threefold. Drum after drum was filled but at a cost. Caritas workers laboured uncomplaining. I came out in a bright red diesel rash. I was not uncomplaining.

Colin, the indefatigable, shopped around and found an available fuel tanker. To speed the operation it was decided to cut through the baffle walls enabling us to fill up without interrupting the flow. A mechanic armed with a hand drill and steel boring bits lowered himself into the tank. Helpfully I rushed off, gathered up a length of cable, found a heavy-duty electric drill, powered it up and presented it to the sweating driller. He looked at it thoughtfully, shook his head and explained patiently the danger of residual gases mixing with electric sparks and went back to his task.

The tanker was a resounding success. The supply plane landed in its designated bay. The fuel hose was connected, the pump turned on at maximum pressure, the tank filled, the hose disconnected and the plane was off. Speed, with the bomber hovering above a full tanker, was of the essence. Turnaround time was slashed.

Problems remained however. Chief among them was security. Fuel was a precious commodity. With our regular nightly supply and full tanks we were in an enviable position. I was made to realise this vividly.

The convoy was stopped outside the control base on the approach road to the airstrip. I jumped out of the jeep and went to find out the cause. A serviceman was calmly siphoning diesel from the front lorry which had been halted at gunpoint by an armed guard.

"What the hell do you think you're doing?"

"I am taking diesel from this tank and siphoning it into this drum." The answer was calm and flat.

"You have no right! That is not your fuel!"

"These are my orders, sir. If you would like to speak to my commanding officer he is in his office."

I stormed into the camp. The officer was waiting for me. He told me to be seated. I stood. "Do you realise what your men are doing?"

"They are siphoning some diesel from some of your lorries."

"On your orders?"

"On my orders."

"You have no right."

"We have no diesel."

"That is *your* problem."

"No, my friend; that is *our* problem. No diesel, no generator; no generator, no radio; no radio, no contact; no contact, no planes; no government planes, no relief planes."

I left. The planes flew in with regularity. The radio was obviously working.

Commandeering of fuel by flight control was annoying but understandable – after all they were supplying us with a service. Highway robbery was another, much more dangerous matter. One of our lorries, straggling behind the main convoy, had been hijacked. The danger facing a full tanker making its way to base was obvious. Colin and I went to see the chief of mobile police, a regular and efficient unit. We laid our case. He was understanding and sympathetic, promising us to double the guard on the supply route.

We had a full road tanker. Despite reassurances I decided to avoid the tarred road, travelling instead by the longer but hopefully safer bush road. The Earl of Kildare was at the wheel. Fitzgerald had come out to see for himself the tragedy that all Ireland was aware of and he had stayed. His help on the airstrip was invaluable. We were in his jeep. The tanker followed. Suddenly he stopped.

"What's wrong?"

"Something ahead."

In the dim light of the shielded headlamps I made out shadowy figures lurking at the side of the road. Hijackers. The indignation, always smouldering, burst into a flame of anger. What in God's name did these people think they were about. Whose war was it? I got down and walked towards them. My language on the airstrip as the tension mounted had been getting riper by the shuttle. I gave them the full blast. They backed off in face of the verbal onslaught. There were three of them, armed. I kept coming. Then I heard the ominous click of a bolt. I stopped.

"Sir, I do not think you understand."

"Understand!"

"We are mobile police. You spoke to our senior officer requesting protection."

For the first time, in the dim light, I saw their shoulder flashes. The speaker was calm, dignified, polite, well spoken. I apologised. There was a tentative titter then a burst of hearty Igbo laughter. We all laughed and grasped hands warmly.

"Brother, I did not know you knew such language." I suspected I was being addressed by a past pupil. Again I apologized. "Na so de world dey be." I edged back into the jeep and we drove off with their farewells. Fitzgerald shook his head. I felt his smile in the darkness.

We parted from the suspected hijackers on good terms but such was not always the case. It had been a particularly heavy and dangerous night at the airstrip. The relief planes came in numbers; we were kept flat out and the bomber was busy. We could hear the rattle of machine-gun fire up among the stars, a new experience and unnerving. Bombs had fallen with unusual accuracy. The first shuttle had not finished before we were drained with exhaustion. The guns opened up again as the bomber circled. We made for the slit trenches and clawed laterite clay as explosions thundered nearer. The cry went up: "Thieves!"

I leapt out of the trench. They were jumping off the back of the salt lorry, sacks on their heads, three of them.

"Get them!" Yelling I plunged after them into the tangled undergrowth bordering the airstrip. They padded swiftly ahead of me up the narrow path, sacks still head-borne. I raced breathless after them. They wheeled off the path. I wheeled after them. We were in their gun emplacement. I was on strictly forbidden territory. The sacks had vanished. They turned on my approach in mock surprise: "Sir?"

I was speechless, panting for breath. Words burst out in incoherent gasps: "Thieves! Thiefmen! Saboteers! I think you be infiltrators. You are working against us. You are stealing food from starving babies. They are dying. You grow fat. Who are you people? Are you the people who shoot at the planes when they are trying to land?"

"Sah, excuse me."

"Do not say 'Sah, excuse me' to me. You are thieves. Bandits. Saboteurs."

One of them made for a rifle. I lunged and grabbed it from him with a roar boiling into babbling rage. The Igbo have a deep-seated caution of a madman. The sight of a screaming, cursing White-man was too much. They turned and fled, from the bunker, on to the airstrip, into a hail of bullets from guards on the perimeter sparking at their heels as they dashed for the safety of the bush. I picked up one of the sacks, slung it over my shoulder, and went back to the lorries.

This was serious, after all they were only kids, drummed into service. I was losing my sense of proportion. My nerves were getting the better of me. We had nightly flights now, on the airstrip night after night with little chance of sleep during the day.

The war was grinding on. The Federal army was closing in. Refugees and more refugees were fleeing before them. More mouths to feed. Less food to spare. The dry season was upon us. Hunger was growing. The seams of discipline that had held the country together for two and a half years were fraying. Lawlessness was growing. I was returning at the end of a busy night after the convoy had gone. Godwin was with me. It had been a quiet night despite the bright moon. One of our trucks stood on the road ahead of us.

"Must be broken down." I stopped and went to investigate. The back was open.

The lorry was empty. The cab was deserted. Blood stained the driver's seat and was splashed across the windscreen.

"Get in the car, Goddy." We raced up to the next roadblock, called out the guard and drove them back to the scene. They cocked their Lee Enfields and crouched into the elephant grass. One of them came with us to Ihiala for reinforcements.

Despite every effort it was difficult to remain disentangled. Military reverses increased. I was in bed fast asleep when I heard the crunch of a heavy lorry on the gravel below. I went down to investigate. The lorry had lost its lights. It was heading for Amaigbo hospital. Could I go ahead and show the way. I shone the torch into the truck. The wounded, broken, bleeding soldiery blinked in the light. We drove to the hospital. One of the Sisters met me on the veranda. It was midnight. She looked at me with glazed eyes. "What is it?"

"Soldiers; wounded."

"How many?"

"I don't know. About twenty."

The door of the theatre opened. An elderly African doctor appeared. He leaned against the wall, his shoulders slumped in exhaustion. He looked at us: "Sister?"

The nun spoke: "Doctor, there are wounded in the lorry."

"Sister, I have been in that theatre since eleven o'clock this morning."

"Doctor, I know. I have been with you."

"Have we beds?"

"We can make room."

"Bring them."

30

Ever-present Danger

I visited the airstrip in daylight. A vehicle had broken down and Colin had arranged its retrieval. It was an unnerving experience viewing in daylight the scene that I had only glimpsed in the dark and the danger and the turmoil of the night. The day was dry; a light wind was blowing, rustling the palm leaves. Hours before, the stars had shone down on a scene of stress and confusion and noise. Now a hazy sun revealed a scene of peace and tranquility. The picture of peace was false. The sun could not gild the tragedy of that strip. Not even the tall elephant grass could hide the shame of the destruction. Signs of wreckage were everywhere: the bombed-out control tower, devastated warehouse, shattered aircraft littering the perimeter, tailplanes showing above the tangled vegetation. It was a sobering sight: eighteen months of destruction, determination and courage. I counted twelve wrecked planes and yet another was to be added before the week was out.

The disaster struck very close to home. It had been a busy night, a dry night, a clear, moonlit night. The bomber came, harassed the relief planes, dropped his bombs and, we hoped, had gone. Des McGlade came up from bottom bay to check that all was going well. It was nearing the end of the first shuttle and things were running smoothly. Despite the bombing, we had had a full complement of planes. The lorries were on the point of leaving for base.

There was a sudden movement among the relief boys. A plane was attempting to land. The guns opened up, warning off the intruder, providing cover for the incoming plane. Above the barking of the heavy anti-aircraft guns we could hear the rattle of automatic fire. The dark mass of a plane was immediately above us, landing lights piercing the light mist. We threw ourselves on the ground. There was a flash, a crash and the roar of a falling bomb. We stood up looking towards the spot where the plane had landed: a column of smoke was spiralling in the moonlight. Des raced for the jeep. I followed; we roared down the perimeter path.

The plane was on fire, smoke pouring from the wings. A lorry was burning close by. Scattered ground staff stood around helpless. Among them I noticed two uniformed White-men, the captain and co-pilot staring into the flames. Des drew them away from the heat.

"Are you all right?"

They nodded. The pilot indicated the burning wreckage: "We've lost two men in there, two good men, flight-mechanic and a passenger. Nothing we could do." The smoke and the flames engulfing the open cargo-hatch emphasized his words. They turned away.

"Who was the passenger?"

"An Italian lad. Called himself Walter. Nice guy . . . was."

I gasped: Walter! My Walter! He had gone over to Sao Tomé to drum up more supplies for his beloved orphans. Walter, the quiet, cheerful, desperate, generous-hearted Walter. Il mio fratello. Now this. I walked blindly into the darkness, up the approach path, unshed tears scorching my throat. Slowly I became aware of figures ahead of me, two shadows silhouetted in the faint moonlight which filtered through the trees. A cigarette glowed.

"Walter! Walter!"

"Jeemy!"

I ran and grabbed him. "You're alive!"

Walter's shoulders sank. He slowly shook his head: "Pilot ees dead. Also other man dead." There were tears in his voice. His companion put a gentle arm around him.

"Come with me," I said. They followed me back down the approach path towards the burning plane. The reunion was ecstatic.

A less happy ending occurred in the days just before the airstrip was shut down. An American Globemaster was shot out of the sky.

Des and I were having a quiet cup of tea in Joe Prendergast's little house on the perimeter of the airstrip. We had our petrol tanker with us and were preparing for a heavy night. The first of the relief planes could be heard circling overhead.

"Sounds like the American. Let's get going." Des was on his feet. Suddenly the even drone of the plane was interrupted by the crackle of machine-gun fire. Des had the door open. The blackness of the night was violently torn by a great orange flash, the silence by a deafening explosion and a roar of something falling on top of us.

"A bomb?"

"The plane!" Des had turned to us, shadowed by the orange glow that filled the night sky.

We were in the jeep, racing towards the source of the glow. The great hulk of the Globemaster lay burning in a clearing of its own making, torn palm trees crackling in the heat. A petrol tank exploded as we approached, flames spiralling up above the trees, the blast forcing us back.

The cargo was cornmeal; we could smell it roasting as flames licked among the sacks. And among the sacks lay the charred bodies of the crew members, black and silent. Father McGlade raised his hand in final benediction. We knew that five brave souls were standing then before the judgement seat of God. God knew why they had died.

I had met some of those men. It was a celebration on the Island. I had been invited. The reason for the celebration was not quite clear but little excuse was needed for a break from the tension and the danger. It was a crew member of the Globemaster who invited me. We were chatting as the plane offloaded its cargo of cornmeal. He was interested in conditions beyond the glare of the landing lights. "Does the stuff really get through?"

"You've got to believe it; we've a Scotsman in charge of distribution. Hasn't been known to miss a manifest yet. He reckons we lose no more than two percent through mishandling and pilfering. And that two percent goes to empty bellies."

I met Alex again on Sao Tomé. The party was in full swing. We shared a beer at a table under a tree bedecked with coloured lights. After the dark and the danger of the airstrip the feeling of comfort and security was pure luxury.

"Sure must be hell in there." Alex was genuinely sympathetic.

"We get used to it. Worse in a sense for you, flying night by night from comfort and safety into that hell, as you call it." I stopped and looked at him. "Why do you do it?"

Alex drained his glass and looked at me: "Do you want to know? Do you really want to know?"

I nodded. There was a pause in the conversation around us. Others were listening. Alex smiled: "Money. Big money and quick."

There was a rumble of laughter around the table. Glasses were drained, refilled. Conversations resumed. I remained thoughtful. Alex remained thoughtful. Suddenly he leaned over. There was a seriousness about his tone: "Tell you something, Jim." He touched my arm. "I've a wife and two beautiful daughters back home in the States, beautiful wife, beautiful daughters. I miss them like hell." He paused. "I mentioned money. I'll tell you something else, pal: I'd get a lot more money back in the States robbing banks and it would be a hell of a lot safer than this job we're on." He stopped suddenly; his eyes took on a faraway look, staring into the distance. Then he snapped back: "Ah, what the hell! Drink your beer. Cheer up. Sing a song. Come on, sing a song."

I was thoughtful and sad beyond words as I stared through the flames at the charred and blackened corpses of the crew of that Globemaster, lying charred and blackened midst the cornmeal they had been bringing. The BBC reported next morning that the plane had been carrying arms.

Father Prendergast had built a little cemetery just off the airstrip and tended it with loving care. There were twenty-five gravestones in that plot, a monument to the airmen who had died.

Danger was not by any means confined to the airstrip. I was on board a lorry taking relief supplies to the edge of no-man's land. A MiG screamed overhead. We leapt out and dived into a roadside culvert. We watched as the plane circled and swung back, roaring low up the road. A line of bullets ripped into the roadway alongside the lorry. The plane flew on. In the distance we heard the crump of rockets.

Not so lucky was a Presentation Sister returning from a round of her clinics. She was with a nurse and driver in an open-top vehicle. The MiG which followed them up the road missed on its first attempt, wheeled in a tight arc and came again. The nurse was wounded. Sister Elizabeth was killed outright.

The Federals had got hold of MiG 19s, night fighters. The stakes were being heightened. Biafra had little in response until a Swedish count flew in with a tiny squadron of Minicons, armed, low-flying and dangerous. They took out two MiGs and an Ilyushin on their first sortie. Skilfully camouflaged, flying at tree-top level to escape detection, they caused panic and destruction in their attacks on Federal airports. I encountered a brace of them on my way to Uga airstrip. Norbert had asked me to contact a relative there of one of his orphans. Puttering along on my little Honda 50, I became aware of a crude engine noise. Thinking it was a heavy motorbike, I was pulling to the side of the road when the aircraft hammered up immediately behind me, above me and away before I recognised anything more than the element of surprise they possessed.

Count Van Rosen had wept at the sight of children killed and maimed in the Umuahia air raids. The Minicons brought solace. It was a futile gesture however. The odds were stacked too high. Moscow had more MiGs for the asking. The Federal army was slowly but surely gaining ground. Uga military airstrip and our own Uli were gradually coming into range.

31

Defeat

Biafra was surrounded.

During the wet season of 1969 the Federals had dug in. The First, Second and Third Armies were centred on Umuahia to the north, Onitsha to the west and Port Harcourt in the south respectively. Supplied as they were with apparently limitless resources: aircraft and field guns from Russia, armoured cars and ammunition from Britain, assorted weaponry from various countries anxious to maintain a surreptitious, friendly posture towards Nigeria, the surprising thing was that the Federals were pinned down at all. Biafran resistance was desperate, avoiding set-piece confrontation, at the same time maintaining sporadic, fierce commando-style attack.

Don McCullin in his memoir *Unreasonable Behaviour* describes one such attack and the debacle of its repulse: the Biafran front line, supplied unbelievably with only two rounds of ammunition per man, advancing in the face of withering, unremitting Federal fire, the unspeakable horror of the wounded lying at his side, faces torn by bullets, stomachs ripped out by mortar shrapnel, the ferocity of the Federal counter-attack, the headlong, desperate retreat, the wounded abandoned, begging to be rescued, grabbing at the legs of those fleeing past, McCullin among them, realising that if captured he could be taken as a mercenary. His was a nightmare world. And he came back. He was there to the end.

There were mercenaries in the conflict as well as reporters; we had a group on the compound. I saw them occasionally returning from night patrol, wiry, tough individuals, South African I guessed but never asked; we kept at a respectable distance. The camp commander, however, did on one occasion bring them to lunch. Introduction of our guests was vague, intentionally so. Their accent as well as the eagerness, the delight with which they accepted my offer of a Castle Lager, smuggled in the night before by my friendly Icelandic flight engineer, hinted at their origin. Conversation was general, centred on the workings of the relief programme. They were genuinely and keenly interested.

Other mercenaries were there, involved in more than troop-training, Rolf Steiner notable among them. His had been the defence of Aba, holding the line with men supplied with no more than a handful of bullets each, relying on the tactic of sudden advance, collecting weaponry left by retreating Federals, resuming a defensive position. Despite their fierce resistance, however, they found themselves surrounded. Steiner fought his way out with grim determination and a staggering loss of men.

Undaunted, he planned an attack on Onitsha, commandeering all available men and weapons. His plan envisaged a subsequent attack on Asaba with, presumably, captured armour, followed by a triumphal progress through the Mid-West. It had been done before. Steiner's men were repulsed at the first stage. The Federal Second Army was deeply entrenched and well armed. Steiner was recalled and dismissed. His men, it was averred, had been interfering with relief supplies. Not done, old chap. He was later captured in the Sudan, again fighting for the underdog. He was imprisoned and tortured horribly.

Other mercenaries in the field, Welsh, Scots, Belgian, maintained the Onitsha offensive with bravery but with little effect. Marc Goosens, a Fleming was killed in a skirmish. Others eventually left the country, some honourably, their contract fulfilled, others with bulging pockets and little to show for the cost to the Biafran treasury.

Biafra fought on, grimly, desperately but as the dry season advanced so did the Federal forces. The Second Army was edging its way inland from the river. We could hear the crump of heavy artillery in the south closing in on the heart of the enclave, Uli with its main supply artery. Once the howitzers were in position it would be all over.

"Where are the Feds?" the constant question of the aircrews continuing to fly. They knew they were working on borrowed time. Supplies kept coming, indeed, increasing but, with the arrival of the MiG 19s, so did the risk. And then came the flares wiping out in their glare the protection of darkness upon which the airlift had depended. I had seen them before as a youngster on Tyneside, onion flares hanging over the shipyards with Dorniers and Heinkels droning in for the kill. And now they were over Uli, leaving us exposed as prey in the beam of a hunter's torch.

McGlade was leaving that night. It was as though the Federals knew and were putting on a special show. He had put up a good fight. With his parish overrun in the early days of the war, he had been arrested and sent to Lagos under guard. While waiting at a checkpoint on the Benue Bridge he had been accosted by a large Hausa soldier who had calmly taken hold of the priest's hand on the sill of his car, bent back the fingers until two of them cracked, smiled benignly and moved on. Deported as an undesirable alien, he had returned to Ireland, recuperated and flew back to Biafra via Sao Tomé. His work on the airstrip had been interrupted after shrapnel had cracked the back of his skull, but again he had recovered and returned. He had been my friend and mentor and now he was leaving. I watched from the top bay as his plane revved for take-off. As it did, a bomb fell, the flash and the crash and the scream mingling with McGlade's plane roaring over our heads. It was a fitting send-off. I saluted him mentally as the DC6 swung around the steeple and headed south.

"Lorries! Fatigue boys! Caritas! Caritas! Plane na bia-o! Come on, boys!" A plane was trundling into our bay. The flare was still burning, the airstrip bathed in its orange light, the bomber overhead. There was a reluctance to venture onto the runway. "Come on, men! Move it! Move it!" How they must have hated the sound of my voice!

Christmas came; we were still in business, airlift as busy as ever. Father McGlade's place had been taken by a jovial young Irish priest with a great sense of derring-do and an even greater sense of humour.

Some of the planes had promised to do a single shuttle. I picked up Father Pat at Ihiala mission. A Christmas party of sorts was in full swing. Everybody was there: German nurses, French doctors, American newsmen; Princess Cecile de Bourbon and her companion of the Knights of Malta were there. We had time to toast the happy–sad occasion, snatch a piece of cake, wish everyone a happy Christmas and dart down to the airstrip before the first plane arrived.

It was a beautiful night, star filled, peaceful. There was no bomber. We sang a happy carol as we bowled along. The roadblock halted us. They did not recognise my companion. "Na who be this man? What of papers now?"

Pat threw his head back and roared with laughter. "Papers! How you say papers, my friend? This be Christmas! Happy Christmas! We three kings of Orient are!" bursting into song, a raucous carol.

The guards stared in amazement and then rocked back with laughter. "Hey, this man, he be too much. Fadder, what ting you get for we? You know it be Christmas."

We knew. We had sweets and cigarettes. We drove on leaving behind a merry band of guards.

Shortly after Christmas the Third Marine Commando under Colonel Obasanjo switched forces from the Aba front, smashed through the Biafran eastern salient, linked up with the First Army centred on Umuahia and prepared for the final assault on Owerri. Once there we knew that Uli would be in direct line of attack. Orders were given for evacuation.

32

Shut-down

The airstrip had been hit hard during the day, strafed and rocketed by MiG 19s, bombed by an Ilyushin. Desperately hard work had repaired the minor damage but little could be done about the crater at the head of the strip. A couple of lorries were positioned to warn incoming planes. We were in business but under severe threat. Federal troops had advanced north of Owerri. We had been warned that a field gun was in position within range of the airstrip. We knew we were working on borrowed time.

Johnsonn was the first to land. His co-pilot leaned out of the cockpit window as the plane taxied to a halt. "Where are they?"

"About eight miles south. What's your cargo?"

"Cornmeal."

Lorries were backed up to the open hatch; offloading went ahead quietly and methodically; we had reduced numbers of helpers but they were our own Caritas volunteers.

Captain Johnsonn climbed down; we shook hands: "How are things?"

"Just a matter of time. Once the shelling starts, this place closes for good. That could be any minute."

"Any passengers?"

I indicated a small gathering on the perimeter.

"Tell them to board. What about yourselves?"

I looked over at Vincent who had returned from an inspection of the bomb crater. He shook his head. "We're staying."

There had been a meeting in Ihioma the previous afternoon, short, sharp and serious. We were joined by officials of the World Council of Churches. Despite the urgency of the matter, it was a warm

Father Jack Finucane, executive director of Caritas relief programme, along with his confreres of the Irish Spiritan Order, responsible for the setting up of one of the biggest relief operations ever

157

and friendly meeting; we had been a good team, the joint churches. The womenfolk were to go. That matter was settled; our German nurses were to be informed; we knew that the nuns would be a different proposition. Lay helpers were to be advised strongly to leave. The World Council members left to report the decisions. Discussion continued. Some of the nuns agreed to leave. The plan was that they would go over to Sao Tomé, wait until the dust had settled and then return, if permission were granted, to continue their work, hopefully in more peaceful conditions. Others in the group were adamant: they were staying.

We knew there were risks involved. The gunfire around us drawing ever closer was indication enough of the physical dangers; what our position would be in the eyes of the Federal civil authorities was more open to question. There was little point in speculation: sufficient for the day is the evil thereof. Jack suggested a beer all round.

There was a tap at the door. The World Council delegation had returned. They had had their meeting. They had outlined the decision made at the general meeting; further discussion had taken place; a final decision had been made: all were to leave.

The disappointment on the part of the delegates was heartfelt. It had been a difficult decision to make after all they had been through: the agony, the danger, the hardship, but it was an obvious decision. They realised they had other responsibilities: their wives, their families. We admired their courage. The parting was equally heartfelt.

Evacuation took place that evening. The bomber, not noted for its accuracy, had obviously been warned off by the advancing Federal troops but the air of tension on the crowded airstrip was high, the exodus desperate but controlled: relief workers, nurses, nuns, television crews, reporters. Our own John Porter was among them, the *Glasgow Observer* editor who had supported us faithfully and generously throughout the conflict; he was leaving at the final moment with stories to file that would have been the envy of the most daring of foreign correspondents.

I had Helga and her friends in the jeep. They were leaving under strong protest but leave they must. Fitzgerald was with us, leaving also under protest; he was given no choice; he had family. "The flight of the Earl," I mused. He had fought a good fight. We picked up a lone reporter looking for a plane. It was Richard Hall; he had no boarding pass. The others were on board. There was trouble: no pass, no flight. "It's all right, Captain, I have his pass. I've misplaced it. I'll find it. Get on board." He did. The plane was off.

It had been a hectic night, supplies coming in, relief workers, reporters, officials flying out. Over a dozen planes landed that night under threat from the guns positioned within range. There seemed no limit to the courage of the aircrews. Their concern was touching. I watched a pilot leave his plane and walk over to a nun hesitating on the perimeter. I watched him gesticulating in his insistence. She walked away. He stood, slowly shaking his head, climbed the ladder. The doors were slammed; the engines burst into life.

A dozen planes, a dozen loads of cornmeal, stockfish, salt and medicines.

The lorries were packed. The convoy departed. The last of the planes flew off. I stayed with a reserve truck. There was always the possibility of a last-minute flight. Some pilots took pride in 'trying harder'. The lorry I had was a new one, flown in from the Sao Tomé, a gift from Caritas Germany, the logo emblazoned on its side.

An army officer approached me. There had been a government plane in during the night but few ground staff to offload. It was easy to guess why. The officer had a request. I nodded guardedly.

"I would like to borrow your vehicle."

"Pardon!"

There had been no such request since the redoubtable Father Finucane, clerical brother of our own director, had forestalled the commandeering of a Caritas lorry. He had grabbed the gun from one of the would-be hijackers, took control of the vehicle, ordered the driver to take them to base camp and handed his 'prisoners' over to their commanding officer, emphasizing the importance of our civilian status and demanding in forceful terms that it be respected. It was.

"I would like to borrow your vehicle."

"No."

"We have a sensitive cargo lying on the airstrip and no lorry to take it. I would like to borrow your vehicle to clear the cargo away."

"What is the cargo?"

"Ammunition."

"Ammunition!"

"If to say the Federals start shelling this place you know what will happen."

I saw his point vividly. What a situation! Personnel were still dotted around the airstrip. There was the possibility of one more of our planes coming in. "OK, but quick. Very quick."

I rounded up Caritas workers, drove up to the government bay and set feverishly to work, box after box of ammunition hoisted up and packed tight. I leapt into the jeep, on ahead through the roadblock, its guardians little suspecting our cargo, and into headquarters. The officer said he would summon a fatigue squad. He left and did not return. We waited then I gave the order to unload. The irony of the situation was beyond words but the job had to be done. Circumstantial evidence would weigh heavily against us. We cleared the truck, reversed at speed out of the compound and raced to the airstrip. A plane had landed. Its cargo had been dumped on the tarmac. We loaded up and drove off. We knew that the next night, if there was another night, would be the last.

Our surmise was correct: Saturday night was our last night on the airstrip. It was unwontedly calm. With no bomber and with willing and orderly helpers the offloading of the plane went smoothly.

Captain Johnsonn waited until we had finished loading the lorries. When it was clear there were no more passengers he prepared to leave. "Room for two more."

We shook hands all round. Johnsonn and the co-pilot climbed back into the cockpit. The engines roared and the plane taxied out of the loading bay. A hand was raised at the cockpit window in salute. We returned the gesture and they were off, hurtling down the runway.

The loaded lorries left for Ihioma. Two more were held in reserve. A Constellation had landed and was parked in the government bay. There was an air of purposeful activity around it though little sign of cargo. A cavalcade drove on to the tarmac. The leading Mercedes flew the pennant of Biafra. I looked over at Vincent. He nodded, mouthing the word 'Ojukwu'. If he was right, the end had indeed come. It was a thought-filled moment.

Our musings were suddenly interrupted by a plane roaring out of the sky fast and low. There was a scattering of feet; it was a relief plane, a DC6 twisting in a tight circle, coming in low again, obviously asking for landing lights. There were none.

"They've lost contact. I'll go and see what's happening."

Base control knew what was happening but were in no hurry. "We will have lights shortly."

I insisted. A plane was trying to land, one of ours, a relief plane. We could hear the roar of its engines as it circled low.

The radio operator looked up and smiled patiently. "Soon we will give him lights." They were obviously acting under orders. "Have a brandy, my friend."

The bottle had been well broached. There was an air of false merriment about the place. I took the proffered glass and saluted them. They were brave men. I knew the fear that lay behind the laughter.

On the way back I was stopped at the approach barrier. There were important documents to be delivered to His Excellency; could I give one of their men a lift to the airstrip? I did so and dropped him at the final barrier.

Progress beyond that point was difficult. The French had arrived and with them: chaos, utter chaos. The landing strip, the sacred landing strip, barred to anything but aircraft and an occasional authorised vehicle was a miniature, compacted Place de la Concorde. I stared in amazement: motor cars, open tops, lorries were everywhere.

The Constellation had left. The landing lights were on. Our cargo plane had landed; I could see its tailplane rising high above the surging, blaring chaos of vehicles.

A Renault open top blocked my way. I blew the horn long and loud. The blaring was lost in the din and confusion around us. I blew again, longer and louder. Again nothing happened; the little bald-headed Frenchman at the wheel sat there. I revved the engine and edged forward till we were nose to tail, bumper to bumper, blasted on the horn and yelled. I was jammed on all sides, a green military vehicle pressing behind me. I felt a wave of deep indignation and of resentment: the controlled calm of the evening, the nightly discipline of the airstrip, the restraint, the harmony, had been rent asunder by this invasion.

Suddenly there was a hammering on the side window of the car. The face of a soldier, contorted in rage, was framed in the glass. I lowered it a little. He was yelling: "Move this car. Move! Move! Move!" All the frustration, the agony and the anger of the night was in his roaring. "Move!"

My own anger and frustration burst out, shouting above the roaring of engines and the din around me: "I'll move when this fat bastard gets out of the way." I turned, jamming down on the horn, revving the engine, yelling. There was a sound of smashing glass and an agonising blow across my windpipe. I turned sharply. An automatic pistol was pointed at my forehead. The face of the soldier behind it was even more contorted. There was deep venom in his snarl: "Nobody calls me a black bastard."

Suddenly a hand, a gentle white hand pushed the gun down: "There has been enough killing."

A gap had been created. I drove through and across to the perimeter, switched off the engine, laid my head gently on my arm on the wheel and sighed a long deep sigh. I owed my life to the wife of Colonel Achuzie.

The chaos on the airstrip seemed to be resolving itself. I struggled over to the plane. The pilot wanted to know what was going on. I signed his manifest. "French are here. Evacuation." Already the cargo was being offloaded, sacks of cornmeal dumped onto the tarmac. "Can you take them?"

"If they're quick."

A high-sided diesel truck had arrived, nosing its way through the throng. The driver was looking for the Libreville plane.

"What's in the truck?"

"Look."

I climbed up onto the cab and peered over the side: babies, dozens and dozens of them wrapped in blankets against the dry-season cold, whimpering. The French had evacuated their orphanage and were taking the children with them to their base at Libreville.

I climbed down. "Driver, that's a Caritas plane over there. He'll take you to Sao Tomé. They've a hospital."

"But we must go to Libreville. You will ask the pilot."

I shook my head: "Sao Tomé. No problem. After, Libreville."

The pilot concurred. "We must start loading straightaway." We started. The lorry was driven up to the open hatch. I knelt on the cab roof and handed the babes from the trailer to willing, gentle hands at the cargo hatch. It was traumatic work: I could feel the little bones beneath the rough and scabrous skin. Little eyes stared up at me with frightened trust. I worked with tears running down my face.

The last little child was handed in. I clambered down. An aeroplane was in the sky, was landing and was whining up the runway towards us.

"Stand by, lorries!" I ran over to the plane. The pilot I did not recognise. "Caritas?"

He shook his head.

"What's your cargo?"

"Ammunition."

"You're joking."

"Government order."

"There isn't any government. The war's over. Take your cargo away. We don't want it. Be quick. The Feds are almost here."

"I've been paid to deliver this cargo. I've delivered it. Sign this manifest and let me get the hell out of here!"

"I'll sign your manifest. You take your cargo and dump it in the ocean."

I was too late; the cargo hatch was open; urgent exchanges were taking place between the French and the cargo handler. Bundles of uniforms were pounding onto the tarmac followed by box upon box of arms and ammunition.

"What the hell's going on?"

"This man says he will take us to Libreville when we unload his plane."

"Do you know what this cargo is?"

"Yes."

"And the children?"

"They will come."

Already the babes were being offloaded from the JointChurch plane and relayed to the arms carrier. I stared in disbelief and walked away.

Our own plane had unloaded its relief cargo, picked up a few last-minute passengers and taxied into position. I watched as it roared down the runway and lifted into the night sky. I watched its afterburners as the plane tilted over Uli steeple and headed for the coast.

The ammunition-plane was loaded; cargo doors were slammed, engines revved and it was off.

I watched as it soared above us with its precious cargo. They had been a heroic band doing sterling work in their camps and clinics and hospital, faithful to the very last minute, almost beyond, independent of the vacillating policy of their government. Their going was an echoing hammer blow. There was a silence on the airstrip.

Vincent had been supervising the offloading. He came over and joined me staring balefully at the pile of arms and ammunition.

"Lorries gone. Last load I reckon."

"That's it."

"What about this?" He indicated the arms dump.

"Not our problem. Let's go."

I looked along the length of the airstrip, silent in the moonlight, deserted. Where planes had roared and lorries had revved, guns had hammered in the night sky and bombs had fallen, now there was silence. The tailplanes of the wrecked aircraft towered above the tangled vegetation at the side, mute testimony of all that had been. I turned the key in the ignition and we drove off, up the approach path and through the roadblock. It was deserted.

33

Alone

Sunday, the 11th of January. The day started with Mass, quiet and prayerful though the words of comfort spoken by the priest were hard to come by. A jet flew overhead in the silence of the Thanksgiving. The guns barked ineffectively; no one moved; the people were drained of panic. We stood outside the little chapel after the service in the chill harmattan breeze and listened to the gunfire now ominously close.

"God will protect us." A young girl standing close whispered the words with heart-felt faith. I put my arm on her shoulder: "We will pray that he does."

Orlu had become command headquarters. Lieutenant-General Effiong, as senior military man in Ojukwu's absence, had assumed command and set up base in our school. The compound thronged with troops, numbers growing as units regrouped in the face of the Federal advance: Third Marine Commando, moving up from the south, Second Brigade from the west, the Northern Army pushing rapidly down from the north. We were surrounded, in the eye of the storm.

Norbert was concerned for his orphans. The purposeful activity on the compound: movement of troops, yelling of commands, revving of engines, piling of arms, suggested battle preparation. If there was to be a last stand, Orlu could be the scene and we were in the heart of it.

Business went on as usual, however; the children had to be fed. Fires hissed and sparked, cooking pots bubbled, food was distributed. I slept lightly during the activity of the morning. It had been a draining night at the airstrip; it was late afternoon when I awoke. Norbert had returned from his tour of the feeding centres and clinics. After a late lunch I went with him to check on the hospital at Amaigbo. In direct line of the Federal advance from the northern sector, the hospital had been evacuated. Norbert was making a final check. I went with him. The road was crowded with refugees moving in front of the advancing Federal army. Among them were soldiers, fleeing from danger into danger. We were driving against the tide.

The guard at the hospital entrance warned us that looters were about. I went to check on the wards. Norbert drove up to the convent. There was little sign of looting at the hospital; supplies had been distributed to the clinics in the interior; the food store was empty and open. The convent was a different proposition. A crowd of looters were pressing forward. When I arrived I found Norbert holding the fort, flanked by an armed guard.

"Go back! Go back!" I could hear the roar of his voice as I approached. "If to say you want chop come to Orlu; I go give you. Here there is no chop. Leave this place and go."

The crowd edged nearer. He was confronted not by hungry refugees but by greedy looters. "Go back!" His Scottish hackles were bristling. "Back!" he yelled. The guards were powerless; their automatics futile. The crowd were used to guards, to guns, to barriers. They edged forward, pushing against the bamboo fence. Norbert lunged, grabbed the rifle from the hands of a startled guard and with a yell that echoed the war cry of his highland ancestors, he charged the mob. They turned and fled. He went after them, yelling, brandishing his weapon, down the pathway, round the hospital building, out of sight.

He returned alone, breathless, shaking his head, laughing. "They'll be back. Not much we can do. It's their country after all." He looked around at the deserted compound: "Let's go." We went, joining the crowds surging towards Orlu, into the unknown and the shadows of night which were beginning to fall.

We sat over a quiet supper with the light of a shaded candle. Godwin had left; an eerie silence enveloped the house and the bush and forest beyond. Occasional bursts of distant gunfire accentuated the silence.

"I suppose the Federals are here."

"Could be down at the marketplace by now."

The gunfire was becoming more insistent.

"That sounds like Umuna. They must have gone down the tarred road."

"So it will be Orlu junction then Ihioma."

"Which will leave us out of the line of fire."

"Meantime. Depends what the troops here do. This could be a battleground."

The conversation had with it an element of the surreal, two schoolteachers discussing enemy tactics.

"What do you suggest we do?"

"I'm off to bed. It's going to be a long day tomorrow."

It had indeed been a long day, beginning in the early hours before dawn with that burst of heavy machine-gun fire, followed by the evacuation of the orphans. The staff meeting in Ihioma with the young Archbishop Arinze had been decisive. It marked the end of our involvement in thirty months of struggle, a struggle to feed the hungry, to harbour the homeless, to succour the sick and the wounded. As we stood in the school compound and watched Arinze's car making off in a cloud of dry-season dust, we knew that the end had indeed come. There was now nothing to do but wait.

Norbert spent the night in his makeshift orphanage, guard over his innocent charges. I spent the night alone in the schoolhouse, alone in the silence of the night with nothing but my memories and the occasional burst of gunfire in the surrounding palm bush to remind me of the reality of the situation. Towards dawn I slept.

34

Arrest

I was awakened by the sound of yelling and shouting. I leapt out of the armchair where I had dozed during the night, rushed downstairs, unbolted the door. A mob was attempting to break through the bamboo fence protecting the house. Godwin, armed with a stick, confronted them alone. I joined him.

This was a matter for the Chief. "Go over to Igwe, Goddy and get help."

I faced the mob. I was angry. The order, with the discipline and the restraint of all those months of hardship was breaking down in the face of defeat. I kept my voice level, loud but level: "My friends!" The noise died down. There was silence. "I think you are very hungry!"

"Ayi!" There was a shouted chorus of affirmation: "Too much!"

"I think you have suffered very much." Again there was loud agreement.

"Now I think our problems are coming to an end. The fighting now is over. No more war. No more air raids."

The crowd was listening quietly.

"If to say you give me chance I go for Okigwi-side I get lorry. I see my Brothers there. I get yam; I get rice; I get corn; I go bring-am here. Plenty. All go chop. Is that good?"

There was a yell of approval.

"If to say you do not give me chance; if to say you go try raid this compound so I no fit leave for go Okigwi-side, then . . ."

I paused for dramatic effect. The listening silence deepened.

"I go curse you!"

My voice rose in the utterance of my wrath. The eyes of the mob were upon me. I raised my hand.

"I go bring bell. I bring book. I bring candle. I go curse you! If to say juju curse be bad thing, Christian curse be bad pass juju long way."

The basis of my anathema was shaky but the effect was dramatic. There was a profound silence then a concerted muttering. The crowd broke. I stood my ground as I watched them retreat.

Godwin returned with a body of men and the compound was quickly cleared.

Norbert arrived and started offloading supplies. "So, we've the compound to ourselves now, Jimmy. We'll clear the technical block and get it ready for the orphans."

A young girl came running. She was crying, sobbing deeply: "You must come. Come with me." She grabbed my hand. I looked at Norbert. He

165

nodded. I ran after her as she hurried back, out of the compound, across the road, through the bush to a brick building set in its own compound. The door was open. The girl stood at the entrance and pointed, still panting, into the interior. I ventured into the shuttered gloom. The smell was intense. A faint murmuring could be heard, then I made out the forms of the little children, many little children, lying on the concrete floor. I walked carefully through them and opened a shutter. Light streamed in and revealed the nightmare: the blood, the urine, the vomit. I had ventured into a baby clinic deserted in the panic and flight.

Norbert had followed. Despite the months of tragedy he had witnessed, his face reflected the horror of the scene. "Go quickly. Get blankets. You will find them in the truck. Send them over. Start cleaning the technical block. Clear it. The women should be there. Swill the place out. Be very, very quick." He was opening the shutters. I sprinted back.

The technical block was open; we found a key for the woodwork room. Many hands had arrived, eager to help. We started ripping down the palm-branch camouflage lining the outside walls. The women arrived with their buckets and brooms, aghast at the extravagance of our gesture. Then the realisation dawned that air raids would be no more and a feeling almost of gaiety descended. Benches were carried out, water was brought, swilled across the concrete floor, brooms were put to work, sweeping the water with the dust and the dirt of months out through the open doors, the women chanting as they worked.

As the last of the palm fronds were pulled away, light flooded into the long, low room. The low rhythmic chant burst into full song; the women were dancing, caught up in the euphoria of the moment. No more aeroplanes, no more war. I found myself dancing step by step with an old mama to the accompaniment of clapping and song and laughter. Beds were carried in, set up in neat rows, the women and helpers working with a merry will. Then Norbert arrived with the babies.

There was silence. His small army of nurses, their tight little bundles of humanity tenderly wrapped in blankets against the cold breeze, waited while we positioned the beds and covered the mattresses with blankets. The babies were laid gently on the beds. More were arriving. Work continued quietly, the women subdued by the sight of suffering in our midst. More beds were brought; more babies were carried over.

We needed extra room. The adjoining wing was locked. Godwin appeared with a bundle of keys. The door creaked open. We stared in amazement. In the dim light filtering through the shuttered windows we saw something that could spell serious trouble: from floor to ceiling, the room was packed with arms and ammunition. We had opened up the armoury.

I went back to Norbert. He glanced up from his task of inserting a saline-drip needle into the temple vein of a small child. "Are you all right?"

I explained the situation. The drip was attached. He straightened. "We'll need to tell Igwe. He would need to take charge of that. If the weapons fall into the wrong hands there could be real trouble. Will you go over?" I nodded.

I told Godwin to relock the door of the arms room and bring the key of the car. I glanced round the room, now glistening in its freshness, rows of beds neatly arranged, each with its pathetic bundle being gently cared for. Now we were in business. Now the work of relieving pain and sickness and hunger could go on unhindered. My heart rose.

Godwin returned with the key. I told him to stay; I would go alone. As I made to leave the room, a small girl lying on a bed near the door held up her tiny bony arm. I stopped. Her large eyes looked into mine and her parched lips moved. I bent to listen. Her words were whispered through pain: "*Biko, agurum miri.*" (Please, I am thirsty.) I called a girl over and told her. I had to leave. Things were urgent. I left, glancing back at the little child, the cup held gently to her lips.

Igwe was in council with his men seated in a silent circle. I greeted them; they returned my greeting solemnly. It was a solemn moment in our lives.

"Igwe, we have a serious problem."

He was listening. All were listening. I informed them about the cache of arms and ammunition lying unguarded in the school across the road, the danger of their falling into the wrong hands, the danger of the Federal troops arriving and finding them in our hands.

There was a silence as all pondered the situation. The Chief spoke: "Brother, what do you suggest?"

"Igwe, I think you know that the Federal troops are at the market crossroads."

"We know, Brother."

"If to say they come here and find these arms, there will be much palaver."

All agreed. There was a general nodding of heads. There was a silence. I felt all eyes upon me.

"I think somebody should go down to the crossroads and inform the Federal troops."

The wisdom of my suggestion was seen by all. The wisdom of pre-empting the situation, of avoiding accusations of active collaboration, the wisdom of someone going down to the marketplace, confronting the Federal troops and bringing back a detachment was seen and approved of. Who was to go? The chief looked round his men. There was no rush to volunteer; there was no volunteer. There was a silence. Eyes turned to me. I had made the suggestion.

"Igwe, if to say you ask me to go, if to say I go with your approval and that of your council-men, I will go to tell the Federals."

Approval was immediately accorded, heartily. We stood. There was a solemn shaking of hands, a murmuring of good wishes. I took my leave.

The road to the market was a lonely one. Little knots of villagers were gathered at intervals but, unwontedly, no hand was raised in greeting. The car shuddered along over the dry-season corrugations, raising a little cloud of dust. I felt a sharp pang of nerves as I approached the outskirts of the market area. I stopped the car and switched off the engine. I sat in the silence quietly collecting my thoughts, muttered a short prayer, let in the clutch and drove forward.

I saw them before they saw me, the military roadblock alive with purposeful activity. Cars were being marshalled into line. A soldier turned, saw me and yelled. An officer whipped round, pistol levelled. He walked towards the car.

"Get out!"

I got out.

"Get away from your car! Move!" I moved.

"Give me your pistol. Raise your hands! Raise them, I say. Your pistol!"

I said I had no pistol.

"You are a mercenary."

I was wearing my soutane. "Missionary."

"Same thing. One of Ojukwu's men."

"I am employed by the Roman Catholic Mission. I have been working for Caritas International. I am a British citizen."

"Caritas, Hah! Palaver people!" He had seen the sign on the side of the car. "Get back in your vehicle."

"Excuse me, I . . ."

"Get back in your car. Now!"

I got back in the car. A soldier joined me. He sat, cradling a sub-machine gun on his knee. "Drive on."

"I have something to say . . ."

"Drive on, I say. Drive!" The gun was pointed at me; I drove on.

I joined the queue of waiting vehicles, all, I presumed, similarly commandeered. A small crowd was gathered around. They were waving little plastic Nigerian flags self-consciously. I recognised the manager from the United Carpenters Workshop. I caught his eye. He came over, leaned in and touched my arm. "Sorry for you, my friend." He rejoined the throng. It was a brave gesture.

"Drive on." The convoy was moving. I followed at the tail end, through the roadblock and on to the road to Owerri. A Saladin armoured car stood over the checkpoint, protective and menacing. I gave it a glance of futile contempt.

"Drive on. Keep up." The pace was brisk. Army trucks passed us filled with troops in full battle-kit, jubilant, shouting greetings to their roadside companions. I heard snatches of song. The light of victory was strong about them.

We stopped at the Njaba Bridge. There had been a battle. Corpses, stripped and bloating, littered the side of the road. I felt a deep, deep sadness at the thought of the futility of it all. A darkness and a depression was settling over me. I was alone, cut off, as defenceless as the corpses about me: a lone white face in a sea of jubilant, triumphant black.

The delay at the roadblock enraged my guard. His indignation was vented in snatches: "Hah, these men! What they think they do?" He, a member of the front-line spearhead, being stopped and questioned by these rearguard amateurs. "Move on. Move on, I say." I moved on, through the barrier, ignoring the raised hand of the guard and into the line now speeding towards Owerri.

The pace slowed to walking as we edged forward in the crowds of vehicles heading towards the centre. A column of troops was marching against us. A number turned as they passed, some with a look of unmistakable contempt, others with a more kindly expression. A number, as I stopped, bent and whispered a word of comfort.

An army command post had been established at Texaco corner. We stopped. My guard got out to report. I watched him speaking to an officer. They walked over. I stepped out of the car and stood at the door. The officer approached, his hand outstretched. He welcomed me, asked me briefly how I was and called over an orderly who left and appeared with a bottle of beer, ice-cold. The captain apologized for the lack of glasses and wished me good health. I sipped the beer gingerly. It was late afternoon and I had not broken my fast.

The officer turned out to be a Catholic, willing to talk and curious, somewhat resentful of the stance that the Church had taken during the conflict. He was also concerned about conditions in the interior.

I assured him that according to all that I had seen, the civilians appeared to be unmolested; indeed I was able to congratulate him on the professional attitude and bearing of his troops and fellow officers, firm but just. He was genuinely pleased, said so and left to deal with some matter that demanded his attention. I gave the rest of the bottle to my guard who took it with delight and sauntered off.

I knew my compliments were correct but superficial. The ubiquitous line of refugees was shuffling past. An old couple stopped to rest by the car. They were tired, very tired. They had walked many miles and still had far to go. I quietly offered them money. I had a bag of Nigerian shillings hidden in the car. The old man shook his head. "No use. The soldiers will take them from us at the next checkpoint." They shuffled on, heads bowed beneath their meagre loads.

Another officer joined me. Despite the bustle and activity about us, the movement of troops and roar of engines, there appeared an inner calm and control that was the fruit of victory. The officer introduced himself, telling me he was from the First Army. His vehicles were on the road opposite. He indicated them guardedly. A line of jeeps stood waiting. The officer, it transpired, knew the Brothers in Okigwi. He asked me if I would like to join them. I said I would, most gratefully.

"Sit in your car. Watch that line of vehicles. When you see the first one move, switch on your engine and follow."

I thanked him quietly and he sauntered over to his mobile detachment. I got back into the car. Things were indeed looking up. The draught of beer had helped to lift the depression, the offer of escort and the promise of rejoining Frank and Harry and James in Uturu that night raised my spirits to the heights. A feeling of relief and optimism filled me with a gentle euphoria. I was watching the lead vehicle with grim intent. Its engine started. I put my fingers to the ignition key ready to turn it when, without warning, a great brown hand descended, covered mine and firmly drew the key from the lock. I turned and looked. A large brown face wreathed in a broad grim smile was framed in the open side window of the car. I recognised the red cap band and the insignia of the Nigerian military police. I was confronted by a provost of the same. His grim smile broadened: "You are going nowhere, my friend. Get out."

I got out.

The height of the provost towered above me. He put out his hand; I handed over the keys of the car. "Stand there. Do not move. Do not move." He signalled to a military policeman who sauntered over, automatic pistol slung carelessly over his shoulder. He took up his stance. I had no intention of moving. "Search this vehicle. Proper." The provost left.

I stood as the soldier went through the car. I knew what he would find. I was in no mood to care. I watched the northern vehicles beginning to drive off; I watched them fade into the gathering dusk.

A deep depression was once more beginning to descend upon me.

35

Detention

The provost was back. He was in a cheerful mood. His man had come across the bag of coins: one hundred pounds in Nigerian shillings.

"You know it is not legal for you to have such money. You could have big palaver. This I will keep safe for you, my friend; I will give you receipt."

He muttered something to his driver who took the money and deposited it in his car, a Peugeot estate, presumably also in 'safe keeping'.

"Get in." The provost's manner was brisk. "Follow me." I sat back behind the wheel. My military guard eased himself in beside me, still cradling his automatic.

"Go!"

I went, the little Volks nosing its way among the maze of military vehicles crowding the area.

"Keep close. Go more fast."

I had difficulty following the car ahead, but eventually we were out of the tangle of traffic and heading south. The sun was setting. We were driving into a darkening land.

"Keep going." My captor was insistent.

It was dark now; I was following the tail lights of the car ahead, bumping over the rutted road, through the sunset into black night, headlights stabbing the darkened forest we were cutting through. The road wound down to the river, to the bridge of which dark tales were told, tales in the early days of the conflict, of bloodshed, Northern blood. The car I was following stopped. I stopped. I switched off the engine and waited in the sudden silence. Below I could hear the dark waters of the Imo tumbling over rocks.

The provost eased himself out of his vehicle. In the dim car lights I watched him approach. One hand was hidden in his tunic grasping something bulky. With his free hand he motioned me to get out of the car. I did so. The guard was out, his automatic levelled at my head. We were alone, in the darkness, on the bridge.

"Move!" The guard indicated with his weapon. I walked slowly towards the provost. He was watching me as I approached, his face, shadowed in the light, expressionless. Slowly he drew his hand from his tunic. I closed my eyes. A feeling of great loneliness swept over me. I felt something pushed against my chest.

"Take some; it's not poison."

My eyes snapped open. In the provost's hand was a bottle, a brandy bottle; he was pressing it upon me. I took it from him. I put the bottle to my lips. I could feel myself trembling. I took a gulp of the brandy, the hot liquor coursing through me.

"Take more." The provost was insistent. "I said it wasn't poisoned. Look." He snatched the bottle from me and gulped a deep draught. "Let's go."

The game was over. The provost had had his fun. We were on the road again speeding towards Aba, mile after mile, past lines of shadowy refugees shuffling past us on the side of the road.

The car ahead stopped suddenly. I jammed on the brakes. The provost's driver was out. He blocked a family group in the line of refugees. I watched their stricken faces in the blazing headlights: a mother, a father, a girl and a young boy. The father was holding a bicycle. The soldier opened the tailgate of the Peugeot and motioned the man to put the bicycle in the car. He protested. The soldier walked up to him, slapped him savagely across the face, took the bicycle, stowed it in the boot and slammed the door. The family stood transfixed with horror. The soldier calmly opened the rear passenger door, walked back to the group, grabbed the girl and pushed her towards the car. The father rushed forward to intervene. The guard beside me was out of the car, his automatic levelled, stopping the man in his tracks. The girl was bundled into the car, the driver resumed his seat and they were off.

"Move!"

I sat motionless.

"Move, I say. Keep up." I heard the click of the safety catch. The car ahead had stopped. I drove off. I was ashamed, unclean.

We approached Aba and stopped at a bungalow on the outskirts of the town. The guard ordered me out, walked me to the entrance, muttered some words to the two soldiers at the door and left. One of the men opened the door and indicated that I should enter. The room was lit dimly by a kerosene lamp. A group were seated at a table. They looked up as I entered; their faces broke into smiles of welcome when they recognised me; three priests from our local seminary, in the same situation, I gathered, as myself. The warmth of their welcome was balm. They made room for me at the table and Martin brought in bread and ham and a flask of coffee. As I ate they plied me with questions. They had been arrested in the first incursion and were anxious to know of developments since. We shared what we knew.

My guard had returned: the provost wanted the keys of the Volkswagen. "Tell him he can't have them." John was laconic but decisive, "These vehicles are not ours to give."

The guard was quietly determined.

I intervened: "He can't go back empty-handed."

A compromise was reached: I was to go back with the car and explain to the provost that such vehicles were not our property. I was too tired to argue. I went.

We found the provost ensconced on the veranda of his house. An oil lamp shone above his head. In its light sat a group of girls. The soldier went across to relay the message.

He returned. "You must get out of the car."

I got out. The military police officer was standing on the steps of his veranda. The girls were watching him. He spoke for effect with great effect. He told me in stinging tones and rising volume that not only could he and would he take my car but he could and he might take a number of other things belonging to me of a much more personal nature. There was a ripple of nervous laughter from some of the girls. The soldier strode over, took the keys from my hand, motioned me back into the car, drove round to the bungalow, ordered me out and left. I walked into the room. They were waiting for me. I leaned against the wall and shook my head slowly. I was tired, very tired. A bed had been prepared on the couch. I took off my sandals, lay down and slept.

It was late the following afternoon before I woke.

"You're awake. Good man. You've had a grand sleep. You must have been tired."

I said I had been.

"You must be hungry."

I said I was. Food was brought. The money they had secreted, American dollars and Nigerian coins, proved invaluable. Martin had soft-talked his way past the guards at the door and made for the local market returning with bread and tinned ham, oranges, bananas, soft drinks and beer. A pot of tea was brewed.

"Indeed, our cup is flowing over," John held up his glass, "let us thank the Lord."

"Do you know why you were brought here, Jim?"

I shook my head.

"We needed a fourth for bridge."

I proved a lame partner but they were patient men, offering mild words of advice when I trumped an ace or unwittingly reneged.

We were about to start the second rubber when a girl entered the room She was a very beautiful girl and obviously very nervous. She stood for a while in silence then sat unbidden on the edge of a seat near the door.

The game continued in silence then John looked over: "Yes, Miss, can we help you? Do you want something?"

The girl's voice was low, shy: "The soldiers told me to come in here, Father."

"What did they say?"

"They said that you might need me."

"Are you hungry?"

"Yes, Father."

Martin came in from the kitchen with a plate of the food that had been left over and set it before her. The girl ate quietly with obvious relish.

When she had finished she stood: "I will wash this dish, Father."

"No, leave it. We can manage. Go well now, dear. God bless you."

"Thank you, Father." She left.

"What next?"

"Two no trump"

The game continued.

The following day dawned bright and clear. A delightful dry-season breeze was blowing through the house. Martin had been on his market expedition. We had fresh bread for breakfast and eggs and coffee. He had also procured a packet of washing powder. We sat in the small garden at the back of the house watching the laundry dry.

"Who's got something to read?"

Martin had *The Naked Ape*. He was harbouring it. A bundle of old *Time* magazines was unearthed. We spent a profitable morning catching up on world affairs. The guards at the door were friendly and polite, happy to arrange shopping for us. We had a pleasant lunch and retired for a siesta. I was beginning to feel richly human.

Evening was drawing in; we set up the table as an altar and Mass was celebrated. It was a prayerful service. Despite the comparative comfort of our surroundings we were keenly aware of the misery about us and dangers facing the men and women we had left in the remnants of the enclave. Our prayers were heartfelt.

Mass was just over when a vehicle pulled up at the door, then another, and another, a convoy, our friends from the interior. Norbert was there, and Lewis, Clara, Vincent and Jack with a score of others

Norbert was overjoyed to see me. He gave me a tight, unbelieving hug. "Jimmy!" I had been given up for dead, gunned down in a wayside ditch. Prayers had been offered for the repose of my soul. We were able to laugh but there were grim tales to be told.

"What about the orphans?"

Norbert shook his head. "Who knows? We were forced out. Even the nurses fled, went into hiding." He told me Anna's story: a particularly handsome girl, she would have difficulty getting past the roadblock between the orphanage and her home. Resourceful as ever, Norbert opened up his second-hand clothing store and supplied her with an ankle-length skirt, a loose-fitting blouse and a pillow to tie round her waist. Anna hobbled home in a state of advanced, instantaneous pregnancy.

With the flight of their nurses, the children were in a parlous state. When Norbert was arrested and driven out, the situation became unthinkable.

They had been rounded up at gunpoint. Dreams of continuing with the work, of relieving the suffering, feeding the starving, succouring the wounded, housing the homeless, were shattered with the arrival of the Federal troops.

There were many tales to tell and to share. Vincent told us of his being waylaid at a roadblock with a car load of sick children making for hospital. He was ordered out of the vehicle. A soldier drove off with the car and the children.

Back at Ihioma the situation had taken on a Kafkaesque quality. The military had assumed command. The major was at breakfast. Conversation at the table, stilted, diplomatic on the part of the community, was interrupted by a commotion outside the dining room. A soldier stamped in, saluted and reported the arrest of a suspect saboteur. "What thing now!" the major stood up, wiped his lips, threw down his napkin and followed the soldier out of the room. A few mumbled words could be heard through the louvered windows. There was a moment of silence then the deafening report of a high-calibre handgun. The major re-entered, holstering his gun, sat and resumed his meal. Conversation, Lewis assured me, was even more stilted.

We were moved on the next day, into convoy under guard to Port Harcourt. Our destination was the Cedar Palace Hotel. If Aba market had provided us with certain comforts, our Port Harcourt accommodation was luxurious beyond dreams. We were under loose house arrest. Money was made available by the Catholic Secretariat. The food was good; the beer was cold; the Lebanese management friendly and helpful. We were even allowed out under loose guard. Lewis organised a football match with the staff in the cool of the evening. After supper we sat in the carefree, pleasant atmosphere of the lounge watched over by an ever-attentive bar staff and we laughed and chatted and joked with nothing but our memories to spoil the illusion.

The calm of the atmosphere was suddenly disrupted by the entry of a German, a young lad. He had been upcountry. He had seen conditions, the misery, the starvation, and the neglect. What were we going to do about it? His voice quivered into near hysteria. The tears in his eyes told the whole story. We sympathised; we knew even more graphically than he how bad things were. At the point when our experience and resources could have made such a difference in the now war-free area, we had been ousted. What could we do? The 'professionals' were taking over, those who had watched from the sideline uninvolved during those thirty months of starvation and suffering, innocent of aiding the stricken, innocent in the eyes of the Federal government. There was a bitterness in our thoughts. Some of those professionals were sharing the lounge with us, sipping their ice-cold drinks.

The next day we were visited by the CID. We were interrogated individually. I had been assigned a novice member of the force. His questions were reasonably to the point but his transcription of my answers was slow and laborious. He could have been one of my Third Year English language students. I offered to do the writing for him. He was pleased. I wrote out a statement. He read it quietly, seemed reasonably happy and offered to read it to me. I pointed out that I had written it.

The following day the senior officers arrived. They had their agenda. I was assigned to one for interrogation.

"You are British?"

"Yes."

"Caritas?"

"Catholic Mission."

"You worked for Biafra."

"I was employed by the Catholic Mission, Owerri Diocese."

"You were working for Ojukwu."

"I was working for the people with whom we were living."

"I see from your papers that you have been to Sao Tomé."

"Yes."

"Many times."

"A number of times."

"With whose permission?"

"Permission?"

"Which immigration authority?"

"State House."

"Which State House?"

"Biafra."

"There is no such thing as Biafra. You understand? There is no such thing!" His voice was loud.

I nodded in acquiescence.

"How could you enter Nigeria without permission of the Federal Immigration Office?"

I said I couldn't.

"But you came?"

"I came."

"You realise that is an offence?"

"It was unavoidable."

"It was illegal."

"Biafra had declared itself a sovereign state."

My interrogator jumped up and glared down at me, yelling: "There is no such place as Biafra. I have told you so. You entered Nigeria without permission of the immigration authority. You had no work permit. You accepted employment. You are guilty on two counts."

"But I have explained . . ."

"Explained! There is no explanation my friend. Look at this!" He opened my passport and stabbed at the Biafran entry permits: "Guilty! Guilty! Guilty! You are an illegal immigrant. A persona non grata."

A lorry was waiting at the hotel entrance. We were given minutes to collect our belongings and hustled down. There were over thirty of us, priests, nuns and brothers, crammed into the truck. Police outriders roared alongside, in front, behind us, racing through the township.

The truck stopped, the tailboard was slammed down; we were ordered out. We found ourselves outside the massive doors of Port Harcourt prison. A guichet opened and we were marched through into the prison yard. The door slammed behind us. We heard the bolts crash into place.

36

Trial

We were not expected. The Governor was not a happy man. He told us so. Remand quarters were not available. We felt almost apologetic at our intrusion.

Intense activity took place while we waited in the prison yard: doors unlocked, brooms and mops noisily set to work, fatigue prisoners bustled, beds arranged.

The nuns were eventually accommodated in married quarters; the men were marched into the warders' recreation room. Conditions were spartan; there was no suggestion of food forthcoming; the beds were bare but at least we were not in the prison proper. Also there were no airport duties, no guns barking, no planes trying to land, no lorries with broken tyres; I lay down and I slept.

I gathered next morning that I had missed a great deal of excitement during the night: Lewis and Vincent escaped. They made their way through the married quarters, out through the back of the prison and on to the hotel. There they had loaded up with bread and drinks, soap and towels, enlisted discreet help and made their way back to the prison where they were received with delight by their fellow prisoners and relief by the warders. The warders' relief, however, was short-lived. Irishmen do not take kindly to injustice. Many an Irish rebel song was sung lustily and with feeling into the early hours of the morning. Even the nuns in the far-away family quarters complained about the noise.

More food arrived during the morning, a cooked breakfast organised by the Irish attaché who, at some personal risk, had undertaken responsibility for our well-being. We had a lot to thank him for.

News arrived shortly after breakfast that we were due in court; a mere formality, our warders assured us, prior to deportation back to our homes. We were whisked round to the courthouse in army trucks and handed our charge sheets. They were all more or less the same. We read them with some amusement not unmixed with a certain trepidation: 'The Federal Government of Nigeria versus James Malia', mine read. I was accused of having entered the country unlawfully and accepted employment without written permission of the Chief Federal Immigration Officer.

"Plead guilty," Jack instructed us; "it's a technical ploy to get us out of the country. The Secretariat will pay the fine and we'll be home for the All-Ireland."

He was right, to an extent. The charge was read; the prosecutor said a few condemnatory words; the judge asked the defendant if he or she had anything to say. Little was said; the sentence was passed: fifty pounds fine and deportation; prisoner to be under house arrest until the fine was paid and transport out of the country was arranged. There were a few hitches: Lewis pleaded not guilty as did also Vincent. They were remanded for trial. One defendant pleaded that he was only 'technically' guilty. The judge assured him there was no such plea as 'technical' guilt. The defendant accepted the charge, was fined and sentenced to deportation.

An elderly priest did have something to say before sentence was passed. His own parish had been in the region where we were being tried, the Rivers State. For many years he had worked with the people of that area. When the fighting broke out and had approached his parish, the people had been forced to move. He had moved with them, away from the shellfire and the threat of violence into the interior. He had moved with them many times under such threat, always in front of the guns, caring for his people, arranging shelter and supplies, succouring the sick, the babes, the aged, attending to their spiritual needs. He spoke well, from the heart, the simple facts. The judge, himself a Rivers-man, was affected. He did impose the now familiar sentence of deportation but he reduced the fine to ten pounds.

The irony, the injustice of it all was beyond plea.

Things were going well from the point of view of the prosecution, indeed too well. The prosecutor was getting bored. There was little need to press his case. The strategy of submission on the part of the defence had deprived him of the opportunity to use his skill. Then an opportunity arose: the defendant had worked on Uli airstrip. We all knew what Uli airstrip was used for: guns and ammunition, supplies for the rebel army. Under cover of bringing in relief to the starving this 'reverend' gentleman was, in effect, nothing better than a common gunrunner. There was a shocked silence in the court. Then one of the accused, a young Irish priest, boiling with rage, sprang to his feet, "Shame!" he yelled, his voice shaking with anger, "and again I say, shame!"

The placid proceedings had been torn asunder. The judge looked through his little spectacles in genuine amazement. Jack was on his feet, his hand to the shoulder of his confrère, gently forcing him to his seat. The judge banged on the desk with his gavel. He stared at the offending priest: "Would you," he asked rhetorically, "would you make such a protest, use such violent language, in a court in your own native land, in a court in Dublin?" Little he apparently knew, thoughts ran, of courts in Dublin but this was no time for argument. Jack spoke up. He apologised unequivocally for the outburst, accepting that it was completely out of order, submitting that the ordeal of the past few days, indeed of the past months, had in fact been the cause of the outburst rather than present circumstances. The judge considered for a moment then looked up. He said he would accept the apology adding that it was timely; it had saved the culprit from a charge of contempt of court and the consequences of that would have been most serious.

Order and a nervous calm appeared to have been restored. The judge turned to Father O'Connor, the accused, waiting patiently in the dock. The judge had heard the case for the prosecution. He intended taking the unusual circumstances revealed by the prosecution into account when considering sentence. Indeed he had already done so. He referred briefly to his notes then spoke out firmly: "Six months' hard labour, both counts, sentences to run concurrent. Next."

Father O'Connor sat down in an atmosphere of stunned silence. Behind me I heard a nun quietly weeping. The next man was in the dock. There was no such grave charge to place against him but illegal entry was sufficient: "Six months' hard labour." The cases were got through with injudicious speed: charge, plea, and sentence. The nuns were fined and sentenced to deportation; the men were given six months in hard labour.

My own case caused a little stir, giving the prosecutor an opportunity to display his rhetoric, bringing against me in effect the same charge laid before my co-worker on the airport: I was a collaborator, an importer of arms, an aider and abetter of rebellion. The judge asked me if I had anything to say before sentence was passed.

I had thought of what I would say. The words of Saint Matthew were ringing in my head: 'You will be dragged before magistrates and governors for my sake'. I spoke with all the eloquence I could muster; I spoke the facts, the bare facts, the true and simple facts. I spoke with some emotion of the work we had been involved in, the simple, urgent work of feeding the hungry, tending the sick, housing the homeless. I spoke of the utterly scrupulous way in which we had avoided any tinge of involvement in the politics of the affair, much more so the mechanics of warfare. I spoke from the heart and at some length. All the while the judge sat at his desk, head bowed, writing.

I stopped. There was a pause.

The judge looked up: "Finished?"

I said I was.

"Six months' hard labour, both counts, concurrent. Next."

We were bundled back into the army trucks and sped through Port Harcourt. Those sentenced to a fine and deportation were escorted to the hotel where they were to be held under arrest pending deportation. We were driven back to prison.

Not for us now the spartan comfort of the outer quarters but bolted doors and locked gates into the prison itself, into a barbed-wire compound and more locked doors.

We had been ritually searched, our possessions taken from us, noted and signed for. There were over twenty-four of us. The operation had taken some time.

It was late evening before we were marched into the inner compound. A double cell afforded accommodation, twelve bunk beds, two latrine buckets and one small window. Protests were vain; the governor was not available. Food was not available. The warders were apologetic, embarrassed, and helpless. Besides, we were no longer in remand; we were prisoners, common, criminal prisoners. We had been given numbers to prove it: I was P1750. The doors were slammed and bolted.

The discipline borne out of training came to the fore. Sleeping areas were assigned; latrine arrangements agreed upon; silence was enjoined. We lay down in the darkness on the bare metal beds and eventually we slept.

37

Imprisonment

Early next morning we were commanded into the presence of the prison governor. The warders had their instructions: we were to be marched into the presence. Commands were barked: "Quickly! Quickly!" We shambled into line. Nobody was in a hurry; everybody felt rather awkward about it, warders included; after all: grown men!

We ambled along to the governor's office. We ambled in. The governor was waiting for us. He was not amused. He stood. He was a short man but he had a strong voice. He began by yelling at us and got steadily louder. We were to understand this and we were to understand it well: we were prisoners, common criminal prisoners, in his prison, under his command. When we were given a command we would obey it and we would obey instantly. Was that understood? We said it was, more or less. Secondly: Biafra was no more; did we understand that? There was a shrugging of shoulders. Did we understand? Yes, we had no problem with that; why should we? Thirdly, as common prisoners, we were not entitled to privileges. We were common, criminal prisoners, we were to be treated as such. Any complaints?

"Yes." The governor glared along the line.

"What?"

"Accommodation."

That was being seen to; the matter was in hand.

"What about food?" Jack was insistent.

"Your food can be brought from outside. There are some of your people in detention who can look after you. Arrangements have been made. ATTENTION!"

The sudden barked command gave us something of a start but produced little response. The two warders in attendance were obviously in a state of some discomfort. Two dozen men in clerical white, some of them large, some of them very large, were not an easy charge.

There was a slight hesitation then one of the seminary professors stepped briskly out of line, turned smartly, stamped to attention: "Right, you lot, let's have you! Eyes front, shoulders back, feet together, chins up. Dress that line. DRESS IT, I SAY! RIGHT . . .! Right turn! Forward march!"

We marched smartly out of the governor's office before his astonished eyes, arms swinging, chins up. "Left, right, left, right!" Warders scurrying to keep up. "LEFT . . . turn!" Through the gate, still swinging. "AND . . . halt!"

We found that we had been allocated a second double cell. A fatigue squad was sent in; beds were moved; cells were swept. We split ourselves into two groups. We had space. Within the barbed-wire enclosure was a grassed area. Tables and benches were set up. It was a pleasant dry-season morning; our spirits began to lift. Breakfast was brought in; spirits soared. The nuns had been hard at work: bacon and eggs, sausage, tomato, toast, coffee and tea. We sat as at a feast.

Lewis and Vincent had stood trial and were found guilty. Lewis's case was clear-cut: working day after day checking manifests, portioning relief, loading lorries, dispatching supplies, medicines to clinics and hospitals, food and clothing to refugee camps, clothing the naked, feeding the hungry: guilty, guilty, guilty! Six months' hard labour. Vincent's case was different; he had been on his way home to England on leave from Cameroon. He had simply slipped into Biafra to see how his Brothers were getting on and hoping maybe to give a helping hand. He'd been in the country for only a few days. His sentence was house arrest in the Cedar Palace Hotel prior to deportation. There he assumed the job of liaison. We found a note among the breakfast plates. Was there anything we wanted? An urgent message was sent back for a bible, a football and a pack of cards. They arrived with the evening meal.

Dinner over, we sat in conference. The months of hectic, demanding activity had produced a mindset; the day's rest we had enjoyed was much appreciated but if we were to face six months of incarceration with little obvious effort to organise us we must organise ourselves. There was no sign or threat of hard labour; we had not even been allowed to wash our own dinner dishes. Activity, mental and physical was therefore planned.

An update on matters ecclesiastical was seen as an urgent necessity; one of the priests admitted that the major source of information he had had on the recent Vatican Council was the Religion section in *Time* magazine. The three men from the seminary undertook to attempt to remedy the situation. Scripture study was added to the schedule along with proposed briefing and discussion on recent liturgical changes.

Three cooked meals a day after a diet of corned beef and flaked potatoes were more than enough. We sent word to our friends in detention to cut back to a late breakfast and an evening meal. Grateful though we were for their care and attention, little did we realise the intense work on the part of our detained friends even that involved. Vincent let it be known that all the hard labour was on the side of himself and the nuns under house arrest. A physical-fitness programme was proposed. Norbert was to devise and regulate the scheme. We rose from discussion with a feeling that the darkness of the clouds about us was indeed tinged with some silver.

That darkness was there, however. Mass was celebrated next morning. It was a lengthy service without the pressure of parish, school or feeding centres. There was even singing: strains of plain chant drifting across the prison walls. In the solemn prayer and thanksgiving afterwards, however, the reality of the situation about us rose painfully to mind: the people we had left, the tiny orphans abandoned to their fate, the little girl who had asked me for a cup of water, the refugees desperately trying to reach their home-place, Godwin and his helpers. What was happening to them under military command? I learned afterwards that our faithful steward did not fare well, arrested and beaten for collaborating with the White-men. We thought of the priests and nuns and helpers still at large, the work they were engaged in brought to a sudden halt, the relief programme interrupted, the hungry, the sick, the careworn left abandoned. We looked beyond our wire fencing and saw the cruelty meted out to some of our fellow prisoners. We offered them all to the Lord.

Breakfast arrived after Mass. It was a leisurely affair. Everything was leisurely, wonderfully therapeutic. We included a note of heartfelt appreciation in our clandestine communication link. Our attentive fatigue boys cleared away the dishes, and we were left to ourselves. Monastic training is an effective preparation for prison life. We had no difficulty in keeping ourselves busy. The desultory conversation after breakfast gave way to serious and intense discussion: scripture, church matters, liturgy, pastoral affairs. All very remote from the reality of the crisis about us in which we had been so deeply involved but very much part of the wider vision and circumstances that would greet us on eventual release.

Laundry followed. The two communal taps, the few buckets allocated and the washing powder sent in by our diligent liaison were put hard to work. Soutanes, dazzling white, socks, shorts and smalls fluttered on our makeshift line in the delightful dry-season breeze. Then our self-appointed sergeant major assumed command: up and out! On to the green, beneath the high prison wall. Norbert took over: arms stretching, knees bending, running on the spot, up down, up down, bend and stretch, bend and stretch. Old limbs creaked, pipe-smoking lungs wheezed. Higher, higher, lower, lower. The drill completed, a cold shower was a pleasant relief. A quiet hour followed. Books had been made available. Men walked in silent meditation, breviaries in hand behind barbed wire, deep in thought.

In the cool of the evening, dinner was brought in. Hidden in the pile of plates was a note from Vincent. News of our arrest and imprisonment had hit the world press: thirty-two priests of the Roman Catholic Mission locked up in Port Harcourt jail. It made good copy. We could imagine how this could be elaborated and the effect upon our friends. We sat over coffee after dinner and discussed the revelation and its possible implications.

Father Milo was concerned. Leaning back upon his bench against the prison wall, he lingered over the filling of his pipe: "Sure it isn't so much the hunger or the deprivation that's getting to me," he struck a match and held it over the bowl of the pipe, emitting a cloud of aromatic smoke, "it's the shame of it all. It's the family I feel for. A son of theirs locked up in prison walls. I can see them scurrying off to early morning Mass to miss the neighbours. God help them."

We knew, despite Milo's ironic humour, that there was a hidden deep concern for the concern the news would cause. I could imagine the effect the newspaper reports would have on my own father, his son locked up in an African jail. I could imagine the extent of the worry it would cause my sisters, the extent of their imaginings of the horror of the situation. I could feel a pang of guilt as I turned the pages of my Desmond Morris in the calm of the evening light.

Eight o'clock sharp we were ushered into our cells. Despite our protestations and promises not to escape, the warders were adamant; the doors were locked and bolted. A smokey oil lamp emitted a dull glow. It was sufficient for the bridge players. After the first night we had divided into two groups, bridge players being allocated to one cell. My prowess at the game had caused some alarm but my snoring guaranteed me a place at the table: if I didn't sleep I didn't snore. The stack was cut; the game commenced.

Despite the banter of the play and the keenness of the scoring, thoughts ran deep. The prospect of six months behind the wire was not appealing. To men who were used to intense activity: church building, school building, parish committees, sacred returns, baptisms and, latterly, the feeding, day by day, of the five thousand, relocating refugees, organising supplies, the enforced idleness was galling. What did the future hold?

There was a lessening of the monotony the next day. Vincent was allowed past the gatehouse. He was able to share with us the news that he had garnered from the press and fill in the details of the brief messages we had been receiving. The world press had indeed got hold of the basic facts. Bishop Whelan of Owerri and the remaining priests and nuns had been arrested, were in detention and were awaiting trial. General concern was uttered at the nature of our summary trial and imprisonment; various diplomatic agencies were at work on our behalf. The Vatican, because of the outrage felt on behalf of the Federal government over Pope Paul's mention of the fear of genocide, was hampered in its efforts to work on our behalf. The Catholic Secretariat based in Lagos, however, had been most supportive, morally and in practical measures, providing the financial assistance that allowed us to dine in such luxury.

We had further visitors the next day: Martin and Francis from Uturu. It was a joyful reunion. We had much to share with each other. Various priests from the missions in the area round about Port Harcourt were given permission to visit. The governor called to see us. He had softened. His attitude was friendly, conciliatory. We felt for him: his was an awkward task.

The prospect of the months stretching ahead became more daunting, as the days passed. March would usher in the rainy season. The carefree activities of the dry season would be curtailed. The thought of lying in our cramped and steaming cells with tropical rain hammering on the tin roof night after night was not pleasant.

Things, we knew, could have been worse, much worse. The glimpses we had of the punishments meted out to certain other prisoners were graphic proof of that. Despite the comparative comfort of our own imprisonment, however, the strain was beginning to tell. The rigid self-imposed discipline of the first days was beginning to prove irksome. Occasional, strongly controlled irritations began to be apparent. The confinement, the monotony were beginning to take their toll, the nights were long and dark; the latrine bucket smelled.

Into the second week the cells were opened earlier than usual. "Quickly! Quickly! Up, everybody!" Fatigue boys rushed in. The hectic work of cleaning the cells began. We were allowed time to shower and shave and then assembled in the yard: the governor appeared. He made a brief but thorough inspection of the area, mumbling instructions to the accompanying staff.

He turned to us as he was leaving: "Today the Attorney General of the Rivers State is coming to visit the prison. He will speak to you. He will ask you if you have any complaints." He eyed us in silence and left.

The Attorney General appeared shortly afterwards. He was accompanied by his entourage. He stopped at our compound, made a silent cursory inspection and stopped in front of us gathered on the lawn. He greeted us and asked us if we had any complaints.

Jack spoke up: as far as treatment in the prison was concerned, considering circumstances and the positive attitude of the staff, we had no complaints. The Attorney General seemed relieved. Jack continued: as far as our trial was concerned, that was a different matter. There were serious irregularities: the nature of the charges, the lack of legal support and the dismissal of extenuating circumstances.

Our advocate was cut short; the trial was not under discussion. The Attorney General with his entourage turned and marched off. We were left standing. Any small flowering of hope was crushed. There was a hurt silence. We moved off to await breakfast.

A sudden flurry at the gatehouse caught our attention. A warder was hurrying up the path. "Quickly! Quickly!"

"What?"

"They are waiting."

"Who?"

"Army lorry, at the gate. For you. You are going."

"Where?"

"To your homes."

"When?"

"Now. Quickly! Quickly! Collect your goods. Come to the gatehouse."

We needed no urging. There was a flurry of excited packing, the few goods we possessed quickly bundled. Scarcely a word was spoken lest the spell should break. We hurried down the path.

Norbert called me back. He was not to be hurried. He was making a last-minute check. "Jimmy."

I turned. He was holding a brass crucifix. "You forgot this."

It was the cross that I had worn around my neck night after dangerous night at Uli. He handed it to me: "Didn't do you any harm on the airstrip." I looked at him and smiled.

The lorries were waiting. We were bundled aboard, whisked round to the hotel where we picked up the detainees and out to the airport. A Fokker Friendship of Nigeria Airways was standing on the tarmac waiting for us.

38

Home

We flew to Lagos in the company of Brigadier Obasanjo. Whether this was coincidence or a policy decision we were not to know. In the circumstances we felt somewhat privileged: he it was who had in effect ended the war thus avoiding even longer pain and suffering. The sudden strike north from Aba, the capture of Owerri, the immediate, continued advance without the normal Federal digging in and reinforcing positions and the dash towards Orlu and Uli had broken all resistance and brought the war to its dramatic and decisive end. The acts of vandalism and cruelty we had witnessed: the commandeering of property – we had seen lorry loads of household furniture heading west – the abduction and presumed rape of young girls, the savage beating we had witnessed in Port Harcourt, these, horrifying though they were, were incidental to the situation. The fighting had ended; there was no genocide; the blockade was over; food supplies could come through normal channels and for this our military fellow passenger could take much credit.

Indeed the formality of the ending of the war was something of which Nigeria could well be proud. Although not accompanied by a ritual handing over of the sword, Lieutenant-Colonel Effiong's presentation of himself to President Gowon and the warmth of his reception along with the goodwill and optimism expressed on all sides augured well for the future, a far cry from the days of the mindless massacres which had occasioned secession and retaliatory attack.

Our flight had about it a feeling of surreal normality. The guards kept a discreet profile; conversation was low-key; normal service was maintained: we were offered a drink. The plane droned over the Niger into what but days before had been hostile territory: forest and creek, scattered villages and townships, all seemingly so very peaceful and normal as we flew above them.

We lost height rapidly over the creeks and landed abruptly in Ikeja. The airport bristled with troops. We were expected and we were watched. Control formalities were minimal; the army was in charge; we were bundled into trucks and driven round to the airport hotel and another world. Archbishop Aggy of Lagos was there to greet us. A meal had been prepared at which he presided. His welcome was heartfelt. We were deeply touched; we knew that our maverick activity beyond the Niger had caused the Church in Federal Nigeria deep embarrassment yet there was no resentment whatever in the Archbishop's words of welcome. Only love and sincere happiness at our release.

We were on our way the following morning. As the Boeing sped along the runway and lifted off above the palms and dust-covered roofs I looked down on the land I had come to love so well and wondered if I would ever return. The plane flew into the clouds, into mist and nothingness.

We landed in Geneva. The stopover had been planned. Our relief work during the crisis had been bound up with that of the World Council of Churches, a partnership that had been forged in a furnace of pain and suffering, danger and love, forming bonds which made an irrelevance of doctrinal differences. We were to visit their headquarters. The welcome we received was warm. Our shared service of thanksgiving and intercession was moving. Pope Paul had been to visit some time before. He had left his crosier as a sign of continuing friendship and respect. We shared his sentiments to the full.

Our next stop was Rome. The party split for the first time but only, we assured each other, temporarily. We were to report to our respective headquarters. Walter was there to greet us, with his friend and fellow worker, Ligabue. It was a joyful reunion. We were met at the Generalate with a warm welcome and a meal where the Frascati della Casa flowed freely into the night.

We had arrived in the midst of a General Chapter. The following day I was asked to address the delegates. Their interest in recent events and the prevailing situation was intense. I spoke in stilted French from a heart still full of the recollection of those recent events and the prevailing situation, and as I spoke the reality and the horror of those events came home to me with a force that made me realise they would be with me forever. The delegates listened in silence.

Happy Re-union

A Mass had been arranged in thanksgiving for our release and in intercession for the hungry and the suffering people we had left behind. Our friends from the prison joined us. They made an impressive sight, vested for the concelebration on the altar of the Chapel of the Mother House. We had a full congregation. The young people were there, members of Walter's youth club who had worked so hard in collecting funds for the starving of Biafra. Again I was asked to speak, this time in Italian. My knowledge of the language was restricted to the opening lines of half a dozen operatic arias but we worked hard. I wrote out the talk in French, Ligabue translated into Italian and we sat with a bottle of wine from the Alban hills laboriously going over the pronunciation until the early hours of the morning.

I told the young people that it was a great joy to thank them personally for the wonderful work they had been engaged in which helped so much to finance the relief which we had had the joy and privilege of distributing among the starving children in the forests of Biafra. A Mexican Brother had written the music for the Mass. As the guitars and drums struck up and the pure voices of the young people responded in strong and tuneful melody I was aware of the bonds of love the suffering of the children unseen in the forests of Biafra had miraculously engendered.

Pope Paul invited us to his home. He wanted to thank us personally for the work in which we had been engaged. As we clattered through the marble

Lewis receiving papal accolade

halls of the Vatican, through portals guarded by gentlemen in feathered hats and trailing swords, I felt how remote it was from the reality and the agony we had left. There was nothing grandiose, however, about the Pope himself. We were ushered into his private audience chamber. He came to greet us, a frail old pontiff, slightly stooped with the weight of the suffering of many on his shoulders. He spoke movingly to all assembled and briefly to each one of us. He gave us a medal and his blessing. Where was Des McGlade, I wondered? Where were Harry, Frank, James and Al? So many others who had worked so hard and long in conditions more dreadful than I had endured. I was with them in spirit but their absence was poignant.

Our stay at the Mother House was short. We were anxious to get home but before parting we arranged a meeting and a farewell service. The venue was discussed: not Saint Peter's, it was felt, but the catacombs, the underground passages carved out of the tufa rock beneath the city of Rome where the early Christians had hidden from persecution and where they had buried their dead. It was a moving ceremony, a quiet Mass in the dim shadows cast by candlelight, celebrated on a martyr's tomb. Our prayers of intercession were uttered with deep feeling, accompanied by an occasional gentle sob. We took leave of each other with no less depth of feeling.

London airport was tetchy. We were taken aside; our passports were gone over page by page; our bags were emptied and examined to the seams; our meagre possessions scrutinized. We were through.

My father met me at Newcastle Central station. His long and silent hug spoke eloquently of the pain he had endured. We repaired to the County Hotel for a pint of ale, a celebratory cigar and a long and earnest chat.

Dumfries was no less warm in its welcome; Glasgow was heartfelt. My first visit was to the Brothers with whom I had lived during my exile, who had recognised and shared the feelings I endured. We had a quiet, tender reunion accompanied by prayer followed by a celebratory drink.

The Marist Club threw open its doors. We were invited along for a welcome dinner accompanied by speeches and the opportunity to thank the many people who had worked with us and for us. One of them was a little girl we met who had written to Harold Wilson and asked him what he was doing about the poor people who had been working for the hungry people in Biafra and who had been put in prison. Mr Wilson wrote back and said he was doing his best. As indeed he was.

After the excitement of our arrival, a quiet time followed. We needed it. In Rome, in expectation of this rest, I had bought a pair of boots, strong Italian leather hiking boots. It was a quiet winter morning. I filled my haversack with a waterproof jacket, bacon rolls and a bottle of fine Italian wine with which I had been presented. I donned the hiking boots and set out for the Highlands. The path to Rowardennan was as I remembered it, lightly dusted in snow;

Loch Lomond was as calm; the snow on Ben Bhreac sparkled in the winter sunshine. A blackbird on a bare branch sang a loud, sweet song. I felt, as I gripped my staff and trudged by the lochside, a gentle peace descending.

It was late afternoon when I reached Inversnaid and its waterfall and darksome pool with floating ice. I sat sheltered from the gentle breeze and opened my pack. The bacon rolls had lost none of their taste, the wine needed no cooling. I let my thoughts wander and the peace of it all entered my soul.

In my pack I had a little battery radio. I took it out, switched it on and tuned it to find some quiet music that would fit my mood. The piece I found was finishing. There was a pause then the orchestra took up the strains of something that I found vaguely familiar. I listened: the growling bass, the shrilling persistent trumpets rising to something I thought I knew, dying before I recognised it, building up to a fury of noise then breaking into calm and silence and out of that silence grew the tune I had come to know so well, the hymn that had been sung by the boys on that night of rain in the school library, their faces lit by a lone candle, knowing they were called to battle; the melody that the lone trumpeter had sounded beneath the blackened palms as the sun went down on the grave of his companion killed in the morning rocket attack; the melody that had been played in the dying moments of Biafra before Effiong's speech of surrender; the melody that had in it all the pathos and the agony of those months of suffering. I listened with a heart that was far away from the Scottish loch by which I was sitting. I listened until the music came to an end. There was a silence. I sat on in that silence by the dark pool with my thoughts which were far away. Then I rose stiffly, packed my bag and set off for home.

The sky darkened as I tramped along; lights came on across the water and twinkled on the still calm loch. A few stars shone in the velvet sky; gentle wavelets lapped at the water's edge; a light wind moaned. I wrapped the scarf tighter round my neck and quickened my step. I had far to go along the lonely lochside path but the memory of that music was in my heart and with me all the way.